Reclaiming a Conversation

Reclaiming a Conversation

The Ideal of the Educated Woman

Jane Roland Martin

Yale University Press
New Haven and London

Designed by Sally Harris
and set in Sabon type by Brevis Press.
Printed in the United States of America by
Vail-Ballou Press, Binghamton, New York.

Library of Congress Cataloging in Publication Data

Martin, Jane Roland, 1929–
   Reclaiming a conversation.

   Bibliography: p.
   Includes index.
   1. Women—History.   2. Women—Education—Philosophy.
I. Title.
HQ1122.M37   1985   305.4'09   85-2372
ISBN 0-300-03324-9

The paper in this book meets the guidelines for
permanence and durability of the Committee on
Production Guidelines for Book Longevity
of the Council on Library Resources.

10 9 8 7 6 5 4 3 2 1

To Tim and Tom

Contents

Acknowledgments

I am profoundly grateful to the Bunting Institute of Radcliffe College for supporting my initial research on women and education. Without the gifts of time, space, and intellectual stimulation it bestowed on me in 1980–81, this book could not have been written. I also want to thank Dean Richard Freeland and the College of Arts and Sciences of the University of Massachusetts, Boston, for granting me a course reduction in the spring semester of 1983, and the University of New Hampshire for an appointment as Visiting Woman Scholar in 1983–84. Without the support of the UNH Women's Studies Program and Education Department this book might still not be completed. I am especially grateful to Cathryn Adamsky and Michael Maxey for making things run smoothly for me and to Kay Munson and Micki Canfield for typing my manuscript.

There are many other individuals to whom I am also indebted. I owe special gratitude to Mary Vetterling-Braggin for realizing that the essays I was writing at the Bunting Institute could form the basis of a book and for persuading me to act on her perception; to Carol Gilligan for encouraging my research on women from the very beginning and for enriching my understanding of the implications of my work during our frequent discussions of women's development and education; to Jane Williams for talking to me at length and with great insight about women's lives and experiences; to Michael Martin for allowing me to test out all my ideas on him and in so many ways for giving this project his wholehearted support.

My thanks go to the many friends and colleagues who read drafts of chapters of this book and discussed my material with me: Kathryn Pyne Addelson for helping me formulate my questions; Ann Diller, Susan Franzosa, Beatrice Nelson, Jennifer Radden, and Janet Farrell Smith for critical readings and stimulating discussions of early versions of the book's central chapters; Mary Vetterling-Braggin for incisive comments on several of these; Barbara Houston for detailed criticisms of the Wollstonecraft chapter; Patricia Thompson for a home economist's perspective and Laurel Ulrich for a historian's perspective on the Beecher chapter; Carol Gilligan, Michael Martin, and Jane Williams for invaluable advice on an early version of the entire manuscript. In addition, the responses to my material of my students at UMassBoston and UNH and of members of the Philosophy of Education Club at Harvard helped clarify my thinking and inform my presentation. Finally, Gladys Topkis of Yale University Press has been a marvelously sensitive and insightful editor.

An earlier version of chapter 2 appeared in Mary Vetterling-Braggin, ed., *"Femininity," "Masculinity," and "Androgyny"* (Totowa, N.J.: Rowman and Littlefield, © 1982), pp. 279–97 (Jane Roland Martin, "Sex Equality and Education: A Case Study"); a portion of chapter 3 appeared first as an article in the *Harvard Educational Review* (1981). Parts of chapter 7 were originally published in: the *Harvard Educational Review* (1982); *Educational Theory* (1981); *Philosophy of Education 1981: Proceedings of the Thirty-Seventh Meeting of the Philosophy of Education Society* (Normal, Ill.); and in Jonas Soltis, ed., *Philosophy and Education: Eightieth Yearbook of the National Society for the Study of Education,* pt. 1 (Chicago: University of Chicago Press, 1981). I thank the publishers of these books and journals for permission to use this material. Quotations from *The Dispossessed,* by Ursula K. LeGuin (© 1974 Ursula K. LeGuin), are reprinted by permission of the author, the author's agent, Virginia Kidd, and Harper & Row. Quotations from "Claiming an Education" and "Taking Women Students Seriously" are reprinted from *On Lies, Secrets, and Silence, Selected Prose 1966–1978,* by Adrienne Rich, by permission of the author and W. W. Norton & Company, Inc. Copyright © 1979 by W. W. Norton & Company, Inc.

Not long ago I was asked to cite the three or four people from whom I had learned the most. After a moment of panic in which names of childhood friends and graduate school mentors, piano teachers and college roommates, philosophical colleagues and feminist scholars rushed into my mind, I realized that my greatest educational debt by far is to my mother, father, husband, and children. It is too late now to tell my parents that I appreciate their gift to me, and I do not have to tell my husband, for he knows. To my sons I dedicate this book so that they will know that it has been shaped as much by what I have learned from being their mother as by any scholarly training I have had.

1 Neglected Conversation

Contemporary philosophers of education ignore the subject of women. In the technical writings of the academy, as in popular polemical works, questions of gender simply do not arise. These theorists analyze the concept of education, discuss the nature and structure of liberal education, construct theories of teaching and learning, set forth criteria of excellence, and debate educational aims and methods without attending to the difference of sex. It has not always been this way. Plato—perhaps the greatest educational philosopher in the history of Western thought and certainly the first systematic one—wrote specifically about the education of females. So did Jean-Jacques Rousseau, one of the few Western philosophers whose educational thought rivals Plato's both in its depth of understanding and in its far-reaching influence. Indeed, throughout Western history both men and women have taken the subject of women's education sufficiently seriously to have written countless treatises about it.

The question arises, then, why educational theorists in our day take no notice of gender and why feminist theorists, in their turn, pay so little attention to questions of educational philosophy. Studies of sex differences in learning and sex bias in educational practices abound, research in the history of women's education flourishes, discussions of feminist pedagogy are numerous, and debates on the best way to incorporate the study of women into the liberal curriculum are commonplace. An examination of educational ideals, however, is seldom found in contemporary literature on women, and the construction of an adequate philosophy of women's education is rarely seen as relevant to the task of developing a comprehensive feminist theory.[1]

Feminist theory has not always been divorced from educational philosophy. Mary Wollstonecraft's *A Vindication of the Rights of Woman* (1792) is a treatise both on woman's place and on woman's education, and Charlotte Perkins Gilman's utopian novel *Herland* (1915) joins a well-developed theory of education to a feminist social vision. But that women now are receiving an education very much like the one Wollstonecraft urged for her daughters does not mean it is the one women *should* be receiving. Indeed, as Adrienne Rich, one of the few contemporary feminists who has written incisively and evocatively on the education of women, has pointed out, that women continue to *receive* an education is itself a matter of concern.

Addressing a group of female college students in 1977, Rich asked them to think of themselves as *claiming* rather than *receiving* an education. The difference between the two verbs is the difference between acting and being acted upon, she said, "and for women it can literally mean the difference between life and death."[2] Why is passivity toward learning a potentially fatal attitude? Rich was not merely echoing the psychologists who tell us that learning must be active if it is to be effective, although she might well accept the validity of the argument. Perceiving the extent to which education can promote or stunt women's growth and development, Rich grounded her thesis on a feminist vision of what women's lives can and should be. She was saying that in becoming mere receptacles for a university learning that excludes their experience and thought, women's lives can be damaged beyond repair.

Rich urged her audience to take charge not just of the manner in which they learn but of the content of their learning: "What you can learn here (and I mean not only at Douglass but any college in any university) is how *men* have perceived and organized their experience, their history, their ideas about social relationships, good and evil, sickness and health, etc. When you read or hear about 'great issues,' 'major texts,' 'the mainstream of Western thought,' you are hearing about what men, above all white men, in their male subjectivity, have decided is important."[3] She might have added that one should not expect to find included among those great issues or in the major texts her topic—the education of women. For although conversation on women's education began centuries before the birth of Christ and has continued into the present time, it has simply been ignored by the standard texts and anthologies in the history of educational thought.[4]

Does it matter that this conversation over time and space is missing?

If females today have access to the same education as males—and in the United States to a great extent they do—what difference does it make that historians of educational thought neglect the topic of women, that Plato's, Rousseau's, Wollstonecraft's, and Gilman's discussions of women's education have not been incorporated into the mainstream of Western thought? Does the discovery in educational history of epistemological inequality—by which I mean inequality in knowledge itself: in this instance, in the representation of women in historical narratives and philosophical interpretations—have any practical significance for those who would follow Rich's advice and claim an education for and about themselves?[5]

Since the early 1970s research has documented the ways in which such intellectual disciplines as history and psychology, literature and the fine arts, sociology and biology are biased according to sex.[6] This work has revealed that on at least three counts the disciplines fall short of the ideal of epistemological equality for women: they exclude women from their subject matter, distort the female according to the male image of her, and deny value to characteristics the society considers feminine. When a discipline does not meet the standard of epistemological equality, not only women but the tasks and functions society associates with them are denigrated. The problem is compounded when the history of educational thought falls short of this ideal because so many parties to the ongoing conversation about female education are women.

To the extent that the major historical texts overlook Plato's female guardians and Rousseau's Sophie, women's lives and experiences are devalued. When the voices of Wollstonecraft and Gilman are unrecorded, students are denied contact with some of the great female minds of the past; the implicit message is that women have never thought systematically about education, that indeed, they may be incapable of serious philosophical reflection on the topic.

I do not mean to suggest that every female educational theorist has been interested primarily in the education of her own sex. Maria Montessori is a notable example of a woman who developed a philosophy of education without reference to sex or gender. Yet many women have focused on female education. For example, with *A Vindication of the Rights of Woman* Mary Wollstonecraft entered the ongoing conversation by questioning Rousseau's theory of the education of girls and women and presenting one of her own. She, in turn, was influenced by the contribution Catherine Macaulay had made to this conversation in her *Letters on Education* (1790). In numerous books and articles written at a later date in another country, Catharine Beecher set forth a philosophy of the education of girls and women that presents interesting contrasts to Wollstonecraft's. And Beecher's grandniece, Charlotte Perkins Gilman, wove into her utopian novel, *Herland,* her educational philosophy for women.

Although these theorists of female education were well known in their own day, it is likely that until recently even Wollstonecraft's name would have been unfamiliar to historians of educational thought. I am able to cite them here because contemporary research on women is in the process of recovering the lives and works of so many who had been lost to history. Yet even if blame does not attach to the authors of the texts that silence women's voices, the fate of the contributions of Plato and Rousseau suggests that had the writings on female education of Macauley, Wollstonecraft, Beecher, and Gilman been known to exist, they too would have been ignored.

The devaluation of women is not the only unhappy consequence of the exclusion from the history of educational thought of all conversation about female education. The noted philosopher of education Israel Scheffler has said that the function of philosophy is to enlighten policy "by pressing its traditional questions of value, virtue, veracity, and validity."[7] These questions need to be pressed in relation to policies concerning the education of girls and women; yet as long as the conversation to which they belong is considered to fall outside the province of philosophy, they cannot be.

In inviting students to take responsibility for their own education, Rich beseeched them to reject those models of feminine weakness, self-denial, and subservience the culture holds up to them:

> Responsibility to yourself means that you don't fall for shallow and easy solutions—predigested books and ideas, weekend encounters guaranteed to change your life, taking 'gut' courses instead of ones you know will challenge you, bluffing at school and life instead of doing solid work, marrying early as an escape from real decisions, getting pregnant as an evasion of already existing problems. It means that you refuse to sell your talents and aspirations short, simply to avoid conflict and confrontation. And this, in turn, means resisting forces in society which say that women should be nice, play safe, have low professional expectations, drown in love and forget about work, live through others, and stay in the places assigned to us.[8]

Every woman has felt the pull of one or more of these negative models. She who is not attracted to the ideal of the self-denying wife and mother may become a woman who denies her intelligence; she who disdains the ideal of silent passivity may find the model of "the slapdash dilettante who never commits herself to anything the whole way" irresistible. Each of us will see mother or daughter, sister or friend, if not oneself, represented on Rich's list. Unfortunately, if a woman does what Rich asks—if she takes responsibility for her own education—she will find herself at a disadvantage. How can a woman avoid shallow solutions to the problems education poses if she never hears what has been said by those who have thought deeply on the subject? How can she know what education to claim if she has never entered into philosophical conversation about this education herself, indeed never even realized that such conversation existed?[9]

Not only women are led astray in this circumstance; men also suffer when they are denied knowledge of the range of educational ideals past philosophers have held up for half the population. In *A Vindication* Wollstonecraft makes clear the disastrous consequences for the man, Emile, of the faulty education Rousseau designs for Sophie. Sophie's case can be generalized. So long as men and women inhabit the same society and live overlapping lives, each sex will be affected by the education of the other. Unenlightened policies of female education will inevitably redound on males.

There is another reason men suffer when past conversation about women's education is ignored. Historians of educational thought are not antiquarians whose sole concern is to preserve the ideas of the past. They justify their inquiries by reference to the insights into contemporary education yielded by a study of past philosophies. "Philosophy, unlike the sciences, never fully outgrows its history," says Scheffler. "The arguments and conceptions of past thinkers retain a fundamental relevance for contemporary philosophy even as it struggles to find new ways for itself."[10] Historical study, then, illuminates educational practice today and guides the development, clarification, and testing of new theories about what education should be.[11]

How much illumination can be shed on the education of boys and men by a historical narrative that ignores girls and women? Philosophers do not construct theories of education in a vacuum. Viewing education as preparation for carrying on societal roles, they tie their proposals to

some vision of the good society. And insofar as the society the philosopher pictures is peopled by both sexes, we cannot evaluate the educational
ideal it holds up for males unless we know its expectations for females.
We will not even know the right questions to ask. Do men and women
in the envisioned society have reciprocal roles, with men carrying out the
functions of citizenship and women those of domesticity? If so, we must
ask not only if the education claimed for males will equip them to be
good citizens but also if it will promote or frustrate the efforts of women
to perform their own functions effectively. Alternatively, do men and
women in this society share roles and the tasks and functions associated
with them? If so, we must ask if the full complement of significant social
roles is reflected in the education claimed for both men and women.

When history neglects past philosophical conversations about wom-
en's education, it follows that the tasks, functions, institutions, and traits
of character that philosophy, as a part of our culture, has associated with
women are neglected. Discussions about marriage, home, family are missing as are discussions about society's *reproductive* processes—a category
I define broadly to include not simply conception and birth but the rearing
of children to more or less maturity and associated activities such as
tending the sick, taking care of family needs, and running a household.

We look to the history of educational thought for guidance. Because
its narrative does not record conversation about female education, it is
implied that the only valid questions about education have to do with its
adequacy as preparation for citizenship and the workplace.[12] No one
would deny the importance of education for society's *productive* processes—in which category I include political and cultural activities as
well as economic ones—but other tasks and functions are just as compelling. In the United States in the late twentieth century, we may reject
a sex-based division of labor, but we must not forget that many of the
tasks and functions that have traditionally been assigned to women are
essential to the existence of society and must be carried on well if we are
to have any chance of creating a better world.[13]

The statistics on child abuse and domestic violence in our society
today[14] belie the assumption that the knowledge, skills, attitudes, and
traits of character necessary for effectively carrying out the reproductive
processes of society occur naturally in people. Education for these processes is not only as essential as education for society's productive processes but also has an overarching political, social, and moral significance.

Jonathan Schell has said that "the nuclear peril makes all of us, whether we happen to have children of our own or not, the parents of all future generations"; he has called the will to save the human species a form of love resembling "the generative love of parents."[15] A historical narrative that neglects conversation about the education of women has little, if anything, to say about this kind of love and cannot serve either sex well.

Men and women need to claim the best possible education for themselves and their sons and daughters. All must listen to and participate in conversation about the ideals governing the education of both sexes. Only then will we understand that the education most of us receive today is too narrow. Only then can we begin to construct theories of education that give the reproductive as well as the productive processes of society their due, and only then can we press our questions of "value, virtue, veracity, and validity" in relation to the whole range of educational concerns. Is education for rearing children and caring for home and family desirable? If so, for whom? Should this education be placed on a par with citizenship education and become a universal requirement or should it be considered a specialty? If it is a specialty, does it properly belong to vocational or professional education? These are a few of the submerged questions that rise to the surface when conversation about women's education is incorporated into public learning.

This book is written, then, not out of some abstract belief in the ideal of epistemological equality but from a concern for the harm done to both sexes because we do not study the ideas of the great thinkers of the past about the education of women. Its object is to retrieve and reflect upon several ideals of the educated woman so that we may make enlightened judgments about women's education and may lay claim to the best education possible for both women and men.

The parties to the conversation reclaimed in these pages are two males and three females separated from one another in time and space. Why these particular participants? Plato and Rousseau are such important figures in the history of educational thought that their inclusion scarcely needs to be explained, but they are especially suited to my purpose here. My image of a conversation derives from the fact that in *Emile* Rousseau was addressing what Plato had to say about women's education in the *Republic* and, in turn, Wollstonecraft, in *A Vindication of the*

Rights of Woman, was directly responding to Rousseau's *Emile.* Thus, history yields a natural conversational triad.

Whether Beecher, our fourth participant, took herself to be addressing its members is not clear, but her ideas on women's education earn her a place in our conversational circle, for they speak directly to the concerns of Wollstonecraft while paralleling Rousseau's ideas on the education of men. Gilman, our fifth participant, undoubtedly meant to be addressing her great-aunt Catharine, among others, but her place in this conversation is assured as much by the bearing her ideas have on the concerns of Plato and Rousseau as by their relevance to Beecher's.

A good conversation is exhilarating. Thoughts are exchanged and ideas are played off against one another. This is what happens when Plato, Rousseau, Wollstonecraft, Beecher, and Gilman come together to talk about the education of women. Hence my case for reclaiming a conversation among these five thinkers rests ultimately on the conversation reclaimed. The conversation, of course, is not unmediated. My task is necessarily one of reconstruction: interpretation is essential if we are to understand these philosophers, as is selection if they are to speak about issues of significance to us today and evaluation if we are to learn from them. Thus, the conversation reclaimed in these pages has six participants, not five, for the act of reconstruction makes me a party to it myself.

It will be noted that I have imposed a chronological order on my reconstruction. Since several members of our circle were in fact addressing their predecessors, this format seems appropriate, but I adopt it also because, remarkably enough, the first of our philosophers is also the one who voiced the opinion many readers today will find especially congenial. In hearing their own views expressed at the outset, they should soon feel able to enter the conversation themselves. Those who do not approve of Plato's theory, however, can join with Rousseau in criticizing it and enter the conversation when he does, or they can wait for Wollstonecraft.

But despite its chronological approach, my reconstruction is not so much historical as philosophical. I leave it to others to trace the sources of Beecher's ideas on domestic education, the reactions to Wollstonecraft's criticisms of Rousseau, the influence of Rousseau's account of Sophie and Emile on succeeding generations. My interest is in the ideas themselves—their "value, virtue, veracity, and validity"—and their implications for us today.

In the case of Plato and Rousseau this kind of inquiry is taken for granted, although it has not in the past been directed to their discussions of women's education and women's place. As we will discover, this failure to acknowledge their theories of female education calls into question the accepted interpretations of the educational philosophies of both men. When the sections on women in the *Republic* and *Emile* are ignored, some of the fundamental insights contained in these works are lost. Thus, in reclaiming Plato and Rousseau's ideas on women's education, we not only gain illumination into education in our own times; new light is also shed on their philosophies.

The three historical female parties to our conversation have seldom if ever been perceived as systematic thinkers whose ideas warrant serious study. Beecher and Gilman have not been considered the authors of philosophical texts, not even by those who have retrieved their lives and works. And although Wollstonecraft's philosophical bent has been recognized, her thought has rarely been treated by philosophers with the respect it deserves. In the pages to follow I hope it will become clear that the fact that a philosophical construction has not been placed on the work of these women is evidence, not that their thought is deficient, but of our ignorance of it. Until recently few of us even knew of the existence of Wollstonecraft, Beecher, and Gilman. Now that historians have recovered their works we need to treat these women as the systematic theorists they clearly were.

Having said this, I should add that the conversation reconstructed here is incomplete. Although each party to it wrote extensively on education, I have focused in each instance on a single text, leaving to others the scholarly task of providing a comprehensive account of the views on female education of the philosophers represented here. This selectivity may not do full justice to *all* their ideas on our topic, but it nevertheless allows the reader to listen to and participate in a richly textured conversation about a wide range of educational ideals for women.

The reader may wonder why we need to reclaim an earlier conversation about the education of women if our conversation today repeats its dominant themes. But, of course, that is precisely the reason we must reclaim it. To adopt one or another position of earlier generations without profiting from the intellectual examination to which it has been subjected is to project its weaknesses into our future. We need to listen to what Wollstonecraft had to say to Rousseau, and what he had to say to

Plato, and what Plato might have said to Wollstonecraft so that we do not repeat their mistakes. We need to know how Beecher's views, for all their divergence from Wollstonecraft's, contribute to the development of the latter's position, as well as how Gilman's views illuminate both Plato's and Rousseau's, and how Rousseau's views, in turn, constitute a check on hers.

Because a variety of ideals is presented here, I use the image of a conversation over time and space rather than that of a debate. The term *debate* suggests that a single question is being argued and that there are two clear-cut positions. Our thinkers do not all focus on the same thesis, some defending and others rebutting it. In rejecting Rousseau's theory of female education, Wollstonecraft does not take up Plato's, although her own theory bears a resemblance to his, nor in rejecting Wollstonecraft's theory does Beecher revert to Rousseau's. Moreover, although Wollstonecraft, Beecher, and Gilman engage in a discussion of women's education, women's place, the good life, and the good society not only with one another but with Plato and Rousseau, there are no winners and losers in this book.

A good conversation is neither a fight nor a contest. Circular in form, cooperative in manner, and constructive in intent, it is an interchange of ideas by those who see themselves not as adversaries but as human beings come together to talk and listen and learn from one another. Using the materials at hand—Plato's *Republic*, Rousseau's *Emile*, Wollstonecraft's *A Vindication of the Rights of Woman*, Beecher's *A Treatise on Domestic Economy*, and Gilman's *Herland*—this is the phenomenon I have tried to capture.

2 Plato's Female Guardians

Alfred North Whitehead once characterized the European philosophical tradition as "a series of footnotes to Plato." This assessment may not do full justice to the originality of Aristotle or the greatness of Descartes, Hume, Kant, and Hegel, but Whitehead's point that Plato is the one who set the agenda for Western philosophical thought is essentially correct. The problems he attempted to solve remained the problems to be solved, and, in addressing them, every generation has had to reckon anew with the solutions Plato proposed. His solutions have not gained universal acceptance—far from it. But if philosophers in the Western tradition have not all been Platonists, they have nonetheless found it necessary to take seriously both Plato's own theories and his objections to the theories he rejected.

In at least one particular, however, the imagery of Whitehead's footnote does not capture reality. Although Plato's social and political philosophy has been taken as the starting point for significant reflection about the nature of the state, his theory of women's place has been derided. And while his educational philosophy has set the stage for future inquiry into the form and structure of an ideal education, his theory of the education of women has been dismissed.

Why have Plato's views on women's education and women's place not remained the touchstones for later thinkers? The most likely answer is that his solution to the related problems of women's education and women's place—female rulers, coeducation, communal living, and child rearing—was too radical. Those of Plato's successors who were inclined to reflect upon these topics were scarcely willing to take the abolition of the traditional female role as their starting point. Indeed, Gilman is the only party to our conversation who explores this possibility. Although she was well aware of the pitfalls of the traditional wife-mother role, even Wollstonecraft, now regarded as the mother of feminism, does not consider its abolition but limits herself to redefining it.

Viewed with suspicion by most people even now, Plato's proposals concerning women's place and education in book 5 of the *Republic* are nonetheless integral pieces of the social whole constructed in that dialogue and, from the standpoint of that larger theoretical structure, are fully comprehensible. From the standpoint of the Western philosophical tradition, however, they are anomalous. Contradicting established practice, they implicitly challenge some of the most deeply entrenched beliefs and assumptions of the Western world—not only those about the irrationality of women and women's incapacity to rule but also those about the necessity of the wife-mother role and the "natural" character of the institutions of private home, marriage, and family.

The disbelief and disregard with which future generations met the proposals of *Republic,* book 5, were anticipated by Plato, who portrayed his spokesman, Socrates, as positively skittish during the unveiling of his program concerning women. We should not be surprised, therefore, to learn that those who came later tried to pretend that he had never formulated his radical policies. Yet if women are to lay intelligent claim to an education and if all of us are to evaluate the education extended to both sexes today, this pretense must finally cease.

Plato's Production Model of Education

In Plato's *Republic* Socrates arrives at his account of the Just State through a thought experiment. To the extent that they are able, Socrates and his companions think away existing institutions and in their imaginations witness the birth of a city. Their starting point is the principle, enunciated by Socrates, that "not one of us is self-sufficient, but needs many things."[1] Implicit in this starting point is the assumption that each person is guided by self-interest and that it is in the self-interest of each to share. The question then arises whether people will specialize, one person producing enough food for everyone and another making the clothes for all, or whether they will simply help one another when necessary, while remaining as self-sufficient as possible. At this point in the thought experiment Socrates introduces an assumption about human nature that is basic to his theory of education.

Each one of us, Socrates says, is born with more aptitude for one task than for others. This Postulate of Specialized Natures does not attribute to each individual at birth the knowledge of how to perform a specific task. Socrates is saying that we come equipped with a talent for one task above all others; but the skill and knowledge and traits of character required for performing that task must be acquired. Although Socrates expects a person's natural aptitude to develop over time, he takes it to be fixed and unchanging. Thus, whereas one's specific nature can flourish or be stunted, a person cannot in mid-life acquire some new aptitude that supplants the original one. Different aptitudes are distributed over the population as a whole, not over an individual's life.

The Postulate of Specialized Natures does not in itself answer the question Socrates asks about specialization. As a further consideration, he adds an assumption about efficiency. Both production and quality are improved, he says, when a person practices one craft rather than several, that one being the craft for which the person is by nature most suited. Yet even this assumption does not yield the answer he gives to his own question. Specialization is the recommended mode of production in the Just State, not simply because in his view it is the most efficient mode, but because Socrates holds efficiency to be highly desirable. Socrates could have witnessed the birth of an inefficient state or of a somewhat efficient state. Without making his preferences explicit, he chooses efficiency.[2]

As it stands, the Postulate of Specialized Natures is purely formal: it does not specify the aptitudes people have at birth. Socrates proceeds to give this postulate content in his thought experiment, not, as one might expect, through a close inspection of human nature, but rather through an examination of the requirements of society. He creates an imaginary city that, when functioning properly, constitutes his Just State and then imposes its needs back onto human nature.[3] In the beginning a city will need farmers, builders, weavers, cobblers, metalworkers, cowherds, shepherds, merchants, and sailors. Eventually it will also need warriors, or auxiliaries, as he calls them, and rulers.

One might expect this mapping of society's needs to be based at least in part on sex, but in book 5 of the *Republic* Socrates argues that sex is not a determinant of a person's nature. He acknowledges that a woman is very different from a man: "But when we assigned different tasks to a different nature and the same to the same nature," Socrates says, "we did not examine at all what kind of difference and sameness of nature we had in mind and in what regard we were distinguishing them" (454b). People are different from one another in many respects, he points out; for example, some men are bald and others long-haired. Would it not be ridiculous to suppose that only bald men—or, alternatively, only those with long hair—could become cobblers? Some differences affect the pursuit a person follows, and others do not. Sex, like baldness, is a difference that makes no difference.

Given his Postulate of Specialized Natures, Socrates could have attributed to human beings talents very different from the ones he does. He could, for example, have said that some people are born with a talent for telling jokes, while others have more aptitude for doing pushups than anything else. He states that some are born with a capacity for bearing children and others for begetting them but draws attention to this latter differentiation only to disregard it. Socrates assumes a one-to-one relationship between human nature and societal needs. This Postulate of Correspondence is crucial to Plato's theory of the Just State.⁴ In that state there are three general types of jobs to be done—those of artisan, auxiliary, and ruler. It is absolutely essential that each person fit into one and only one category and that each person do his or her own job and no other.

One might ask why Plato does not consider the bearing of children a societal need. A fascinating feature of the experiment in thought in which Socrates and his friends construct the Just State is that the reproductive processes of society are all but ignored. Socrates knows that in addition to cobblers, shipbuilders, and cowherds a state needs to have children born and reared, houses cared for, the sick and elderly tended, and everyone fed. Yet he mentions wet and dry nurses, chefs and cooks (373c)—occupations traditionally performed by females—only in passing. The Just State appears to be derived from society's productive needs, not from its reproductive needs.

From a historical standpoint there is nothing surprising about this. But whereas Socrates minimized the importance of the reproductive processes of society by omitting them from his plan for the Just State, he did not take it for granted that the task of performing them belonged by nature to women. If he had, Plato's theory of women's place and his resultant theory of female education might have received as much acclaim from future generations as the rest of his philosophy has. Insisting that in regard to being a guardian of the Just State, in which category he includes both rulers and auxiliaries, he says no pursuit belongs to women because they are women or to men because they are men. "Woman by nature shares all pursuits, and so does man"—although, admittedly, woman is a physically weaker creature (455e). Moreover, Socrates does not apply this point to his guardians alone but extends it to all, adding, "One woman, we shall say, is a physician, another is not, one is by nature artistic, another is not." Herein lies the reason later thinkers have discounted Plato's ideas about women: quite happy to emulate Socrates in relegating the reproductive processes to what political philosopher Lorenne Clark calls the "ontological basement," they have been unwilling to follow him in refusing to place women there.[5]

Plato places responsibility for the reproductive processes of society outside the guardian class. Because he considers private property in general and private home and family in particular to be potentially divisive institutions, and because he wants to ensure that rulers and warriors function as a cohesive unit, keeping in mind at all times the good of the state rather than their own private interests, he substitutes for them communal living and child-rearing arrangements. In doing so, however, he does not deny the necessity of reproductive processes.

Plato speaks of nurses who take care of children born to the guardians, and we are surely justified in assuming that the cooks he mentions will prepare the guardian meals and that there will be launderers to look after their clothes. Exactly who these nurses, cooks, and launderers will be is not entirely clear. In view of Plato's perception of the difficulties— perhaps even the impossibility—of a woman's performing the traditional female tasks while being a guardian of the Just State (451d) and the fact that it does not occur to him that a male guardian could perform them, we must assume that, except for the begetting and bearing of children, the reproductive processes required by the guardians will be carried on by others. The Postulates of Specialized Natures and Correspondence, as well as the passages from the *Republic* just cited, lead one to expect that those others would not necessarily be women. Because Plato does not explicitly address the issue of who is to perform the duties historically associated with females, however, we cannot know if he really would have thought of men doing "women's work."

The begetting and bearing of children remain the responsibility of the guardian class. That by Socrates' own account these processes fail to be reflected in a person's nature does not mean that he refrains from mapping societal needs onto human nature. Construing the begetting and bearing of children as bodily functions, he does not project them onto human nature because he does not think they belong there. For Socrates, remember, human nature is composed of talents and aptitudes that do not develop on their own but require education. Because the capacities to beget and bear children emerge naturally as people mature and, in Socrates' eyes, can be accomplished quite well without education, there is no reason for him to project them onto human nature.

As we have seen, the Postulate of Specialized Natures asserts that each person is born with more aptitude for one task than for others, and the Postulate of Correspondence asserts a one-to-one relationship between the natural aptitude of an individual and that person's role in society. Because justice requires that each individual perform his or her own job in society and because Socrates assumes that no person is able to do from birth or simply by maturing the task for which he or she is naturally suited, the objective of education in Plato's Just State becomes apparent: education must equip people with the knowledge and skill and traits of character that will enable them to perform the societal tasks or roles for which nature suits them.

Plato's is a production model of education par excellence. The human being is the raw material of the educator. Like other raw materials, human beings are malleable within certain fixed limits. The object of education is to turn this raw material into a finished product or, more precisely, into one of three finished products. The educator must discover, not decide, to which finished product nature has suited the individual. From the educator's point of view, the composition of the raw material is a given, as are the specifications for the three kinds of end product. In their thought experiment Socrates and his friends have little to say about the good artisan, but the specifications for good auxiliaries and good rulers emerge in the course of their discussion.[6] Thus, for example, in a famous passage, Socrates likens those who will be warriors to pedigreed dogs: they must be high-spirited and brave, yet gentle with their own people.

Plato recommends that young children be allowed to play. As they move about freely in the Just State, their true natures will reveal themselves. Once these natures are discovered, the production of artisans, auxiliaries, and rulers can begin. The task of education is not simply to turn out these three kinds of people, however, but to produce people who will fill certain necessary roles in society. In other words, a Functional Postulate is implicit in the account of education contained in the *Republic*. Education is a servant of the state, which equips the individuals born into it to perform the functions preassigned to them by nature.

For Plato's state to be just, education must do its job well. Socrates simplifies the educator's task enormously by introducing in book 5 the assumption that all people who will perform the same task must have the same education. The Postulate of Identity directs educators to ignore individual differences within each of the three functional groups. It is this postulate that leads Socrates to assign to the female guardians of the Just State the same education the male guardians are to receive: an education consisting of intensive physical activity in the teens; the systematic study of arithmetic, geometry, astronomy, and harmony beginning at age twenty; and the study of dialectic beginning at thirty. Those born to play different societal roles are to be given different educational treatment. In conjunction with the Postulate of Identity, this Postulate of Difference directs educators to determine one course of study for artisans, one for auxiliaries, and one for rulers—three separate curricula, but one and only one version of each.

The Identity Postulate: Male-based Methods and Subject Matter

Once the underlying structure of Plato's educational philosophy is exposed, one realizes that recent commentary on *Republic*, book 5, has tended to concentrate on Plato's Postulate of Specialized Natures and its partner, the Correspondence Postulate. Responding to the misunderstandings of traditional scholars,[7] this work takes seriously Socrates' claim that being female does not bar a person from being a guardian of the Just State, but it is of two minds on the issue of Plato's commitment to sex equality.[8] Such philosophers as Christine Pierce and Christine Garside Allen—attempting in very different ways to show, despite the disparaging remarks about women to be found in book 5 itself, in other sections of the *Republic,* and in Plato's other dialogues, that Plato's thought is coherent—conclude that he builds equality of the sexes into the structure of the Just State. In contrast, Julia Annas, Lynda Lange, and Jean Bethke Elshtain, among others, conclude that, because Plato's primary concern in constructing the Just State is efficiency, not equality, only a few token women will belong to the guardian class.

For scholars on both sides of this argument the question has been primarily whether Plato really considers females qualified by nature to rule the Just State. For the most part the education he prescribes for the guardian class and his Identity Postulate of same role, same education have been considered unproblematic. The guiding assumption has been that if women—or, rather, enough women—are allowed into the guardian class, sex equality will prevail.

In recent years political theorist Susan Moller Okin has devoted the most attention to Plato's theory of female education. In *Women in Western Political Thought,* Okin argues persuasively that whereas many scholars have maintained that the disappearance of private home and family for the guardians of Plato's Just State is a result of his emancipation of women, the opposite is true: Plato emancipates women because he abolishes private home and family. Once these institutions disappear from their lives, she says, women cannot be defined by the traditional female role. Okin goes on to discuss Plato's account of the guardian education at some length, but the need for a detailed analysis of his production model, as well as for an evaluation of the adequacy of the Platonic educational ideal for the guardian role, remains.[9] Because Gilman implicitly treats this latter issue in *Herland,* let us wait until she enters our conversation to address it. Here let us examine two of the most troubling aspects of Plato's production model—the Identity and the Functional postulates. When Rousseau, Wollstonecraft, and Beecher enter the conversation there will then be ample opportunity to reflect upon Plato's deliberate rejection of an education to equip his guardians to carry on society's reproductive processes.

The Identity Postulate is part of our Platonic heritage, but it should not for this reason be embraced uncritically. For the sake of argument, suppose that Plato did envision a population in which 50 percent of those suited by nature to be guardians were female. It is not at all obvious that the system of education he prescribes for his Just State would enable those females to carry out the guardian role successfully. And even supposing it did, it is certainly not obvious if Plato prescribed "an androgynous character for all guardians," as Okin has claimed, or if, as Elshtain implies, he fashioned a male persona for his female guardians.

Distinguishing between the possible and the desirable, Lange has attributed to Plato the thesis that although it is possible for women and men to function as equals, it is not desirable for them to do so. One need not posit sexist intentions or the belief that nature favors the male, however, to reach the conclusion that Plato's guardian class might in fact contain few women. Just as there is a distinction to be drawn between the possible and the desirable, so there is one to be drawn between the possible and the probable. Give Plato the benefit of the doubt and grant he assumes that as many females as males are by nature suited to rule; then examine the Identity Postulate of his production model of education. It will be clear that even though Plato provides women in his Just State with equal *role opportunity,* there is reason to believe that he denies them equal *role occupancy.*

From Plato's postulates of Correspondence and Identity it follows that in the Just State females who are by nature suited to rule will receive an education identical to that given males who are by nature suited to rule. For women in the Just State, then, both equality of *role opportunity* and equality of *access to identical education* exist. However, there is no guarantee whatsoever that identical education will yield identical results.

Consider this example. Tennis instructors are fond of saying, "Watch my racket as I serve the ball." I, for one, can watch till doomsday without its having any apparent effect on my serve, while my more visually oriented colleagues proceed to hit aces. No doubt some of these fast learners have more aptitude for the game than I. But not all. When finally the instructor analyzes the serving motion verbally, introduces a meaningful metaphor, tells me to listen to the sound the ball makes, or takes hold of my arm and puts it through the correct motions, my serve will equal my colleagues'. Where education is concerned, natural talent is only part of the story. People with similar talents often learn in different ways.

To the extent that people learn differently, they require different educational treatment to attain the same ends. The question is whether there is any reason to suppose that females learn differently from males. No research has yet been done that shows conclusively that being female affects the way one learns, but I submit that in view of everything we know about the differential socialization of males and females it would be foolhardy to assume that it does not.

Let us return briefly to our tennis example. Many beginning female tennis players have more difficulty then their male counterparts do in acquiring an adequate serve. Why? Because the serving motion is similar to throwing a ball, and most females have had much less experience with this activity than males have. If the structure of the serving motion is not, in general, as immediately accessible to females as it is to males, to give women the same instruction in serving as men almost guarantees that the women will fail to learn an adequate serve. To reach this goal they must be given special instruction, which takes into account their past experiences.

We are talking here, however, about the guardians of Plato's Just State, not about tennis. It will be recalled that the intensive physical and intellectual education of his future rulers comes relatively late in life. If the early socialization of girls in Plato's Just State parallels that of girls today, it is unlikely that an identical education for male and female auxiliaries and rulers would yield equal numbers of capable males and females in those roles, for many of the females would, as in our tennis example, be starting their training with handicaps. Unless they were given special treatment, many potential female warriors and rulers would probably not be able to finish the obstacle-course curriculum in physical skills, mathematics, and abstract thinking that Plato sets for these groups.[10]

When Socrates proposes that men and women who have the same natural talents be given the same education, he is extending to women the kind of education designed for future male guardians.[11] However, there is no reason to suppose that male-based educational methods will transform most potential female guardians into actual ones. Socrates insists that sex is a difference that makes no difference. But he maintains this in relation to the *possession* of the natural talents for performing societal roles without recognizing that sex might make a difference to the *learning* of those roles. Furthermore, he fails to distinguish between the biological category of sex and the social-psychological-cultural category of gender.[12]

Claims about the existence of sex differences are today associated in the public mind with theories of biological determinism. Because the argument that biology is destiny has been used throughout history to keep women in the home, to justify women's subordination in marriage, and to deny women full citizenship, many contemporary feminist thinkers have been reluctant to acknowledge even the possibility that differences between females and males, beyond the obvious biological difference, exist. But suppose we grant that biological sex—which at present is considered a matter of chromosomal pattern and hormonal states as well as anatomical features—is not a determinant of an individual's aptitudes, or hence of that person's capacity to perform some societal role. It does not follow that the social, psychological, and cultural implications of being born a girl or boy—that is, being gendered—have no relevance to the way a person performs certain tasks or learns them in the first place.

In a 1978 talk to teachers of women, Adrienne Rich said:

> Long before entering college the woman student has experienced her alien identity in a world which misnames her, turns her to its own uses, denying her the resources she needs to become self-affirming, self-defined. The nuclear family teaches her that relationships are more important than selfhood or work; that "whether the phone rings for you, and how often," having the right clothes, doing the dishes, take precedence over study or solitude; that too much intelligence or intensity may make her unmarriageable; that marriage and children—service to others—are finally, the points on which her life will be judged a success or a failure. In high school, the polarization between feminine attractiveness and independent intelligence comes to an absolute. Meanwhile, the culture resounds with messages. During Solar Energy Week, in New York, I saw young women wearing "ecology" T-shirts with the legend: CLEAN, CHEAP AND AVAILABLE; a reminder of the 1960s antiwar button which read: CHICKS SAY YES TO MEN WHO SAY NO. Department store windows feature female mannequins in chains, pinned to the wall with legs spread, smiling in positions of torture. Feminists are depicted in the media as "shrill," "strident," "puritanical," or "humorless," and the lesbian choice—the choice of the woman-identified woman—as pathological or sinister.[13]

The young woman sitting in a college classroom, she concluded, "is already gripped by tensions between her nascent sense of self-worth, and the battering force of messages like these."

It is implausible, to say the least, that the cultural construct of gender—encompassing, as it does, not simply mannerisms and dress, but interests, expectations, behavior, ways of perceiving others and being perceived—has no bearing on a person's learning. Treated differently almost from birth, and with different expectations held up to them within the family and in the early years of schooling, children become aware at an early age of their culture's distinctions between masculine and feminine roles and of their culture's higher valuation of men and masculine roles.[14] This process of socialization, begun in infancy, continues through childhood and adolescence into adulthood. Would it not be astonishing if it had no consequences for learning?

Rich directed the teachers she was addressing to look at their classrooms:

> Look at the many kinds of women's faces, postures, expressions. Listen to

the women's voices. Listen to the silences, the unasked questions, the blanks. Listen to the small, soft voices, often courageously trying to speak up, voices of women taught early that tones of confidence, challenge, anger, or assertiveness, are strident and unfeminine. Listen to the voices of the women and the voices of the men; observe the space men allow themselves, physically and verbally, the male assumption that people will listen, even when the majority of the group is female.[15]

No one who has ever noticed the details of life in classrooms can have confidence in a thesis that denies the relevance of gender to learning in our own society. Insofar as there is differential socialization for girls and boys in Plato's Just State, there too we should expect gender to make a difference, even if biological sex in itself does not, in the *way* females learn, in their *motivation* to learn, and in the degree of *readiness* they possess when their formal education for ruling begins.

There are two reasons for believing that in the Just State differential socialization according to sex will not occur. One is that because Plato abolishes private home, family, marriage, and child rearing, there would seem to be no societal need to mold children into traditional sex roles. However, it is not clear whether these institutions—and with them, presumably, the associated female role of wife and mother—disappear in the Just State for everyone or only for the guardian class. If the latter, the prospects are slight of there being no socialization according to sex in that state. Of course, if Plato had proposed positive measures to ensure that baby boys and girls would not be perceived, spoken to, and handled differently; that the toys children play with would not project different adult roles; that the portrayals of males and females in literature would not transmit differential valuations of the sexes; that adult men and women in the society would be treated equally; that the language itself would cast no aspersions on females—if he had done all this, we might assume that the differential socialization according to sex that permeates our own society would not occur in the Just State. But Plato did not take these precautions for the Just State.

The second argument for believing that differential socialization will not occur is that in book 5 of the *Republic* Plato speaks of giving males and females destined for the same role in society the same upbringing as well as the same education. Does this not mean that he would expose potential male and female guardians to identical experiences from birth, so that by the time their formal education begins in their teens the sexes would have had identical socialization? In books 2 and 3 Plato outlines a program of education in literature and the arts for the early years. Assuming that it is meant for both boys and girls, still nothing in the *Republic* suggests that in the Just State people will behave in exactly the same way toward male and female infants and children, let alone that they will speak to them and evaluate them in exactly the same way. Given the data we now have on early socialization, we are certainly justified in doubting that potential male and female guardians will be sufficiently alike when they begin their formal education to benefit equally from identical treatment. Unless a positive program—for which there is no evidence—is instituted in the Just State to ensure that being male or female is irrelevant to socialization, the future guardians will not be the same.

The Identity Postulate itself, or even in combination with the differential socialization of girls and boys, does not put females at a disadvantage vis-à-vis role occupancy. It does place females at a disadvantage *when educational methods are determined by what works with males.* Then, equality of role occupancy is by no means assured, because females may not, for example, have as strong a desire to succeed as males, or may not be in an equivalent state of readiness to learn, or simply may not find the learning activities congenial. Consider those small female voices and the female silences in the classroom. They suggest that even that seemingly egalitarian method, the classroom discussion, will be experienced differently by females and males, and so have different effects on the two sexes.

When an identical education received by males and females consists of methods of teaching and learning that are male-based, equality of role occupancy is not assured. When the content of that education "validates men even as it invalidates women,"[16] this goal is further jeopardized. Moreover, supposing that an equal number of each sex graduates into Plato's guardian class, so that there is equality of role opportunity; it cannot be assumed that women will be perceived or treated as the equals of men.

Plato is one of the few philosophers of education who has demonstrated an awareness of the informal learning, or socialization, that occurs in a society. In particular, he recognizes how powerful an agent of socialization literature can be. Assuming that young children acquire traits of character and behavioral dispositions informally through unconscious imitation—an assumption shared by those who today condemn the sex stereotyping in school texts and confirmed by studies of television violence[17]—Plato recommends an extensive program of censorship for his Just State. Thus, for example, he urges banning stories portraying the gods quarreling with one another or committing impious deeds and those depicting the lamentations of famous men. One searches the *Republic* in vain, however, for caveats about exposing children to stories that perpetuate traditional attitudes toward women.

Considering the way in which Socrates and his companions tend to speak of women, the absence of such warnings is not surprising. For example, here are Socrates' comments on female behavior, from his discussion of the dangers of impersonation and imitation:

> We shall then not allow those for whom we profess to care and who must grow up into good men to imitate, being men, a young or older woman who is railing at a man, or quarreling with the gods, or bragging while thinking herself happy, or one in misfortune and sorrows and lamentations, even less one in illness or in love or in labour. (395e)

There is also Plato's use in the *Republic* and elsewhere of the term *womanish* to denote behavior he disapproves of, be it cowardly, stupid, or unduly emotional. And in the dialogue bearing his name, Timaeus tells Socrates that of the men who came into the world originally—and only men did—"those who were cowards or led unrighteous lives may with reason be supposed to have changed into the nature of women in the second generation."[18]

In view of his own conditioning, we have little reason to believe that Plato would perceive sex stereotyping in the stories children are told. Yet an upbringing that through its literature portrays females as irrational, untrustworthy, and generally inferior to males will very likely have a differential effect on the self-confidence and the aspirations of girls and boys.[19] When the stories children are told transmit the message that men are the shapers and thinkers of the world and women are passive prey, we must anticipate that girls will encounter problems boys do not in the course of becoming the rational, autonomous individuals Plato's rulers must be, indeed, that many girls, even though suited by nature to rule the state, will never overcome the special obstacles they face. We must expect also that those girls who achieve the educational goals set for the guardian class will not be perceived in the same way as his male guardians or be accorded the same treatment and respect.

The problem of the differential representation and valuation of males and females in the subject matter of guardian education extends beyond the stories children are told to the various fields of formal study. The subjects of the guardian curriculum are abstract and theoretical. Because, unlike history and psychology, they do not purport to describe and explain human experience, we need not ask whether they ignore or distort women's deeds and lives. Contemporary scholarship on women has shown that, by defining itself as the record of public and political events of the past—the very aspects of life from which women have for the most part been excluded—history effectively excludes women from its narratives. It has shown that the system of periodization history has invented—the Renaissance, the Enlightenment, and so on—is largely determined by the interests of men; that even when an issue concerns women as well as men—as fertility certainly does—it is treated as a masculine issue; that cherished explanations such as Turner's frontier thesis apply to men only.[20] Similarly, in psychology the experience of females is assimilated into that of males, and theories of female personality are constructed out of the investigator's prejudices.[21] These comments do not apply to Plato's curriculum, but analyses of philosophy and the theoretical sciences do.

Recent research on gender and science reveals the extent to which metaphors tied to our cultural definitions of masculinity are associated with science. The more objective a science, the "harder" it is; the more subjective, the "softer." Facts are "hard," feelings "soft." Scientists are "he," nature is "she." Scholars maintain, moreover, that the fundamental scientific norm of objectivity is itself a reflection of the cultural image of masculinity, involving, as it does, a distance or separation between the knower and what is known, the setting aside of feeling, and the rejection of immediate sensory experience.[22] Philosophy is classified as a humanity, not a science; but there, too, the imagery and ideology are related to our cultural definitions of masculinity, with "tough-mindedness" considered a virtue and "softheadness" a vice. Tackling an argument or wrestling with a problem, the philosopher first pins it down and then dissects it and gets to its heart. Attacking his opponent's theories at their weakest points, he never pulls his punches but, rather, produces knock-down-drag-out arguments, thereby destroying the other's position. These metaphors of war and violence make the claim of one feminist philosopher, that the approved form of philosophical reasoning incorporates aggressive behavior through its adversary methodology, seem gentle and cautious.[23]

We need to know more than we do about the study of mathematics, astronomy, harmony, and dialectic that Plato's guardians undertake in order to determine the extent to which those studies invalidate females. However, because nature and matter are feminine and Ideas masculine in Platonic symbolism,[24] we can assume that those being educated to leave the world of nature and enter the realm of Ideas would receive the same message transmitted to students of philosophy and theoretical science today: the most valued and valid ways of thinking, acting, and being are masculine.

We may never know enough about the curriculum of Plato's guardians to determine all the respects in which males and females are represented differentially in its subject matter. But one thing is clear. Insofar as the subjects studied and the literature learned do validate males while invalidating females, one would expect to find differences in the way members of the two sexes perceive themselves and one another. If stories portray women as irrational and immoral, will not students of both sexes come to believe that males are superior and females inferior human beings? If abstract disciplines employ masculine imagery and set masculine norms, will not students of both sexes come to believe that females are abnormal human beings? Epistemological inequality surely has destructive effects on the students of a field. How difficult it is for any group to be seen as the equals of others, or even to see themselves as such, when they are not accorded equality in knowledge itself!

The assumption of same role, same education has a plausible ring to it. Yet this Identity Postulate does not express a necessary truth about education. Those today who wish to claim an education for women need to approach the Postulate of Identity cautiously, recognizing that it extends a male-based pedagogy and subject matter to women, making it difficult for women to achieve equal role occupancy and all but impossible for them to be perceived and treated as the equals of men.

The heart of this concern about the Identity Postulate is that identical education is not in every instance equal education. Whereas potential female guardians in the Just State are to be given the *same* education as potential male guardians, potential male and female guardians will not necessarily be given *equal* education. Imagine two people, one of whom has appendicitis and the other tonsillitis. Perform a tonsillectomy on both and they will each have been given identical treatment. They will not, however, have received equal medical care, because what was appropriate for the one illness was not for the other. Plato's production model of education makes no provision for differential treatment according to sex; in fact, the Identity Postulate expressly forbids it. Plato's future female guardians might, however, require different treatment than his future male guardians in order to arrive at the point where they can capably carry out their assigned roles in the Just State. Even if they have equal access to education, they will not have equal educational opportunity unless they have *equal access to equal education.*

A production model of education could contain a *Postulate of Equivalency* instead of an Identity Postulate. Who knows, had Plato been aware of the limitations of the Identity Postulate, he might have provided equivalent, rather than identical, education for male and female future guardians. Then, assuming that roughly equal numbers of each sex were by nature suited to be guardians, there would be good reason for supposing that in his Just State there would be equal role occupancy. The Identity Postulate is not the only problematic element of Plato's production model of education, however, for if Plato is forcing future female guardians into a masculine mold, the question of equal respect and treatment arises anew.

The Functional Postulate: Whose Role?

According to Arlene Saxenhouse, "Socrates attempts to turn women into men by making them equal participants in the political community."[25] She argues this thesis on the ground that he ignores the sexual female and, in particular, the peculiar biological qualities of women: women's natural role in the preservation of the city through the procreation of the next generation is left unconsidered; the female is brought into politics through disregard of her body, although the thing she can do better than anyone else—hence the thing that should be considered her specific nature—is to bear children.

Elshtain, on the other hand, suspects that Plato allows women to be rulers of the Just State for the very purpose of procreation. She, too, deplores their loss of female identity, which, like Saxenhouse, she attributes to Plato's "denial of biological integrity."[26] Understanding, as few of Plato's commentators do, that the Identity Postulate is no guarantee of identical results, Elshtain foresees Plato's female guardians speaking in their own voices, rather than in philosophic speech, even after being educated to grasp the form of the Good. Their previous "privatization and silence" will not, presumably, have been overcome by their male-based education.

One need not adopt Saxenhouse's account of the de-sexed female to agree with her that in admitting women to the guardian class Plato imposes a masculine mold on them. Nor need one share Elshtain's beliefs that women can escape biological imperatives less easily than men, and that no woman would accept parity with an elite group of men on Plato's terms, to agree with her that women suffer as men do not by being admitted to the guardian class of the Just State.

Historically, warriors and rulers have been predominantly male. No doubt this explains why Socrates and his companions never entertained the possibility that members of the male sex might not qualify by nature to be guardians; only females are problematic in their eyes. It does not follow from the fact that females are given entry into roles traditionally occupied by males that a masculine mold must be imposed on them. In principle, the entrance of women into traditional male roles could be accompanied by a redefinition of those roles. However, although Plato does redefine at least the role of ruler in relation to the Just State, the qualities or traits he assigns his guardians were considered in his day and are still considered masculine. By this I do not mean that males possess these traits and females do not, or even that males are more likely than females to possess them, but simply that the traits of Plato's guardians belong as much to his cultural stereotype of the male as they do to ours.

The physical qualities of the guardian are clear, Socrates says: guardians must be quick to see things, swift in pursuit of what they have seen, and strong to catch the enemy and fight to the end. Guardians must also be brave and high-spirited, because a high spirit makes the soul fearless. They must love wisdom. If they are to be rulers, moreover, they must be rational thinkers, able not only to distinguish the Good by their reason but to argue their case according to reality rather than opinion, while surviving refutations of it. The capacity for rational thought is not enough; reason must rule the individuals who rule Plato's Just State.

As readers of *Republic* know, the impetus for this dialogue is the search for justice in the individual. Only after considering and rejecting several accounts of the just person did Socrates decide to construct a perfect state in imagination and locate justice within it. Claiming that because the state is a larger unit justice will be more readily discerned there, he convinces his comrades in book 2 that once justice is found in the state it can easily be discovered in the individual. They therefore embark on their thought experiment, returning to the question of justice—first in the state, and then in the individual—in book 4.

In that book Socrates assures his comrades that the Just State is completely good; hence it is "wise, brave, moderate, and just" (427e). Where is wisdom found? In that smallest group of citizens, the rulers, of course, for they are the ones with knowledge of guardianship. Where is courage found? In the warriors, who have been trained in what and what not to fear. And where is moderation found? Resembling a kind of harmony, this virtue, consisting of the agreement "between the naturally worse and the naturally better as to which of the two must rule," is spread throughout the whole state (442a-b). Having located these three virtues in the state, Socrates concludes that whatever remains is justice. What is justice then? Without doubt, it is doing one's own job. If a carpenter should attempt to do the work of a cobbler, no great harm is done, but "the meddling and exchange between the three established orders does very great harm to the city and would most correctly be called wickedness" (434c).

The Just State, then, is the one in which artisans, auxiliaries, and rulers perform those tasks, and only those, for which they were born and educated. Transferring this finding to the individual, Socrates says: "If it corresponds, all will be well. But if it is seen to be something different in the individual, then we must go back to the city and examine this new notion of justice. By thus comparing and testing the two, we might make justice light up like fire from the rubbing of firesticks, and when it has become clear, we shall fix it firmly in our own minds" (434e–435a). He argues at length that the soul of the human individual has the same parts as the State—reason, spirit, and appetite—and that the four virtues are found in the individual in the same places as in the State: wisdom in the rational part of the soul, courage in the spirited part, moderation in the obedience of both spirit and appetite to reason, justice in each part doing its own job and no other.

We can see now that Plato's rulers do not simply possess a highly developed capacity for rational thought. They are also individuals in whom the spirited part of the soul comes to the aid of the rational part in order to exercise authority over the appetite, "which is the largest part in any man's soul and is insatiable for possessions" (442b). In other words, they are people of moderation, where this virtue is understood as a harmonious relation between the ruling and the ruled parts of the soul. They are also just individuals, where this virtue is understood as a state of the soul in which each part is performing its own function and no other. The ideal Plato holds up for his rulers, both male and female, is that of a person

> concerned with himself and his inner parts. He does not allow each part of himself to perform the work of another, or the sections of his soul to meddle with one another. He orders what are in the true sense of the word his own affairs well; he is master of himself, puts things in order, is his own friend, harmonizes the three parts like the limiting notes of a musical scale, the high, the low, and the middle, and any others there may be between. He binds them all together, and himself from a plurality becomes a unity. Being thus moderate and harmonious, he now performs some public actions, or private contract. In all these fields he thinks the just and beautiful action, which he names as such, to be that which preserves this inner harmony and indeed helps to achieve it, wisdom to be the knowledge which oversees this action, an unjust action to be that which always destroys it, and ignorance the belief which oversees that. (443d–444a)

Plato's guardians have been called androgynous because they are required to be gentle as well as courageous. Androgyny is not achieved, however, simply because, as one commentator has put it, Plato saw the need to temper with gentleness the qualities his guardians had to develop in their education for battle.[27] Plato's guardians must be gentle with their own people so that they themselves do not destroy the city they are supposed to protect. But when one examines the qualities the guardians need for battle, the kind of thinking they must exhibit to discern the Good, the moderation they must display at all times, and the self-control involving the subordination of feelings and emotions to the rule of reason they must attain, it becomes clear that the predominating traits of the guardian involve qualities that are usually considered masculine.

Some might argue that so long as females as well as males are allowed to occupy a role and that role is defined in terms of traits that both sexes can possess, then, even if the role is described by traits considered to belong to our masculine stereotype, sex equality is achieved. As the philosopher Elizabeth Beardsley has shown in her work on language, however, traits that can be possessed by both sexes are often appraised differently in males and females.[28] Consider one of Beardsley's examples, the trait of aggressiveness. The authors of a book on assertiveness training for women report that in the first meeting of their training courses they ask their students to call out the adjectives that come to their minds when they hear the terms *aggressive woman* and *aggressive man*.²⁹ Here is the list of adjectives the women used to describe an aggressive man: *masculine, dominating, successful, heroic, capable, strong, forceful, manly.* And here are the adjectives they used to describe an aggressive woman: *harsh, pushy, bitchy, domineering, obnoxious, emasculating, uncaring.* Thus, even supposing that the traits Plato's guardians will possess are judged to be highly desirable ones for males, we must not assume that they would have been evaluated so highly when possessed by females. I will call this differential appraisal of traits according to sex *trait genderization.*

Are the traits to be possessed by Plato's guardians, like aggressiveness, genderized in favor of males? That they are in our society cannot be doubted. The physical courage and fearlessness the guardians must display are considered positive virtues when possessed by males. For women to be swift enough to catch and fight the enemy, however, they not only must dress in ways that are perceived as unfeminine and hence abnormal but must display a fierceness and tenacity considered unnatural to the "weaker" sex.

Perhaps, however, there is no need for all guardians to be equally fast and fierce. Perhaps in the Just State the guardian role will develop specialized functions, with some guardians performing the task of catching and fighting the enemy and others performing less rigorous duties. This position finds support in the *Republic* in the allusions of Socrates and his companions to the physical weakness of women and in their apparent willingness to assign the lighter duties of guardianship to women.

Females who failed to acquire the physical traits Plato assigns the guardians would indeed escape the negative effects of their genderization. However, it is far from obvious that one who did not possess those traits could qualify as a full-fledged guardian, for it is not clear that such a person could possess the soul of a guardian as outlined in book 4 of the *Republic.* According to Socrates, a fit body is no guarantee of a good soul, but it is essential that the body be as fit as possible if the soul is to be good. In any case, not only the physical traits of Plato's guardians are genderized.

The portrayal of Rosalind Franklin by James Watson in his bestselling book, *The Double Helix,* demonstrates that when a woman displays the rationality and autonomy that are attributes of Plato's guardians, she is derided for what are considered negative, unpleasant characteristics even as her male colleagues are admired for possessing them.[30] A brilliant, highly trained scientist and an expert in x-ray analysis, Rosalind Franklin contributed more than she was initially credited for—indeed, more than she realized she had—to the discovery of the structure of DNA. Invited to build up the x-ray diffraction unit of King's College, London, she arrived there in January 1951, some months before James Watson and Francis Crick began the collaboration at Cavendish Laboratory, Cambridge, that led them to the Nobel Prize. In November of that year she gave a seminar on her work on DNA, which Watson and about fifteen others attended. Watson comments on the way Franklin comported herself on that occasion: "There was not a trace of warmth or frivolity in her words. And yet I could not regard her as totally uninteresting. Momentarily I wondered how she would look if she took off her glasses and did something novel with her hair."[31]

Although seriousness of purpose is essential for first-rate scientists, Watson here belittles Franklin for possessing this trait. He also holds her autonomous behavior against her. Deriding her for refusing to think of herself as Maurice Wilkins's assistant—something she was not hired to be—he says: "Clearly Rosy had to go or be put in her place. The former was obviously preferable because, given her belligerent moods, it would be very difficult for Maurice to maintain a dominant position that would allow him to think unhindered about DNA."

This is only one side of the coin. The other is that Watson judged Franklin to be unfeminine: "By choice she did not emphasize her feminine qualities. Though her features were strong, she was not unattractive and might have been quite stunning had she taken even a mild interest in clothes. This she did not. There was never lipstick to contrast with her straight black hair, while at the age of thirty-one her dresses showed all the imagination of English blue-stocking adolescents."[32]

"The best home for a feminist," Watson concludes, is "in another person's lab." Rosalind Franklin was not a feminist. She was simply a woman working at the highest levels of science who expected to be treated as a scientist. She believed in the rule: same role, same treatment. In the Paris laboratory where she worked before going to King's and later at Birbeck College, London, her expectations were realized. But as the possessor of traits genderized in favor of males, she is described in Watson's book less as a colleague than as a freak. And because of his book's popularity, that is the way she has come down to us.

The phenomenon of trait genderization, which lies behind Watson's portrayal of Rosalind Franklin, is not simply a function of free-floating stereotypes. As Beardsley has pointed out, genderization has its source both in the differential allocation of responsibilities in society and in the differential assessment of the capabilities of males and females. According to tradition and the ruling ideology of her time, Rosalind Franklin was supposed to devote her days and nights to children, home, and family— in other words, to carry on the reproductive processes of society. She therefore was expected to be nurturing and caring, warm and sympathetic; above all, she was expected to put her own purposes and plans aside to help her children and husband carry out theirs. She was not supposed to be an abstract, rational, critical thinker; she was not supposed to pursue her own projects single-mindedly—traits that were considered appropriate only for carrying on the *productive* processes of society.

Rosalind Franklin consciously chose the laboratory rather than "women's sphere." The traits she possessed were certainly not dysfunctional there; quite the contrary. Yet she was perceived by some of her scientific colleagues as a trespasser, an alien who could not be taken seriously no matter what her personal qualities might be. If she was so perceived, would not Plato's female guardians be perceived similarly? Because Plato abolishes reproductive processes other than conception and childbearing for the guardian class in his Just State, it might seem that his female rulers would not suffer the fate of Rosalind Franklin. Perhaps they would not be viewed as aliens because there would be no reproductive processes for them to carry on. Tradition should not be forgotten, however; nor should we overlook the fact that Plato explicitly abolishes home and family only for the guardian class. Given that in Athens, where we presume the founders of the Just State live, the place of almost all women was in the home, would not the traits of Plato's guardians remain genderized in the traditional way?

So long as the guardian role is defined in terms of traits that are considered masculine, in Plato's Just State potential female guardians would be in a no-win situation. They would have to acquire traits thought to be masculine in order to meet the requirements of the guardian role.

Yet if they acquired those traits, they would very likely be viewed as abnormal and be derided or belittled for possessing them. The heart of the matter, as far as the Functional Postulate is concerned, is that although they are attached to social roles, traits can remain genderized even when the social roles to which they belong are detached from gender. Assuming that Plato sincerely wanted his Just State to have a significant number of female guardians, one can say that occupancy of this most important social role is not tied to gender. Yet so long as a role is defined in terms of genderized traits, male and female occupants of the role can expect to receive differential treatment and to be accorded differential respect for possessing these traits.

Plato's female guardians could try to escape the fate of a Rosalind Franklin by performing the ruler role differently from their male counterparts. Once they are included in the class of guardians, who is to stop women from redefining their role? Who is to keep them from eschewing traits genderized in favor of males and attaching to the tasks assigned them traits genderized in favor of their own sex? First, their education will stop them; it is designed not merely to instill the very traits they want to avoid but to extinguish the ones they want to assume. Second, the fear of ridicule will stop them. Were women in Plato's Just State to perform the ruler role differently from men, they would surely be considered as abnormal in their way as Rosalind Franklin was in hers.

For his male and female guardians to be treated equally, Plato would have had (1) to define the role of guardian in terms of traits other than the ones he used or (2) to sanction measures for changing people's values and attitudes so that these traits would not be genderized in favor of males in the Just State. It is doubtful that he could have defined the guardian role in markedly different terms without radically revising his entire philosophy; for the qualities of rational thinking, self-control, and autonomous thought and action are absolutely central to his system of thought. The second alternative would not have had serious repercussions throughout Plato's philosophy; but whether he would have wanted to adopt it and could in reality have proposed measures for turning around the attitudes and values of the people who would inhabit the Just State is highly speculative.

The purpose of this speculation about the measures Plato could have taken to ensure sex equality in his Just State is not to blame him for his failure to guarantee sex equality but to further our understanding of the kind of education women should claim for themselves. It is unlikely that Plato would have thought to adopt an Equivalency Postulate because he most probably was unaware of the limitations of the Identity Postulate outlined here. It is also unlikely that he could have addressed the problem that his definition of the guardian role raises for true sex equality because it is improbable that he could have known of the existence of genderized traits. Thus, it is not fruitful to condemn him for doing less than he should have for his female guardians. It is fruitful, however, to take to heart for our own lives the lessons we can learn from the way in which Plato's production model of education functions in his theory of the Just State.

"If there is any misleading concept," Adrienne Rich said in her talk to teachers, "it is that of 'coeducation': that because women and men are sitting in the same classrooms, hearing the same lectures, reading the same books, performing the same laboratory experiments, they are receiving an equal education."[33] Although identical education does not have to mean coeducation—it could be translated, instead, as separate but identical education—Plato takes coeducation for his guardians to be a corollary of his Identity Postulate. Those today who ponder the pros and cons of coeducation must understand that not only coeducation but the assumption of same role, same education upon which it rests needs to be questioned. Certainly, coeducation presents special problems in relation to the goal of equal education because the two sexes tend to be treated differently in the classroom, and, moreover, students often act differently in mixed-sex settings than they do in single-sex settings. Still, whether females and males are given the same education together or separately, the possibility that this "same" education may validate one sex at the expense of the other remains, as does the possibility that the methods used will not work equally well for both sexes.

But that is not all. As Rich makes clear, classroom methods and formal curriculum content are not the only factors to consider in deciding the issue of equality. If outside the classroom women are perceived "not as sovereign beings but as prey," can they have the sense of self that an equal education requires? Rich's answer to this question bears repeating:

> The capacity to think independently, to take intellectual risks, to assert ourselves mentally, is inseparable from our physical way of being in the world, our feelings of personal integrity. If it is dangerous for me to walk

home late of an evening from the library, *because I am a woman and can be raped,* how self-possessed, how exuberant can I feel as I sit working in that library? How much of my working energy is drained by the subliminal knowledge that, as a woman, I test my physical right to exist each time I go out alone?[34]

John Dewey is credited with repudiating the dichotomies between school and society, education and life, so often taken for granted today. Plato rejected these too. He knew that a society itself is educative—or miseducative. He knew that it makes no sense to provide for people a formal education that is at war with their informal one. Unfortunately, he did not realize that he was making the future female guardians of his Just State the victims of just such a war. Few people in history have realized this, and most of those who have, have done so only dimly. Today, however, as new research on women reveals the hidden curriculum of both school and society in the feelings of inferiority and "otherness" of women, we no longer have ignorance as an excuse. If sex equality is what we want, then, knowing what we do, we must start to worry less about the sameness of the education of girls and boys, women and men, and more about its equivalency.

We must also start to worry more than we have in the past about trait genderization. Otherwise we can expect females to continue to be caught in the middle of a war between educational goals and processes based on the assumption that sex is a difference that makes *no* difference, on the one hand, and cultural images and expectations that assume sex is *the* difference that makes a difference, on the other. Remarkably enough, the next party to our conversation understands that traits are genderized. But instead of telling Plato's female guardians to go ahead and redefine the guardian role, claiming an education designed for themselves rather than settling for the one designed for their male counterparts, Rousseau would have them function within traditional gender boundaries. His strategy for preventing the war whose unwitting victims Plato's women will be is to deny the validity of holding up educational goals for females that embody traits genderized in favor of males.

Let us listen to what Rousseau has to say to Plato. Rousseau's misogyny is so pronounced as to make Socrates' belittling of women seem inconsequential. However, behind his unflattering comments about Sophie, and by implication about women in general, lies a theory of society and of education to which those who would claim an education for women must pay heed. Although many of the conclusions to be drawn from Rousseau's conversation with Plato are negative, there are also positive lessons to be learned from the genuine insights contained in the story he tells of Sophie and Emile.

3 Rousseau's Sophie

            In the introduction to his translation of *Emile*, Allan Bloom says that what Rousseau attempts "is to present an egalitarian politics that rivals Plato's politics in moral appeal." In imagination, Rousseau "takes an ordinary boy and experiments with the possibility of making him into an autonomous man—morally and intellectually independent, as was Plato's philosopher-king."[1] In contrast, Rousseau himself says, "Read Plato's *Republic*. It is not at all a political work, as think those who judge books only by their titles. It is the most beautiful educational treatise ever written" (p. 40). In fact, the *Republic* is both a political and an educational treatise, and so is *Emile;* moreover, if Plato's title has misled generations into supposing his greatest dialogue to be solely a political work, Rousseau's title, *Emile, or On Education,* has led them to the opposite error of supposing this great book to be solely about education.

            To understand fully the political and social dimensions of *Emile*, it is necessary to do something seldom done, namely to read carefully what Rousseau has to say about the education of Sophie. Then the darker side of the egalitarian politics unfolded by Rousseau in *The Social Contract,* his explicitly political treatise published in the same year as *Emile,* is revealed, and the irony of Bloom's judgment that Rousseau's egalitarianism does not debase man "for the sake of the will-o'-the-wisp, security" (p. 6) becomes apparent. Plato's guardians, upon whom Emile is modeled, are destined to contemplate the Good and rule the state. Stripped of private home, family, marriage, and child rearing, their lives are to be dedicated to the specific role for which their education prepares them. Emile too is destined to rule, albeit as a citizen in a democracy rather than as a philosopher king. The big difference between his life and that of Plato's guardians, however, is that Rousseau restores the very institutions Plato abolishes. Thus, Emile is destined to live in a traditional home as a patriarchal husband and father. Who, then, is to take care of Emile's home and rear his children? In Rousseau's philosophy man is not debased for the sake of security; woman is. The price Rousseau pays for his autonomous man, Emile, is Sophie, Emile's wife. For the sake of his security she is hidden away in the "ontological basement."

"It is not good for man to be alone. Emile is a man. We have promised him a companion. She has to be given to him. That companion is Sophie. In what place is her abode? Where shall we find her? To find her, it is necessary to know her. Let us first learn what she is; then we shall better judge what places she inhabits" (p. 357). So begins book 5 of *Emile*. It takes Rousseau almost a hundred pages to reveal what Sophie is and the place she inhabits. When he is finished, we have not only become acquainted with Sophie; our impression of Emile, gleaned from our reading of books 1–4, has been transformed.

The Difference of Sex

"Everything that characterizes the fair sex ought to be respected as established by nature," Rousseau says (p. 363). As book 5 proceeds, however, it becomes clear that in attributing traits to Sophie and calling them "natural," Rousseau is selective. What exactly are Sophie's characteristics? To know the answer to this question, one need only recall the song Irving Berlin wrote in 1946 for *Annie Get Your Gun*. The girl that he marries, sings the hero of that musical comedy, must wear lace, satin, nailpolish, and cologne. Soft and pink, she must be a doll he can carry.[2]

Rousseau's Sophie "awaits the moment when she will be her own doll" (p. 367). She has an agreeable and nimble mind. She loves adornment. Guile is a natural talent of hers, as is the art of coquetry. Rousseau, however, does not envision these or Sophie's other "natural" characteristics as emerging full-blown at birth. Like the traits of fierceness and gentleness Plato attributes to his future guardians, Sophie's natural qualities at birth are simply aptitudes or potentialities that require training and education so that they will be neither stunted nor abused.

In Sophie's case Rousseau clearly embraces Plato's Postulate of Specialized Natures: Sophie's nature is for him as inborn, fixed, and specific as the natures of the inhabitants of the Just State are for Plato. Rousseau also embraces the Postulate of Correspondence: Sophie's nature suits her for one and only one role in society, that of wife and mother.³ Her proper purpose, Rousseau says, is to produce not just a few but many children. If this appears to be a biological rather than a societal role, let it be understood that Sophie must also give the children she bears to her husband; that is to say, she must make it clear to him and the world, through her modesty, attentiveness, reserve, and care for his reputation, that he is their father. The unfaithful woman, Rousseau says, "dissolves the family and breaks the bonds of nature. In giving the man children that are not his, she betrays both" (p. 361). Thus Sophie is destined to be not simply the bearer of children but the preserver of family bonds. She is destined also to govern her husband's household, oversee his garden, act as his hostess, rear his children, and above all please him. In sum, she is to play the traditional female role in the traditional patriarchal family.

Rousseau speaks the language of nature, but his conception of education is, like Plato's, that of production. Sophie is raw material to be turned by education into a finished product. The product happens to be one that Plato rejects, at least for the guardian class of his Just State; also Plato's assumptions about his raw material are quite different from Rousseau's. Nonetheless, the basic structure of Rousseau's account of the education of Sophie is identical to that of Plato's account of the education of the artisans, auxiliaries, and rulers in his Just State. Plato's is not a pure production model of education and neither is Rousseau's. Sophie's education has the task of equipping her for her societal role. "Whether I consider the particular purpose of the fair sex, whether I observe its inclinations, whether I consider its duties, all join equally in indicating to me the form of education that suits it" (p. 364). Rousseau thus embraces the Functional Postulate as well as the Postulate of Specialized Natures and the Postulate of Correspondence. And when he says, "Once it is demonstrated that man and woman are not and ought not to be constituted in the same way in either character or temperament, it follows that they ought not to have the same education" (p. 363), it becomes quite clear that he also embraces Plato's postulates of Identity and Difference. As Plato formulates these postulates they connect educational treatment with societal roles. Because, for Plato, societal roles correspond to people's natures, he ultimately connects educational treatment with people's natures. That is just what Rousseau does when he prescribes different educational treatments for Sophie and Emile according to their natures.

Historians of educational thought see Rousseau's guiding metaphor as growth: he conceives of the child as a plant whose development is determined by nature, and of the educator as a gardener whose task is to ensure that corrupt society does not interfere with the predetermined pattern of development.[4] But if a conception of education as growth were implicit in his account of Sophie, Rousseau would not devote so much attention to the possibility of Sophie's acquiring characteristics that he says are not by nature hers. Roses may fail to blossom if their gardener does not tend them, but whatever the gardener's skill and diligence, a rosebush will not bear avocados. For one who directs his readers time and again to follow nature, Rousseau is inordinately concerned that Sophie might become something other than the obedient wife and nurturant mother he wants her to be. Will Sophie "be nurse today and warrior tomorrow?" Rousseau asks. "Will she suddenly go from shade, enclosure, and domestic cares to the harshness of the open air, the labors, the fatigues, and the perils of war?" (p. 362). Not if Rousseau has his way. Yet the very questions acknowledge that she might were her education not strictly supervised. "To cultivate man's qualities in women and to neglect those which are proper to them is obviously to work to their detriment," he continues (p. 364). In Rousseau's concern to tell mothers not to make men out of their daughters, a production interpretation of his theory of education finds its vindication.

As Rousseau imagines Sophie, she is born with a wide range of capacities and potentialities. The traits he calls natural are those that, in his view, *should* be developed, but they are certainly not the only ones that *could* be developed. Because Sophie can acquire any number of traits that Rousseau would rather she did not, it is not plausible to attribute to him a conception of the teacher or tutor as a gardener who provides the proper conditions for a plant to flourish. Rousseau's educator must attend to every detail of Sophie's education so that the traits Rousseau deems inappropriate to the role of wife and mother in a patriarchal context are frustrated and those he thinks belong to that role are fostered. Rousseau appeals to nature, but he does not trust it. Just as Plato insists that positive steps be taken to shape his future guardians to meet relatively clearly defined specifications, so Rousseau does this same thing in regard to Sophie.

Thus, the education of Sophie constitutes an anomaly for the standard interpretation of *Emile*. What Rousseau has to say in book 5 is not merely left unexplained; it *cannot* be explained by an interpretation that abstracts education from societal influences and constraints and pictures it as a process of natural growth and development. Nor can it be explained by an interpretation that assumes, as this one does, that Rousseau posits autonomy as a universal ideal.

The object of the education Plato claims for his female guardians is to develop reason to the point where it can grasp the most general principles and ultimately discern the Good, so that the individual can rule herself and her fellow citizens. The education Rousseau would provide women could not be more dissimilar. Sophie, the prototype of a woman, is to be educated not to rule but to obey. She is to learn to be modest, attentive, and reserved; to sew, embroider, and make lace. Works of genius are out of her reach, Rousseau says, nor does she have the precision and attention to succeed at the exact sciences. The end product that Sophie is to become is Emile's dependent wife. Small wonder that historians of educational thought ignore Sophie or else dismiss her as an aberration. Rousseau's account of her education raises serious questions about the emphasis on growth and autonomy in the traditional interpretation to which they subscribe.

How could such radically different proposals for the education of women be arrived at by philosophers who make the same fundamental assumptions about education? As we have seen, the postulates of the production model of education are purely formal. Plato gives them content by positing three distinct societal roles. Instead of singling out for Sophie one of these roles distinguished by Plato, Rousseau specifies the traditional female role in a patriarchal society and maps its associated traits and skills onto her nature. The nature of the future female guardians suits them to rule the state, whereas Sophie's suits her to obey her husband. Because both Plato and Rousseau conceive of the task of education as fitting people into slots in society, it is to be expected that Sophie and Plato's female guardians will receive very different educations.

Why do Plato and Rousseau give such radically different contents to the postulates of the production model of education? As we know, the role Rousseau assigns to Sophie is not available to Plato. He could perhaps have made his female guardians responsible for carrying on the reproductive processes required by the Just State. Had he done so, he might have designed an education for them that would overlap Sophie's: one that would prepare them to care for and rear children, if not preserve family bonds; to cook and clean, if not protect a husband's reputation and obey his commands. But he did not, for what he considered good reasons. Plato and Rousseau, philosophers who make the same fundamental assumptions about education in general, have given us divergent theories about it for women because Rousseau consciously rejects two elements in Plato's philosophy. Against Plato he argues that if the family is removed from a society, the bonds of love which Plato wants to establish among members of the guardian class and the attachment he wants them to have for the state cannot develop. It is "by means of the small fatherland which is the family that the heart attaches itself to the large one," Rousseau says (p. 363). Also contrary to Plato, Rousseau maintains that sex is *the* determinant of a person's nature.

Aware of Plato's opinion on the difference of sex, in *Emile,* book 5, Rousseau argues that being male or female *is* a difference that makes a difference in determining a person's place in society; indeed, a close reading of book 5 suggests he believes sex is the *only* difference that makes a difference. "Sophie ought to be a woman as Emile is a man," Rousseau says. "That is to say, she ought to have everything which suits the constitution of her species and her sex in order to fill her place in the physical and moral order" (p. 357). The implications of this statement are clear: Sophie has one place to fill, Emile another, and their education ought to equip them for their respective places. Because the places of the two sexes are different, it seems evident to Rousseau that the education each is to receive must also be different.

Rousseau's Production Model

How is one to explain the fact that the standard interpretation of Rousseau's educational philosophy as one of growth and autonomy does not fit what he says in book 5 of *Emile* about the education of girls and women? Some psychological theories that have difficulties incorporating findings about females have turned out, upon investigation, to have been derived from male data.[5] Similarly, this interpretation of Rousseau's philosophical theory can be seen to be based on books 1–4 of *Emile,* in which he discusses only the education of boys.

In the past few years commentators on Rousseau have turned to the study of *Emile,* book 5.[6] Documenting thoroughly the sex bias not only in his theory of female education but in his political ideals, such feminist scholars as Zillah Eisenstein, Lynda Lange, and Susan Moller Okin have shown that Rousseau does not intend his proposals for Emile's education to apply to Sophie's, indeed does not even extend to women his political ideals of liberty and equality. Yet, while this new scholarship on Rousseau reveals the inadequacies of a growth interpretation of his philosophy of female education and his failure to hold up for women the ideal of personal autonomy, it has tended to assume the validity of the standard interpretation for Emile if not for Sophie. In the past, those commentators on *Emile* who have recognized Sophie's existence have usually taken it for granted that Rousseau makes fundamentally different assumptions about the education of males and that of females; indeed, that the education he proposes for men and women is based on directly conflicting principles. Recent scholarship does not challenge this perception of Rousseau as an educational dualist committed to two distinct theories of education, one for males and one for females.

The view that Rousseau embraces a growth model of education and the ideal of personal autonomy for Emile and Plato's production model and the ideal of dependency for Sophie is undoubtedly preferable to one that ignores Sophie altogether or misrepresents what Rousseau has to say about her. We should not attribute such a marked conflict in educational philosophy to a thinker of Rousseau's stature, however, without first determining if a unified interpretation of the education of Sophie and Emile can be given.[7] Granted, we have now established that his proposals concerning Sophie do not embody a growth model of education. How sure are we, however, that the production model implicit in his account of her education is not also to be found in his account of Emile's? And if it is, what consequences has this discovery for the vision of Emile as Autonomous Man?

At the beginning of book 1 of *Emile* Rousseau says that on leaving his tutor's hands a pupil will be neither magistrate nor soldier nor priest; rather, he will be a man. If we take Rousseau at his word, we must conclude that a narrow, vocational mold is not to be imposed on Emile. It does not follow, however, that Rousseau places no mold at all on him. Despite the imagery of plants and shrubs, Emile's tutor is not to allow every aspect of his student's potential to flourish; on the contrary, Rousseau's attitude toward Emile's education is anything but laissez-faire.

Rousseau wants Emile to be a morally autonomous individual—a rational man who joins thought and action, whose judgments are objective, and whose beliefs are formed independently of others—and he would have the tutor arrange each detail of Emile's education toward that end. In Emile's training to be as self-sufficient as possible—"Let the child do nothing on anybody's word," Rousseau says (p. 178)—it is no accident that the first book he is allowed to read is *Robinson Crusoe*.

The mold Rousseau imposes on Emile of the rational, moral, self-governing, self-sufficient individual may seem independent of any function Emile is supposed to play in society. It matches Rousseau's definition, however, of what he takes to be the most important role of all—namely, that of citizen in his ideal city state. *Emile* should be read in conjunction with *The Social Contract,* for the two works are complementary. *Emile* provides the educational theory that any account of an ideal state requires but that is not to be found in *The Social Contract* itself; *The Social Contract* enables one to understand how Rousseau solves the problem he poses at the beginning of *Emile*—educating Emile simultaneously as an autonomous man and a citizen.

The fundamental philosophical problem Rousseau tries to solve in *The Social Contract* is reconciling individual autonomy or freedom with membership in civil society. How can a person be free, Rousseau wants to know, if the person is a member of a civil society and hence subject to its laws? Rousseau's solution lies in his concept of the General Will. In contrast to what Rousseau calls the Will of All, which is the sum of the private wills of all citizens and as such disregards the common good, the General Will has the common good as its object. It is the result of deliberation in isolation from one another by citizens who are rational, impartial, and sufficiently informed about the issues.[8] Individual autonomy and obedience to law are reconciled in Rousseau's ideal state because the laws of that state are expressions of the General Will and because each citizen participates in that Will. The laws that each citizen must obey, which would seem to limit individual freedom, are enactments of the citizens' own objective deliberations about the common good. Thus, in obeying the laws of the state, each citizen in effect governs himself. Freedom is therefore preserved even as the state rules its subjects.[9] Moreover, because for Rousseau the General Will is always right, the individual's moral integrity as well as his autonomy is preserved in the state.

As Bloom says, Emile is, in effect, taught *The Social Contract*.[10] In educating Emile to be a man, Rousseau would equip him with the traits and skills that a citizen of his ideal city state must have. True, in the opening pages of *Emile* Rousseau contrasts man and citizen and questions whether it is possible for a given individual to be both at once. Yet in book 3 he has Emile learn a trade on the ground that "rich or poor, powerful or weak, every idle citizen is a rascal" (p. 195). Clearly, Rousseau's assumption is that Emile will be a citizen; he simply is not to be an idle one. In reading *Emile* one must distinguish between the role of citizen in the actual states Rousseau knew and that role in his ideal city state. Because his concept of the General Will was not embodied in any actual state, Rousseau believed that in an actual state an educator who wanted to raise a citizen would indeed be raising him to obey others. In Rousseau's ideal state, however, an educator would not have to choose between raising a free man and a citizen, for they would be one and the same.

Sophie's function as wife and mother, on the other hand, was well entrenched in the states with which Rousseau was acquainted, and there is no reason to suppose that he intended her function to disappear in the ideal city state of *The Social Contract*. Rousseau's arguments alone against Plato's abolition of the family are enough to suggest that Sophie would play the same role in that state as in Rousseau's own France. Moreover, in insisting that she is by nature subordinate to Emile's authority Rousseau makes it both necessary for her to remain in the traditional female role and impossible for her to be a citizen of the ideal state.[11] Okin has said that Emile is educated to be his own man, and Sophie is educated to be his own woman. It certainly seems this way; as his own man, Emile can be a citizen—that is, a participant in the General Will—without sacrificing his freedom. As Emile's own woman, Sophie can be neither a citizen in Rousseau's sense nor free in the sense of being an autonomous person.

Rousseau makes the same fundamental educational assumptions about Emile and Sophie. Both are born with certain aptitudes and capacities—different ones because Emile is male and Sophie is female. Since no one's natural talents are fully developed at birth, education is necessary for both. Their educations serve the function of equipping them to perform their respective societal role. Emile's education is totally different from Sophie's because, having a different nature, she is to have a different role. Were their natures and their roles the same, Rousseau would no doubt propose the same upbringing for them. The five postulates of the production model of education, which Rousseau embraces in relation to the education of Sophie, are also implicit in his account of the education of Emile.

Given the production model underlying Rousseau's account of Emile's education, Rousseau's definition of Emile's nature is not as open-ended as some have suggested. Emile is not "free to become whatever he can and will."[12] Just as Sophie must develop attractiveness, Emile must develop strength; as she must endure injustice, he must revolt against it. If Emile were really free to become anything at all, he would have no need for a tutor to control his total environment. Rousseau says to Emile's tutor:

> Do you not dispose, with respect to him, of everything which surrounds him? Are you not the master of affecting him as you please? Are not his labors, his games, his pleasures, his pains, all in your hands without his knowing it? Doubtless he ought to do only what he wants; but he ought to want only what you want him to do. He ought not to make a step without your having forseen it; he ought not to open his mouth without your knowing what he is going to say. (p. 120)

Readers of *Emile* cannot help but notice that the tutor manipulates Emile. In fact, Rousseau requires the tutor to perfect that art. Let your pupil "always believe he is master, and let it always be you who are," Rousseau says. "There is no subjection so perfect as that which keeps the appearance of freedom" (p. 120). Rousseau wants Emile from an early age to believe he is his own man. Manipulation is necessary, not because Emile's nature cannot flourish untended in a corrupt society, for until late adolescence or young adulthood Emile is to be educated in virtual isolation from all society, but because a citizen in Rousseau's ideal state is both a person who can transcend private interests and a person of independent judgment who is subservient to none; hence a range of vices and other weaknesses, from lying to arrogance, is denied Emile.[13] He has no more the option of becoming a gentle person and acquiring Sophie's keen powers of observation than of becoming a thief, for his education must equip him not only to be a participant in the General Will but to be head of the family Sophie serves. *Emile* ends when, a few months after the marriage of Emile and Sophie, Emile informs his tutor that he will soon be a father. If Sophie is destined to be wife and mother in a patriarchal family, Emile is destined to be the patriarch.

Recent commentary on *Emile,* book 5, has delineated the societal role Rousseau assigns to Sophie. It has overlooked, however, the significance for Rousseau's educational philosophy of the fact that, since Emile is to be Sophie's husband, to him belongs the societal role of patriarch. Thus, insofar as Rousseau's definition of Emile's nature is more open-ended than his definition of Sophie's, it is because his dual role of patriarch and citizen is more open-ended. Emile is not free to become anything at all. He is the one who exercises authority in the family, who has the ultimate say in decision making, who represents the family in its dealings with the outside world. He has no choice in these matters; he cannot decide to be Sophie's subordinate or to keep the house and garden and rear the children.

I emphasize Emile's patriarchal role here for, although Rousseau never explicitly links Emile's education to his participation in the General Will, book 5 leaves no doubt that Emile will play the dominant role in "the small fatherland which is the family" and that his education must equip him for this task. Thus, if proponents of the standard growth interpretation of *Emile* want to deny my claim that Emile's tutor is training him to be a citizen in Rousseau's sense of the term, they will still have to contend with Emile's other role as head of family. That role, which they can scarcely deny belongs to Emile, lends additional credence to a production interpretation of Rousseau's educational thought.

The conclusion is inescapable that the definition of Emile's nature, as of Sophie's, is selective. Emile has at birth a wide range of talents and potentialities, but Rousseau considers to be natural only those that he wants to see fully developed. These are the traits and skills he associates with the double role he assigns Emile: as head of family and citizen. One perceptive philosopher of education has said that if Rousseau's child "is to walk the path of nature, it will not be because there is a natural affinity between the child and this path, but because his tutor has led him along it."[14] It should be clear by now that the path along which the tutor leads Emile is defined by Emile's function, indeed, that Rousseau maps Emile's function onto his nature as surely as he maps Sophie's function onto hers.

Whether one takes Rousseau to be determining Emile's nature or discovering it, the principles governing the boy's education reveal Rousseau's disdain for traditional pedagogy. "I hate books," says Rousseau. "They only teach me to talk about what one does not know" (p. 184).

The senses alone should guide the first operations of the mind, he explains: "No book other than the world, no instruction other than the facts. The child who reads does not think, he only reads; he is not informing himself, he learns words" (p. 168). The principle that experience should precede verbal studies is important to Rousseau. In particular, books should be avoided until an age at which secondhand experience will amplify rather than substitute for firsthand experience.

It has been said that Rousseau discovered childhood. He certainly does tell Emile's tutor to respect childhood and to treat Emile according to his age. Rousseau understood what modern psychology now tells us, that children have their own ways of seeing, thinking, and feeling. "Nothing is less sensible," he says in book 2 of *Emile,* "than to want to substitute ours for theirs" (p. 90). That education must take age into account and, in particular, that the child's cognitive structures and emotional states must be respected are as central to Rousseau's philosophy of education as is the principle of delayed verbal learning.

Books 1 to 4 of *Emile* contain a number of important educational principles, many of which will sound familiar to those acquainted with the open classroom movement of the late 1960s and early 1970s and with the writings of radical school reformers of that period.[15] Rousseau maintains that educators should discard the distinction between work and play. Of Emile he says, "Whether he is busy or playing, it is all the same to him. His games are his business, and he is aware of no difference" (p. 161). In disregarding the dichotomy between work and play accepted by most educators, he maintains that education comes to us from nature and things as well as from men, and that in the early years, at least, learning should be a by-product of the child's daily occupations.

In book 3 of *Emile* Rousseau gives a wonderful example of the education he has in mind. When Emile's tutor lectures him, the boy is extremely bored and asks, "What's the use of that?" The tutor is sensible enough to stop the lesson. The next day they go for a walk before lunch. Time passes, tutor and pupil lose their way, and the boy becomes hot and hungry as they wander about. Emile does not realize that a simple copse hides the gate of Montmorency from them and begins to cry. At last the tutor asks, "My dear Emile, what shall we do to get out of here?" A Socratic dialogue ensues in which the tutor leads Emile to discover the direction of Montmorency. The two then take the path Emile proposes and arrive home in time to dine.

On this walk Emile acquires knowledge about the heavens without studying astronomy and without perceiving that he is learning the subject. The astronomy lesson illustrates Rousseau's belief in the efficacy of indirect learning as well as several other of his principles of good teaching. The teacher's first duty, Rousseau says, is to be humane and love childhood. He is to avoid excessive severity and excessive indulgence equally, and the primary instrument of teaching is to be well-regulated freedom. How many instructors consider a pupil's boredom to constitute part of the daily regimen! If Emile's tutor is not so inhumane as to insist that his ward endure his lectures, he is far from being overprotective. When Emile becomes hungry and frightened in the woods, the tutor does not pamper him by showing the way home. Furthermore, although the tutor allows Emile to turn away from a boring lecture, as well as to walk where he will and talk about what interests him, he also makes sure that Emile suffers the consequences of whatever choices he makes. Emile's hunger and fright in the woods are his own fault: he would not have lost his way had he listened to the astronomy lecture—or so his tutor reasons. Having chosen his course of action, Emile must not look to the tutor to bail him out of the trouble he brought upon himself.

The elements of books 1–4 of *Emile* that so many educators have found attractive are compatible with the unified interpretation of *Emile* presented here.[16] Indeed, the principles of teaching and learning set forth in these books can be understood as specifying the content of the educational treatment ordered by the Identity and Difference postulates. This interpretation preserves these important features of Rousseau's educational philosophy while making clear their relationship to other elements of his thought. It also explains why manipulation plays so large a part in Rousseau's educational thought. Once it is understood that the task of Emile's tutor is to produce an end product to predetermined specifications, the principle that the educator should give the pupil the illusion of freedom while controlling carefully what the pupil learns is what one would expect of an educational theory that tells the teacher to be humane but gives that teacher a hidden agenda.

The educational metaphor of growth is said to embody "a modest conception of the teacher's role, which is to study and then indirectly to help the development of the child, rather than to shape him into some preconceived form."[17] Given the total control the tutor exercises over Emile's education, it is difficult to understand how the standard texts in

the history of educational thought could have attributed a growth conception of education to Rousseau. The growth metaphor has been criticized for masking the fact that the educator must make choices no
gardener ever faces.[18] I would add to this the criticism that in drawing
attention to the development of the child, the growth metaphor conceals
the social and political dimensions of education. The opening pages of
Emile testify to Rousseau's awareness that the educational is the political.
He uses the language of growth, but he is not fooled by that language.
His interpreters *have* been fooled by it and have done Rousseau the injustice of supposing that the large political concerns with which he wres-
tled all his life play no part in the education he prescribes for Emile.

A production interpretation of Rousseau's educational thought acknowledges his concern for the political. It enables one to see beyond the
isolation in which Emile is to be raised to the theoretical standpoint from
which Rousseau, like Plato, envisions education as an enterprise linked
closely to political purposes and ideals. As we have noted, while Emile is
to be educated for the role of citizen, and hence for the political realm,
Sophie is not. Given the Difference Postulate, does this not mean that
Emile's education will be governed by one set of principles and Sophie's
by another, hence that a unified interpretation is not valid after all?

There are real differences in the education Rousseau proposes for
Sophie and Emile but the same principles govern both. For example,
Sophie is not given as much freedom as Emile. Because idleness and
disobedience are a girl's most dangerous defects, she must learn to conquer herself. Instead of allowing dissipation, frivolity, and inconstancy to
arise, as they will if her tastes are indulged, Sophie's teachers must see
to it that she is industrious and vigilant. "Always justify the cares you
impose on young girls, but always impose cares on them," says Rousseau
as he tells Sophie to work all day alongside her mother. Sophie is to be
subjected early to constraints Emile never knows, because all their lives
girls "will be enslaved to the most continual and most severe of constraints—that of the proprieties" (p. 369). Still, she is not to be subjected
to undue severity either; she ought not to live like her grandmother,
Rousseau says, but rather ought to be "lively, playful, and frolicsome, to
sing and dance as much as she pleases, and to taste all the innocent
pleasures of her age" (p. 374).

Similarly, Rousseau's dictum that, in learning, work and play ought
not to be separated applies to Sophie as well as to Emile. Sewing is

Sophie's work, but it is also her play; she wants to sew and learns how to do it in order to adorn her doll. The principle of delayed verbalization holds for Sophie's education as well. The uses to which reading is put will vary for Emile and Sophie, and this in turn may dictate a different choice of books; one can be sure that *Robinson Crusoe* will not be given to Sophie. Rousseau says, however, "If I do not want to push a boy to learn to read, *a fortiori* I do not want to force girls to before making them well aware of what the use of reading is" (p. 368).

Furthermore, Sophie's age must be taken into account in determining what is suitable. Thus, to the extent that boys and girls think, feel, and see in different ways, the principle that childhood must be respected is not to be abandoned in Sophie's education, but is to be applied in the light of her particular modes of thinking, feeling, and perceiving the world.

The difference between the education Rousseau proposes for Sophie and the one he proposes for Emile is accounted for not by a difference in its governing principles but, as we have seen, by the differences in the societal roles he assigns males and females. Thus, his urging that teachers be humane is not countermanded in Sophie's case; her role simply requires that the humanity of her teachers take particular forms. Even the fact that Emile is to be educated in isolation and Sophie is not can be explained without positing a conflict of principles. Since the role of citizen exists in society only in corrupted form, Rousseau deems it necessary to remove Emile from society. But since Sophie's role exists in at least some segments of society in its pure form, there is no need to remove her from family and friends. As Rousseau says: "In order to love the peaceful and domestic life, we must know it. We must have sensed its sweetness from childhood. It is only in the paternal home that one gets the taste for one's own home, and any woman whose mother has not raised her will not like raising her own children" (p. 388).

Rousseau is ambivalent about whether it would be possible for Sophie to acquire the rationality, objectivity, and independence he demands of those who participate in the General Will. Even as he insists that a woman is by nature incapable of grasping abstract truths, Rousseau warns that "a brilliant wife is a plague to her husband, her children, her friends, her valets, everyone" (p. 409). Even as he claims that Sophie is necessarily a dependent being, he expresses the fear that a woman will "abruptly and regularly change her way of life" (p. 362). This ambivalence is neither here nor there, however, for if she is indeed capable of acquiring the attributes Rousseau associates with the good citizen, Sophie's education will ensure that she does not.

The Union of Sophie and Emile

Although Emile is to fill the role of patriarch, Bloom considers the relationship between Emile and Sophie to be a union of complementary equals.[19] It is not at all clear that a union in which one person must always obey the other, as Sophie must obey Emile, can be one of equals, although Catharine Beecher will try to convince us of just this when she enters our conversation. Bloom, however, seems to think that Sophie's nature and education will make it so: "Rousseau argues that woman rules man by submitting to his will and knowing how to make him will what she needs to submit to. In this way Emile's freedom is preserved without Sophie's will being denied" (p. 25). There is no doubt that through the use of her "native" guile, Sophie will acquire power over Emile that will serve as a counterforce to his authority. He will be the one with the right to command; she will have the skills of manipulation. However, since Rousseau does not grant Sophie the authority to make her own decisions, let alone Emile's, it follows that the egalitarian ideal for which Rousseau is famous is to hold in the political, not the domestic domain. Since the political domain is not open to Sophie, the limits to Rousseau's egalitarianism are clear: equality is a principle intended to govern relations among males, not relations between males and females.

Although it is not a union of complementary equals, the marriage of Sophie and Emile is definitely one between individuals possessing complementary traits. "A perfect woman and a perfect man," says Rousseau, "ought not to resemble each other in mind any more than in looks" (p. 358). In the union of the sexes, he continues, each contributes in different ways to the common end: "One ought to be active and strong, the other passive and weak. One must necessarily will and be able; it suffices that the other put up little resistance." The partnership between a man and woman produces "a moral person of which the woman is the eye and the man is the arm." If the man were as good at details as the woman, and she could grasp general principles as well as he, "they would live in eternal discord" (p. 377). The moral person created by the marriage of Sophie and Emile is supposed to be a harmonious whole. Its two parts, while perfect of their kind, are not in themselves complete, for Emile lacks those traits belonging by nature to females and Sophie lacks those belonging by nature to males. In their union, wholeness is achieved, not because each finds fulfillment in the other's love, but because the two sets of traits when joined together form a perfect whole.

Rousseau's theory of marriage was given its modern expression in Marabel Morgan's *The Total Woman* (1973). "It is only when a woman surrenders her life to her husband, reveres and worships him, and is willing to serve him, that she becomes really beautiful to him. She becomes a priceless jewel, the glory of femininity, his queen!" Morgan says.[20] Like the girl the hero of Berlin's song would marry, the Total Woman is a reincarnation of Sophie. Sophie's modesty might preclude her from being the seductive lover the Total Woman is supposed to be and would certainly keep her from donning the outfits with which Total Woman greets her husband when he comes home from work. One suspects, too, that Sophie would lack the mercenary motive of Morgan's Total Woman:

> I have been asked if this process of adapting places a woman on a slave-master basis with her husband. A Total Woman is not a slave. She graciously chooses to adapt to her husband's way, even though at times she desperately may not want to. He in turn will gratefully respond by trying to make it up to her and grant her desires. He may even want to spoil her with goodies.[21]

Yet the Total Woman is as dependent on her husband's good will and her own guile as is Sophie. She may think of herself as her husband's queen, but she cannot help but know that she lives her life under the rule of a king.

Behind these twentieth-century variations lies Rousseau's assumption of complementary traits and spheres. The girl the man of the song marries must be soft, cuddly, and kittenish because he is tough, worldly, and rational. The Total Woman must admire, adapt, and acquiesce because her husband is strong and independent. She acquires her freezers and furs, not because she has deliberated about her family's needs, its financial situation, and her own desires, but by means of her manipulative skills. The Total Woman has the potential for rational thought and autonomous action, but, just as Sophie is not allowed to develop her potential because reason and independence are qualities reserved for Emile, so the Total Woman must deny hers.

The problem with this vision of marriage is that Rousseau's complementary-trait theory of gender, when buttressed by his theories of the education of Sophie and Emile, makes a harmonious union highly unlikely, if not impossible. For two people to live in harmony some traits must be shared. If a woman is not herself a rational, autonomous being, her marriage will be doomed. Wollstonecraft argues this point so well that I will leave it to her to pursue Sophie's side of the matter.[22] It would be a mistake, however, to suppose that for their union to be harmonious Sophie requires some of Emile's virtues but he requires none of hers. Sophie possesses not only the negative characteristics of coquetry and guile, docility and a willingness to obey even Emile's unjust commands. She is the one who teaches Emile to love his children. She is also the one who is by nature patient and gentle, tender and caring, and concerned above all to make the lives of her loved ones "agreeable and sweet" (p. 365). How harmonious can a marriage be in which all these virtues belong to one partner and not even one of them belongs to the other?

For Sophie, caring for Emile is its own reward. He will not—indeed cannot—reciprocate. For how long can unreciprocated tenderness and care last? Will Sophie not come to resent the absence in Emile's behavior toward her of those dispositions she displays in such abundance? Will she not lash out at him in anger or else, turning her anger inward, silently withdraw? If, emotionally, Emile is no more mature than a child, will Sophie not come to perceive him as just one more of her boys? And if he does become in her eyes a figure of scorn, will she be able to maintain the level of concern required to make his life agreeable and sweet?[23] In particular, will she be able to do this when he exhibits no concern at all for the quality of her life?

We need do no more than remark on the fact that without Sophie's virtues Emile himself will be a defective individual, for Rousseau knows this. The marriage he arranges is intended to correct Emile's emotional deficiencies—not by teaching him to be tender and caring but by giving him a tender, caring mate. Unfortunately, Rousseau does not have George Eliot's insight into the characters of his hero and heroine. He does not realize that just as the emotionally impoverished Mr. Casaubon, in *Middlemarch,* found his young wife's displays of tender devotedness increasingly distateful, so Emile may find it more and more difficult to receive Sophie's spontaneous exhibitions of care and concern; and that just as in the absence of reciprocating warmth Dorothea's patience and sympathetic understanding for Mr. Casaubon turned into silent criticism and even resentment, so Sophie may find herself becoming alienated from Emile.

Eliot's description of the plight of Dorothea Brooke and Mr. Casaubon is all too likely to apply to Sophie and Emile:

> If he would have held her hands between his and listened with the delight of tenderness and understanding to all the little histories which made up her experience, and would have given her the same sort of intimacy in return, so that the past life of each could be included in their mutual knowledge and affection—or if she could have fed her affection with those childlike caresses which are the bent of every sweet woman, who has begun by showering kisses on the hard pate of her bald doll, creating a happy soul within that woodenness from the wealth of her own love. That was Dorothea's bent. With all her yearning to know what was afar from her and to be widely benignant, she had ardour enough for what was near, to have kissed Mr. Casaubon's coat-sleeve, or to have caressed his shoe-latchet, if he would have made any other sign of acceptance than pronouncing her, with his unfailing propriety, to be of a most affectionate and truly feminine nature, indicating at the same time by politely reaching a chair for her that he regarded these manifestations as rather crude and startling.[24]

True, Rousseau maintains that Emile loves Sophie. Will he not, then, be as gentle and tender toward her as she is toward him? Bloom claims that "judiciously chosen comparisons presented at the right stage of life" will make Emile a gentle and beneficent man, and others, too, have attempted to trace the route Rousseau would have Emile take from *amour de soi* through *amour propre* to other-regarding virtues. One acute commentator, however, has pointed out that given Rousseau's definition of *amour de soi* as absolute self-love in the sense that it involves no reference to other beings, no path from it to a concern for others can be traveled.

John Charvet's discussion of individual identity and social consciousness in Rousseau's thought is complex.[25] For our purposes, however, two of his most significant findings can be detached from the whole argument. The first of these derives from the fact that until relatively late adolescence Emile's education is designed to give him virtually no knowledge of others or even of himself in relation to them. Rousseau sees childhood as a time simply to know oneself and something of the natural world. Thus he wants not only to separate the young Emile from society but to deny him knowledge of history, politics, human nature, and religion. For many years, then, Emile is supposed to exist for himself alone. If his education succeeds, he will know that other people exist, but he will not view them as individuals possessing an observing and judging consciousness. Thus, the educational problem facing Rousseau is that of transforming an absolutely nonsocial being into a social one. The crucial first step in this process is for the tutor to present Emile with cases of suffering. Activating his pity and love, these will cause Emile to identify emotionally with others and so, ultimately, to become a social and moral individual. Yet since it has not been allowed any chance to develop in childhood, out of what does Emile's capacity for pity and love arise?

In Rousseau's theory the very identification with others needed to develop these sentiments presupposes their prior existence. Furthermore, supposing that Emile were able to identify with others, Charvet makes it clear that he would be responding to them, not in all their particularity, but only in relation to those aspects of humanity he shares with them. As a social being, Emile would base his relations to others "on the abstract essence of men"—a notion Charvet finds incoherent.

Incoherent or not, a social relation in which people exist for one another as undifferentiated human beings rather than as particular individuals poses unresolvable problems for the union of Sophie and Emile. Since Sophie's nature is radically different from Emile's, one wonders if it would even be possible for him to identify with her essential self; that is, if he would be able to discern in Sophie qualities sufficiently like his own to permit the identification Rousseau has in mind. Charvet does not discuss Rousseau's theory of complementary traits in conjunction with his theory of social and moral development. Had he done so he might well have concluded that even if a route from self-love to gentleness, tenderness, and care could be constructed, it would not bring Emile close to Sophie. For Rousseau, sex makes such a difference that the identification with others, which in Emile's case is at once so necessary and so problematic, seems bound to be restricted to individuals of one's own sex.

If Emile cannot identify with Sophie—or, for that matter, with any woman—then, according to Rousseau's psychological theory, he cannot be expected to be tender and caring toward her. But, supposing now that Emile can identify with Sophie as a human being in essence no different from himself, one must ask if the consequent gentleness and beneficence he feels toward her is appropriate to the marriage relation. After all, Emile marries the unique person, Sophie, and not some abstract essence of humanity, and if he responds to her emotional needs at all, he is going to have to respond to her in all her particularity. As Eliot makes so clear in the case of Mr. Casaubon and Dorothea, that Emile feels beneficent to all mankind, and hence to Sophie, will scarcely satisfy Sophie's need for him to be tender on a certain morning or evening of her life. Whether Sophie's tenderness toward Emile turns to scorn or, as in the case of Dorothea Casaubon, to pity, the prospects are slight that her union to Emile will produce the "resonant, vibrant, constant" family life that Elshtain[26] claims Rousseau makes a precondition for his ideal polity. Elshtain captures Rousseau's intent, but his gender-based complementary theories of traits and of education defeat his own ends. The "private world" formed by the marriage of Sophie and Emile is as likely to be the arena of violence and hate contemporary sociologists perceive the modern home to be as a haven of warmth and love; as likely to be silent, gray, and claustrophobic, in the manner of that of Dorothea and Mr. Casaubon, as resonant, constant, and vibrant.[27]

The quality of the marriage of Sophie and Emile is of interest here not simply because their happiness is at stake but because the very possibility of their being completely moral depends on the success of their union. Only in marriage, or at least in heterosexual pairing, can Rousseau's males and females be perfectly whole. Yet surely, if the marital relationship is characterized by discord and strife, the union of traits required for the moral life will not be accomplished. But it is not only the moral perfection of Sophie and Emile that is in doubt. Remember that in Rousseau's philosophy "it is by means of the small fatherland which is the family that the heart attaches itself to the larger one." Since marriage provides the foundation upon which the family rests and the family, in turn, provides a "natural base" upon which the "conventional ties" of the state rest, the marriage of Sophie and Emile is bound up not only with their personal fates but with the destiny of the state itself.

In maintaining that love of one's nearest is the principle of the love one owes the state, Rousseau explicitly challenges Plato's removal of private family, home, and marriage from the lives of the guardians of the Just State. "That noble genius had planned everything, foreseen everything," he says (p. 362), yet he forgot that it is "the good son, the good husband, and the good father who make the good citizen." Rousseau was not the first to criticize Plato's social policies concerning the family. Aristotle, for one, had argued that Plato's aim of the greatest unity possible for the state was unacceptable and that, in any case, the result of the Platonic policies "would be the opposite of what Socrates intends: for it will weaken the ties between people."[28] Rousseau's disagreement with Plato is particularly instructive, however, because he accepts Plato's ideal of unity and places ultimate responsibility for achieving it on Sophie.[29] If the good state requires the good son, surely the good son requires the healthy family that it is Sophie's duty to create and maintain.

An inharmonious marriage may make a healthy family impossible, but supposing the latter to be achievable within the terms of Rousseau's philosophy, there is then a puzzling problem to be resolved regarding his claim for its educational function. While the hearts of Rousseau's citizens must be attached to the state, the thoughts and actions of these men are supposed to be both autonomous and governed by reason. So far as reason and autonomy are concerned, however, Rousseau takes the family to be a corrupting influence.[30] Why, after all, does he give up Emile's education entirely to a tutor? Why is Emile to be reared in virtual isolation? The goal of autonomy Rousseau holds up for Emile requires, in his view, not only that the boy's environment be tightly controlled but that Emile himself be kept from entering into intimate relationships with others.

If Emile does not grow up within a family, says Rousseau, he will not be able to develop the ties that as a citizen he must have to the state. If, on the other hand, he does grow up with parents and siblings, he will not be able to develop the rational autonomy a citizen must possess. He is thus damned if he does and damned if he doesn't. And so is Sophie, for if Emile does not become a self-governing person, he will not constitute her "other half"; on the other hand, if Emile does not learn to be affectionate as a child in a loving family, he will not be able to develop the ties he must have to Sophie, let alone to his state.

Even if life in families is conducive to the development of the autonomy Rousseau wants Emile to acquire, the prospects of the small fatherland's fulfilling its educational function in the state are dim. We must not forget that in this fatherland ruled by Emile, Sophie is the one who binds father to children, exhibits care for others, works to sustain relationships, and keeps in mind the interests of the whole family. She is the one who exemplifies what Nancy Chodorow refers to as "nurturing capacities"[31] and what Carol Gilligan has called an "ethics of care."[32] As we shall see, Wollstonecraft argues that Sophie's education makes it all but impossible for her to develop "other-regarding" virtues. But if, for the sake of argument, Sophie is granted the qualities she must have for the family to carry out its task of preparing citizens, it then appears that the wrong family members will receive the training in citizenship Rousseau intends the family to provide. It is "the good son, the good husband, and the good father who make the good citizen," says Rousseau (p. 363). Yet if Sophie is the nurturant, caring parent, we must expect her daughters, rather than her sons, to follow her example. In the family ruled by Emile but cared for by Sophie, is not a hypothesis of differential socialization for boys and girls the most plausible one to entertain? But if so, will not Sophie's sons develop over time their father's, not their mother's, traits and qualities?

One does not have to rely on a theory of socialization to reach the conclusion that only the girls born to Sophie and Emile will develop nurturant capacities and an ethics of care. Rousseau's complementary theory of traits and his philosophy of male and female education guarantee this. The qualities Sophie possesses by nature and education Emile does not. If educated properly, her daughters will share Sophie's qualities as her sons will share Emile's. We have already glimpsed the damage Rousseau's gender-based division of traits will do to the marriage of Sophie and Emile over time. That theory also contains the seeds of destruction of Rousseau's ideal state.

Rousseau considers the family a training ground for citizens because his state is to be a genuine community. Objecting to Plato's proposals about women and family, and also rejecting his elitist premises regarding ruling, Rousseau nonetheless embraces an essentially Platonic political vision. Like the guardians of Plato's Just State, his citizens are not intended to be unconnected, atomistic individuals of the sort posited by Hobbes in *Leviathan* but are to be tied to one another by bonds of mutual sympathy. Like Plato's rulers, they are supposed to be able to put aside their own purposes and postpone their own satisfactions for the good of the state itself.

The question, of course, is whether Emile's sons must acquire Sophie's other-regarding virtues to be good citizens. As any survey of educational programs for citizenship would reveal, the qualities of nurturance, care, and concern for others are not usually taken to be essential for citizenship, or even relevant to it. Yet just as Sophie must sustain relationships within the family, Rousseau's citizens must do this within the polity; and just as she must strive to preserve her family's life, they must strive to preserve the state's. As citizens, Sophie's sons must do and feel for one another and for the state what she does and feels for her husband and children. Unfortunately, however, as replicas of Emile they will lack the habits of mind, the repertoire of behavior, and the qualities of character this role requires.

Imagining a state whose citizens must possess Sophie's virtues and a home in which these flourish, Rousseau defends the private family against Plato's attack by assigning it the function of political socialization. Yet the family he envisions cannot fulfill this function because those members who at Sophie's knee will learn to be nurturant and caring are not the ones Rousseau destines for citizenship. How ironic! By his own theory, the people Rousseau claims to be suited by nature to be citizens—males—do not possess by nature and are not allowed to acquire by education or socialization characteristics he himself deems essential for the good citizen. At the same time, the very people who do, or at least can, possess these characteristics by nature and education—females—are barred by his theory from the citizenship role.

Dependent Women, Dependent Men

Rousseau's small fatherland, then, is incapable of performing the task that, in his argument against Plato, he makes its raison d'être. It cannot provide the political socialization it is supposed to offer because the community-oriented virtues the citizens of Rousseau's ideal state must have are tied in his philosophy to the wrong gender. Worse still, instead of demonstrating that the family is a precondition of the ideal state, the union of Sophie and Emile vindicates Plato's belief that the private family is a divisive institution.[33]

In Rousseau's ideal state citizens must have the good of the whole in view; they must not act on the basis of their own private interests. Consider, however, that through long experience as the object of his tutor's manipulative tactics Emile has been trained to be pliant while, at the same time, Sophie has been trained to be manipulative. Add to this the fact that although Sophie's education is perhaps intended to make her sensitive to the good of her family, it is designed to keep her ignorant of the political, economic, and social issues a citizen of the ideal state must decide. Furthermore, as Okin points out, nothing in the education Rousseau prescribes for girls "leads to the expectation that patriotic loyalties will take precedence over personal or selfish ones."[34] Thus, a pliant Emile, whose manipulator is Sophie, will not be able to fulfill his function as a citizen, for Sophie's power over him will be turned to her own advantages. Since she is a good wife and mother, her private interests will presumably encompass the well-being of her family, but they will not necessarily include the well-being of the state.

Chiding Plato for insisting that the institution of the family be abolished for his guardian class in the interests of the unity and preservation of his Just State, Rousseau fails to see that Plato's script about divided loyalties will be acted out in Emile's living room. Sophie's domain is the home. By nature and education she is prevented from caring about any larger realm. Thus the only needs she will feel, the only desires she will have, the only aims she will pursue, will be personal and familial. When these are consonant with the public good the fact that she is accustomed to manipulating Emile to her own ends will be of no consequence. But when private and public purposes clash, as they inevitably must, Sophie's considerable manipulative skills will be directed to causing Emile to favor familial interests over his public obligations. Rousseau evidently admires Sophie for the power she will wield over Emile, and Bloom attributes her freedom to it. Both men apparently forget that in manipulating Emile, Sophie is manipulating not just her husband but a citizen.

This is not to say that the influence Sophie exerts over Emile will necessarily incline him to evil. There is no reason to believe that when public and familial purposes diverge the public ones should always take precedence. Rousseau insists, however, that the citizens of his ideal polity must set aside their private interests, and it is not at all clear that Emile will be able to do so. Assuming that he himself discerns the public good, he cannot hope to convince Sophie by rational persuasion to sacrifice her private wants for it: rational argument is not her strong point, and the public good is not her concern. It might seem that he could command her to do so and that she would have to submit, but we should not underestimate her manipulative powers and Emile's susceptibility to them. When her own or her family's interests are threatened by the state's, we can be confident that she will find a way around whatever inclination Emile may have to act in the public interest without his realizing that she has done so. Thus, as Plato could have told him, the private family Rousseau constructs acts as a centrifugal force in a state whose goal is unity.

Even if Rousseau's citizens are not induced by their wives to place private advantage over the public good, they will inevitably fail in their attempts to be good citizens. As we have seen, although his definition of the citizen role incorporates some traits he assigns by nature and education to males—for instance, independent judgment—it includes others he assigns to females—for instance, caring for others. His females would do no better in the citizen role, however, for while they would possess some qualities males lack, they would in turn lack other significant ones. In truth, the only people in Rousseau's philosophy who could conceivably fill the role of citizen, as he defines it, are the male-female pairs created by marriage. Rousseau never contemplates this alternative, for it implies that Sophie would have to be educated in public issues and taught to make the state's purposes her own. And if Sophie were so dedicated, then the question would arise of how two individuals could act as a single citizen; in particular, whose opinion would be decisive if Sophie and Emile disagreed on what ought to be done? Furthermore, this preparation for citizenship and her participation with Emile in the citizen role would place her in the midst of the very political processes Rousseau wants to maintain as a male preserve.

Instead of proposing a scenario in which married couples rather than individuals are citizens, we could, of course, adjust Rousseau's theory so that citizenship education would be allowed to compensate for the failings of nature by fostering in Emile such traits as gentleness and patience. But if education were allowed to be compensatory for one sex, why not for the other? If it is legitimate to educate Emile in the emotional capacities he lacks by nature, would it not be legitimate to educate Sophie in the capacities for abstract reasoning and independent judgment she lacks? Once a wedge is inserted between Rousseau's complementary-trait theory of gender and his educational theory, there is no basis for denying Sophie an education in the traits belonging to Emile by nature. But then this proposal backfires as a strategy for saving Rousseau's theory, for it would allow *both* Emile and Sophie to possess the qualities needed to be not only citizens of the ideal state but also heads of families. A compensatory theory of education grafted onto Rousseau's complementary theory of gender would entail the collapse of his patriarchal philosophy.

Rather than allow education to compensate for the deficiencies of male and female natures, we could simply interpret Rousseau's complementary-trait theory of gender as allowing some traits to belong by nature to both sexes. Such an interpretation is plausible since Rousseau never denies that Sophie and Emile share certain qualities, for example, an aptitude for reading. Thus, it would seem that we could allow Emile the luxury of acquiring the other-regarding virtues essential for maintaining Rousseau's polity. But this strategy is also doubled-edged. For if some traits belong by nature to both sexes, why not those of abstract reasoning and independent judgment? If we are free to build Sophie's virtues into Emile's nature, why not Emile's into Sophie's? A compensatory theory of human nature serves Rousseau's purposes no better than a compensatory theory of education. It may make Emile better fit to be a husband and citizen, but it will also make Sophie fit to be a citizen and head of family.

The problem Rousseau's political philosophy faces is that by virtue of his theory of education and his theory of gender *neither* Sophie *nor* Emile will be qualified for citizenship. And if these theories are modified, then *both* Sophie *and* Emile will qualify for that role. In order to ensure that Emile alone is fit to be a citizen, Rousseau must give up his theory of the ideal state as a close-knit community and his characterization of Sophie as manipulative. Then it will not matter that Emile is unable to possess the traits belonging to an ethics of care or that Sophie has no concern for the state. This strategy, however, would make Rousseau's assertions of Sophie's power even less convincing than they already are. It would also make Rousseau's political philosophy much less original and compelling than it is. Moreover, it would further undermine his arguments against Plato for the preservation of the institution of private family, for that rests on the claim that individuals must be socialized to the virtues of community.

Earlier I cited Okin as saying that Emile is his own man and Sophie his own woman. That is the way Rousseau intends matters, but when Rousseau's account of the educations of Sophie and Emile are read together, one can see that the hidden curriculum in manipulation Rousseau arranges for Emile may well counteract Emile's explicit curriculum in self-governance. If in theory Emile is to be his own man, he is likely in fact to go through life as Sophie's marionette. As such, of course, he scarcely deserves the label Autonomous Man.

The autonomy Rousseau attributes to Emile actually has two aspects: Emile is to be self-governing in the manner of Plato's rulers and self-sufficient in the manner of his fictional hero Robinson Crusoe. However, just as Emile's self-governance is limited by Sophie's manipulative impulses, so his self-sufficiency is limited by his need of her. In loving Sophie, if he does, Emile becomes dependent on her loving him in return.[35] But apart from the question of love, Emile's dependence on Sophie is marked. He needs her not just to love him but to feed him, run his household, bear his children, rear them, even teach him to love them. He can do none of these himself. Nor by himself can he be a complete moral person. For this, too, he needs Sophie, as he does if he is to possess the attachment to the state he must have in order to be a good citizen. What greater dependency than Emile's can there be?[36]

We have already seen how, in relation to the accepted growth interpretation of Rousseau's philosophy of education, Sophie constitutes an anomaly. We are now in a position to see that Sophie's existence also calls into question the standard interpretation of Emile as an autonomous person. So long as Emile's relation to Sophie remains hidden, as it does when *Emile*, book 5, is ignored, this interpretation of his nature and destiny may seem warranted. Once Sophie's place in Emile's life is revealed, however, it can be seen that her manipulation of her husband undermines all claims to his being a self-governing person, just as his dependence on her for the material and emotional conditions of morality, citizenship, and, indeed, of life itself undermines the claims of his being a self-sufficient person.

Recent commentary on book 5 has made clear just how dependent on Emile Sophie is. Let us not forget that Sophie manipulates Emile because, possessing neither economic nor political power of her own, her sole alternative is to channel his resources to her ends. One who can get what she wants only by indirection, who must act the coquette, flatter and dissimulate to achieve her purposes, is no more a self-sufficient agent than is the person she manipulates. Denied access to the role of citizen, prevented from developing her intellectual powers, confined to her home, trapped in a marriage to an untender mate all of whose decisions she must abide by, Sophie is profoundly dependent on Emile. Nonetheless, we must not overlook the fact that in Rousseau's philosophy the dependency between females and males runs in two directions. Sophie's dependence on Emile is neither deeper nor more fundamental than Emile's on her. Just as in Plato's Just State no individual is self-sufficient and every person needs the services others provide, so in the land of Sophie and Emile no one is absolutely self-sufficient and everyone is dependent on at least one other human being.

The difference between Plato and Rousseau is that Plato builds human dependency into his social philosophy by means of his tripartite division of human natures and, consequently, of human labor and by his three-track system of education. His guardians need the artisans if they are to have food, clothing, and shelter, let alone the luxuries of life. His rulers and artisans need the auxiliaries to defend their land from invaders. His auxiliaries and artisans, in turn, need the rulers since they themselves are incapable of knowing the right thing to do. In contrast, Rousseau builds human˙ dependence into his social philosophy by means of his gender-based theory of complementary traits and division of labor and his two-track system of education. Furthermore, Plato would have us recognize the dependence on others of every individual in his Just State for what it is—a fundamental premise of social existence—whereas Rousseau is evasive about the dependence of males on females.

Obviously, Rousseau is aware of Sophie's place in Emile's life even if some of his interpreters are not. Why, then, this double standard according to which Sophie's dependency on Emile is repeatedly brought to our attention, whereas his dependency on her, although well documented, is minimized? Correctly perceiving dependency to be a necessary condition of being human, Rousseau builds the dependency of males on females into his account of Emile's nature.[37] Yet although Emile's education is supposed to follow nature, it does not fit him for a lifelong attachment to the person on whom his well-being by nature depends. Moreover, in trying to make a Robinson Crusoe of Emile, Rousseau does not seem to appreciate the extent to which Emile's self-sufficiency is circumscribed by his gender-based theories.

One answer to the question of why the double standard with respect to dependency is that Rousseau, like so many other political thinkers, assigns both women and the reproductive processes of society to the ontological basement and therefore does not consider Sophie's services important enough to classify Emile's reliance on them as an instance of dependence. Rousseau certainly has reason to be blind to Emile's dependency on Sophie, for this enduring fact of Emile's life calls into question the appropriateness of the ideal of self-sufficiency Rousseau holds up for males. But it must be acknowledged that Rousseau reveals a greater understanding of the social and political significance of the family and its associated processes than many Western philosophers have. Had he not blurred the two faces of autonomy, he might have been willing to say explicitly that the relationship of Sophie and Emile is one of reciprocal dependence. After all, Rousseau's primary concern is that Emile be a self-governing individual, for only then can he participate in the General Will. Had Rousseau understood, as Plato does, that autonomy in the sense of self-governance is compatible with extreme dependence on others, he could have accepted Emile's dependency on Sophie without fearing that his ideal of a self-governing man would be called into question. Of course, in being Sophie's marionette Emile falls short of attaining the ideal of self-governance, but that is another matter. At issue here is the fact that in making Emile dependent on Sophie and consequently not self-sufficient, Rousseau mistakenly assumes that Emile's autonomy, in the sense of self-governance, is necessarily sacrificed.

Anyone who doubts that dependence on others is compatible with self-government should read the play *Whose Life Is It Anyway?*[38] Paralyzed from the neck down, Ken Harrison, the protagonist, is completely dependent on others for the performance of everyday tasks. Despite his almost total lack of self-sufficiency, however, he is as capable as anyone of making his own decisions, even that most fateful one of whether to continue living. Whether or not one agrees with his decision to take his own life, whether or not one sympathizes with the doctor who tries to prevent him in that one instance from being a self-determining agent, one cannot doubt Ken Harrison's capacity for self-governance. The play can thus be interpreted as testing to its very limits Plato's insight that human dependency and individual self-governance can go hand in hand.

Perceiving any dependence on others to be a failure of autonomy, Rousseau is loath to acknowledge Emile's dependency on Sophie. He does not deny Sophie's dependence on Emile because he never attributes autonomy in general or self-governance in particular to her. In treating the dependency of Sophie and Emile in different ways, he is thus consistent. Unfortunately, Rousseau's interpreters have allowed themselves to be misled by his talk of self-sufficiency. Never having read books 1–4 of *Emile* in conjunction with book 5, they have not understood that Sophie's services lie hidden beneath the ideal of Autonomous Man that Rousseau holds up for Emile. If all goes according to his tutor's plan, Emile's security will be assured by his marriage to Sophie, and the myth of his self-sufficiency, which Rousseau would have us embrace, will be sustained. Never looking in the ontological basement, no one will discover that Emile's dependency on Sophie is at least as great as hers on him.

Recent feminist commentators have remarked on Rousseau's fear that men will be enslaved by female sexuality.[39] If, as they argue, he designs the relationship between Sophie and Emile so as to avoid this, his gender-based theories of complementary traits, division of labor, and education make it certain that his men's lives will still be governed by their need for the services only his women can supply.

Upon first reading *Emile,* book 5, one is tempted to say that historians of educational thought have done women a favor by ignoring a pernicious ideal. However, we need to ask, as did Adrienne Rich in her 1978 speech to teachers of women: what does a woman need to know if she is to think of herself, not as one of the boys, not as a neuter or an androgyne, but as a woman? Rich responded to her own question:

> Does she not, as a self-conscious, self-defining human being, need a knowledge of her own history, her much politicized biology, an awareness of the creative work of women of the past, the skills and crafts and techniques and powers exercised by women in different times and cultures, a knowledge of women's rebellions and organized movements against our oppression and how they have been routed or diminished? Without such knowledge women live and have lived without context, vulnerable to the projections of male fantasy, male prescriptions for us, estranged from our own experience because our education has not reflected or echoed it. I would suggest that not biology, but ignorance of our selves, has been the key to our powerlessness.[40]

In claiming their education, women need to know about the negative ideals held up for them as well as the positive ones. Since Rousseau's program for Sophie is a part of our history, it needs to be studied in detail; its relationship to his political and social visions must be understood if we are to claim more adequate ideals for women's education. And it is important to study Rousseau's account of Sophie's education in conjunction with his account of Emile's, for some of the defects of the latter are revealed and illuminated only in the comparison.

There is a danger of overreacting to the story of Sophie and Emile by despising Sophie in toto while embracing Emile's image for both sexes. Wollstonecraft is about to tell us that Sophie's education is so atrocious that it does not even fit her to be the good wife-mother Rousseau wants her to be. Moreover, as we have seen, that education is not well designed for one who is to pull the strings of a participant in the General Will. But the deficiencies of Sophie's education are matched by the deficiencies of Emile's. It is his education, after all, that prepares him to be Sophie's marionette rather than a self-governing citizen. It is his education that makes of him an inadequate husband, father, and community member.

Upon hearing Wollstonecraft's contribution to our conversation, we will discover what a strong attraction Emile has for even the most vociferous critic of Rousseau. Let us, therefore, remember that Emile is at best a partial human being and that Sophie possesses virtues he desperately needs but can never attain. Let us remember also that many of the societal tasks she is to perform for Emile are essential and that Emile is qualified neither by nature nor by education to carry them out. This is not to say that we should accept a gender-based theory of complementary traits such as Rousseau sets forth. That theory not only imprisons Sophie in the home, but threatens to destroy both Sophie and Emile and the ideal state itself. It is precisely because the ideal Rousseau holds up for Emile is grounded in his complementary-trait theory that we who reject the destiny Rousseau marks off for Sophie must also reject Emile's education for both men and women. An education intended for a person who is dependent on Sophie's services should hardly be claimed by those who consider that dependency exploitative and oppressive. Nor should an education designed for incomplete men such as Emile be claimed as the best possible one for either sex.

If we reject the particular form dependency takes in Rousseau's philosophy, we must not embrace in its stead the goal of absolute self-sufficiency Rousseau posits for Emile. As both Plato and Rousseau know, that goal is illusory. Rousseau's mistake is not that he fails to understand that dependency is an inescapable fact of life but that he considers it an evil and so does not acknowledge the implications of Emile's dependency, either for Emile's education or for Sophie's. Like Rousseau, Beecher constructs a theory of female education based on the interdependency of males and females, but rather than hide the fact of men's dependency on women, as Rousseau tries to do, in her social vision she focuses attention on it. Stressing Emile's insufficiency in domestic affairs, she transforms the arena of male dependency into a domain of female autonomy. Before we give her opinion of the matter a hearing, however, let us listen to what Wollstonecraft has to say to Rousseau about the havoc women like Sophie can wreak on dependent men like Emile.

4 Wollstonecraft's Daughters

No writer has made it clearer than Mary Wollstonecraft what it will cost Sophie to keep her "femininity" intact. No writer has constructed a better brief for ignoring the difference of sex in education. Of this remarkable English woman, whose *A Vindication of the Rights of Woman* was published in 1792, just thirty years after *Emile,* and who died in childbirth five years later, Virginia Woolf has said:

> Many millions have died and been forgotten in the hundred and thirty years that have passed since she was buried; and yet as we read her letters and listen to her arguments . . . and realize the high-handed and hot-blooded manner in which she cut her way to the quick of life, one form of immortality is hers undoubtedly: she is alive and active, she argues and experiments, we hear her voice and trace her influence even now among the living.[1]

Not all readers have shared Woolf's enthusiasm for Wollstonecraft the person or the philosopher. In 1946 the authors of a psychoanalytically oriented text wrote: "That Mary Wollstonecraft was an extreme neurotic of a compulsive type there can be no doubt. Out of her illness arose the ideology of feminism, which was to express the feeling of so many women in years to come."[2] Echoing Rousseau in saying that "whatever else men and women may be in relation to each other, they are not equal, identical. They are similar in species, different individually, and always complementary,"[3] these writers reduced Wollstonecraft's concern for the equality of women to an attempt to achieve masculinity, and they diagnosed her as "psychically ill." Did they not realize that the view of human nature underlying their analysis was the very thing Wollstonecraft was questioning?

Sophie Rejected

A Vindication of the Rights of Woman represents one long rejection of Rousseau's definition of Sophie's nature, the education he would give her, and the person he would have her become. Had historians of educational thought read this book, they could not have constructed their interpretations of Rousseau's philosophy. Unfortunately, although upon publication Wollstonecraft's commentary on *Emile*, book 5, reached a large audience, over time it became as invisible as Sophie herself. Thus, until the new scholarship on women brought Wollstonecraft's work once again to our attention in recent years, *A Vindication* could not serve as a corrective to those who mistakenly read Rousseau's account of the boy Emile as applying to both sexes.

A celebration of the rationality of women, *A Vindication* constitutes an attack on a view of female education that would render women artificial and weak by subordinating cultivation of understanding to the acquisition of some "corporeal accomplishment" (p. 23). The character of Sophie is undoubtedly captivating, says Wollstonecraft to Rousseau, but "it appears to me grossly unnatural." It is not Sophie's "superstructure" that concerns Wollstonecraft most "but the foundation of her character, the principles on which her education was built" (p. 24). Truth is hidden from women, she says, "and they are made to assume an artificial character before their faculties have acquired any strength" (p. 44). Like despots, women have perhaps more power now than they would "if the world were governed by laws deduced from the exercise of reason" (p. 40), but in obtaining that power the character of women is degraded.

In her novel *The House of Mirth*, written more than a century after the publication of *A Vindication*, Edith Wharton traced this process of degradation to its tragic conclusion. On what turns out to be the last morning of her life, Lily Bart lies awake considering her situation.

> She had learned by experience that she had neither the aptitude nor the moral constancy to remake her life on new lines, to become a worker among workers and let the world of luxury and pleasure sweep by her unregarded. She could not hold herself much to blame for this ineffectiveness, and she was perhaps less to blame than she believed. Inherited tendencies had combined with early training to make her the highly specialized product she was: an organism as helpless out of its narrow range as the sea-anemone torn from the rock. She had been fashioned to adorn and delight; to what other end does nature round the rose leaf and paint the humming-bird's

breast? And was it her fault that the purely decorative mission is less easily and harmoniously fulfilled among social beings than in the world of nature? That it is apt to be hampered by material necessities or complicated by moral scruples?[4]

Lily, a young woman struggling to maintain a place for herself in turn-of-the-century New York society, is a fictional representation of Sophie, or rather of *one* of the images of Sophie contained in *A Vindication*. Making pleasure her business, Lily reaps the very rewards Wollstonecraft imagines for Sophie. While pleasure continues to be the business of woman's life, Wollstonecraft says,

> little can be expected from such weak beings. Inheriting, in a lineal descent from the first fair defect in nature, the sovereignty of beauty, they have, to maintain their power, resigned the natural rights, which the exercise of reason might have procured them, and chosen rather to be short-lived queens than labour to obtain the sober pleasures that arise from equality. Exalted by their inferiority (this sounds like a contradiction), they constantly demand homage as women, though experience should teach them that the men who pride themselves upon paying this arbitrary insolent respect to the sex, with the most scrupulous exactness, are most inclined to tyrannize over, and despise, the very weakness they cherish. (p. 55)

Lily has inherited more than her fair share of beauty and has enjoyed the homage it has commanded without ever having been willing to acknowledge that there is a price to pay for being a sea-anemone, a rose leaf, a humming-bird's breast. "Ah!" Wollstonecraft continues:

> why do women, I write with affectionate solicitude, condescend to receive a degree of attention and respect from strangers, different from that reciprocation of civility which the dictates of humanity and the politeness of civilization authorise between man and man? And, why do they not discover, when "in the noon of beauty's power," that they are treated like queens only to be deluded by hollow respect, till they are led to resign, or not assume, their natural prerogatives? Confined then in cages like the feathered race, they have nothing to do but to plume themselves, and stalk with mock majesty from perch to perch. It is true they are provided with food and raiment, for which they neither toil nor spin; but health, liberty, and virtue are given in exchange. (pp. 55–56)

Wharton's lily of the field eventually exchanges not only health, liberty, and virtue for the sovereignty of beauty, but life itself.

Lily Bart exemplifies an ideal of the educated woman Wollstonecraft rejects on two related grounds. To be a moral individual, she says, one must exercise one's reason: "The being cannot be termed rational, or virtuous, who obeys any authority but that of reason" (p. 191). The exercise of reason requires, in turn, that knowledge and understanding be cultivated. In other words, an education of the mind is essential for the rationality that is the mark of the truly virtuous person. In denying Sophie such an education, Rousseau makes it impossible for her to be a moral creature. Insofar as the traits of character he allows her to develop—docility, coquetry, and the like—can be considered virtues at all, they are not moral virtues. Rousseau does not simply deny Sophie the possibility of being moral, however. He denies her immortality. "If woman be allowed to have an immortal soul," Wollstonecraft says, "she must have, as the employment of life, an understanding to improve" (p. 63).

If the requirements of morality and immortality demand that Sophie's education develop her reason as fully as possible, so, according to Wollstonecraft, do the requirements of the wife-mother role. Thus, she argues, Sophie's education is ill designed to fit her for the very societal role Rousseau assigns her. Wollstonecraft warns her readers, "The woman who has only been taught to please will soon find that her charms are oblique sunbeams, and that they cannot have much effect on her husband's heart when they are seen every day" (p. 27). Will Sophie be able to look to herself for comfort "when the summer is passed and gone"? It is more rational, says Wollstonecraft, to expect her to try to please other men, in order to forget the mortification her pride has received, than to cultivate her dormant faculties. "When the husband ceases to be a lover," Sophie's desire to please will become "a spring of bitterness" as love gives place to jealousy or vanity. In sum, Wollstonecraft rejects Sophie's education in the art of pleasing on the ground that it can be useful only to a mistress; a chaste wife and serious mother—as Rousseau wants Sophie to become—should consider her power to please simply as "the polish of her virtues" (pp. 27–28).

Wollstonecraft also rejects the education in dependency Rousseau prescribes for Sophie. A woman must be intelligent in her own right, Wollstonecraft argues, because she cannot assume that her husband will be intelligent. What if she never finds an Emile and must settle instead for a rough, inelegant man? "Husbands, as well as their helpmates," she says, "are often only overgrown children; nay, thanks to early debauchery, scarcely men in their outward form—and if the blind lead the blind, one need not come from heaven to tell us the consequences" (p. 22). And if

Sophie does find an Emile, she cannot assume that she will always have him. What if Emile dies? What if he leaves home to seek more agreeable society?

Sophie's education for dependency leaves her unfit to be a mother as well. "Meek wives are, in general, foolish mothers," says Wollstonecraft (p. 152). "If women be educated for dependence; that is, to act according to the will of another fallible being, and submit right or wrong to power, where are we to stop?" (p. 48). Will they not in turn make their children endure *their* tyrannical oppression? Just as women must submit without reason to their husbands' commands, "having no fixed rules to square their conduct by," they will be kind or cruel as the whim of the moment directs.

Supposing Sophie to be well disposed to carry out the duties of a mother, Wollstonecraft concludes that the education Rousseau designs for her will nonetheless make her unfit to perform them adequately, for a woman whose understanding has not been cultivated is "a slave in every situation to prejudice" and will either neglect her children or spoil them (p. 151). But, Wollstonecraft reminds us, a being taught only to please may not even care to mother her children. "What an example of folly, not to say vice, will she be to her innocent daughters!" she exclaims. Instead of making friends of her daughters, "the mother will be lost in the coquette" and will view them as "rivals more cruel than any other" (p. 49). An exhaustive list of the domestic miseries Sophie's family will endure, be she well or ill disposed to carry out her societal role, would fill pages. Inattention to her health during infancy and youth will keep Sophie, as a mother, employed guarding against her own sickness. Inattention to the formation of her character will make her unable to educate her sons or impress them with respect. Inattention to the enlargement of her mind will cause her to deprive her servants of innocent indulgences, to devote her motherly attentions to "the frippery of dress" instead of the management of family.

The fate Wollstonecraft foresees for Sophie, Emile, and their children—a fate Lily Bart perhaps foresaw for herself had she taken advantage of the opportunities for marriage that presented themselves—is not a happy one: the marriage will not be the harmonious union Rousseau desires; the private world of their family will not be resonant, vibrant, or constant. We must not be misled, however, by Wollstonecraft's efforts to demonstrate the incompatibility between Sophie's education and the place Rousseau reserves for her in society. Scornful as she is of what Sophie will become, Wollstonecraft agrees with Rousseau that woman's nature suits her for the traditional female duties. "Whatever tends to incapacitate the maternal character, takes woman out of her sphere," she says (p. 177). She leaves no doubt that this sphere is women's natural place when she insists that "the care of children in their infancy is one of the grand duties annexed to the female character *by nature*" (p. 151; emphasis added). If this passage suggests that Wollstonecraft assigns women to the wife-mother role only during their children's earliest years, numerous others make it clear that they must also care for their children and instruct them throughout childhood.

Clearly, Wollstonecraft's quarrel with Rousseau is not that he reads the traditional female role back onto Sophie's nature but that his definition of this role is wrong-headed. She wants to convince her readers that from the standpoint of his own theory the education Rousseau prescribes for Sophie is counterproductive in that it will not yield the end product he himself envisions: a chaste wife, a well-organized housekeeper, a tender mother. But Wollstonecraft is not satisfied simply to provide an internal criticism of his philosophy. She argues that Rousseau's conception of the wife-mother role is itself misguided, that the qualities of gentleness, docility, and "spaniel-like affection" make Sophie merely "the toy of man, his rattle" (p. 34).

Rational Women

"What gives her book its timeless appeal is not primarily the originality or the profundity of her ideas (for they have neither), not the eloquence of her prose (which is not always eloquent), but her devotion to her fellow men and her concern for their well being." Thus Charles Hagelman, Jr., introduces a 1967 edition of *A Vindication.*[5] Had he understood that Wollstonecraft wrote this book out of devotion for her "fellow" women, not her fellow men, Hagelman would not have been able to dismiss her ideas so easily.

It cannot be denied that the conceptual framework of *A Vindication* is derivative. Wollstonecraft is a daughter of the Enlightenment, a true eighteenth-century rationalist whose world view is indebted to John Locke and his intellectual descendants. Reason serves as the starting point for Wollstonecraft's political philosophy, as for Locke's. She believes that

there are rights that human beings inherit because they are rational creatures; that rationality forms the basis of these rights because reason, itself
God-given, enables them to grasp truth and thus acquire knowledge of
right and wrong; that the possession of reason raises humans above brute
creation; and that through its exercise they become moral, and ultimately
political, agents.

A *Vindication* belongs to the same powerful intellectual tradition as
the American Declaration of Independence. In its emphasis on the rationality of man and on the connections between reason, on the one hand,
and virtue, natural rights, and equality, on the other, Wollstonecraft's
political philosophy is neither more nor less original than Thomas Jef-
ferson's. Both thinkers share the Enlightenment belief in the efficacy of
knowledge and the reign of reason in the state as in the individual; both
understand that although man is born rational, his reason does not mature by itself but must be cultivated through education. Yet while Wollstonecraft embraces a world view shared by others, she is the one who
argues systematically for bringing women into its domain. The originality
and profundity of her ideas are not to be found in her eighteenth-century
rationalism per se but in the way she extends the fundamental tenets of
that philosophy to women. In A *Vindication* Wollstonecraft sets herself
a threefold task: to rebut the presumption that women are not rational
but are slaves to their passions; to show that if the rights of man are
extended to females, women's domestic duties will not suffer; and to
propose an education and upbringing for females that will sufficiently
develop their ability to reason independently so that they will clearly
deserve the same political rights as men.

In carrying out her first task Wollstonecraft's strategy is brilliant;
she puts her opponents in the awkward position of being committed to
the thesis that women are not human beings. This is accomplished by
her claim that there are only two possibilities: either women are human
beings or they are brutes; there is no middle ground. Since her opponents
presumably believe, as she does, that rationality is the defining characteristic of being human, the trap is set; those who would deny female
reason automatically relegate their wives and daughters to the realm of
brute creation.

Wollstonecraft knows better than to expect all her readers to shrink
from classifying women as brutes. Given the choice of attributing reason
to women or assigning them to a lower order of creation, some will

undoubtedly prefer the latter option. Thus, she does not rest content to force her opponents to choose between two unpalatable alternatives; she also shifts the burden of proof onto those who would deny the rationality of women.

To this end Wollstonecraft distinguishes between female appearance and female nature. Readily granting that most women do not seem to be rational creatures, she acknowledges that Sophie is not merely a figment of Rousseau's imagination but is alive and well in the England of her day, as she was in the France of his.[6] However, Wollstonecraft attributes the existence of Sophies in the world to their upbringing and environment rather than to their nature. Look at the way girls are raised! Look at their education! She argues that women are social constructions; therefore, whether by nature they are rational creatures or mere brutes one cannot say, for in the majority of cases their experiences, their training, and their instruction positively forbid their development of reason.

Wollstonecraft documents for her readers the details of what today we call female socialization. In so doing she reveals a sensitivity to the educative powers of the community perhaps matched only by Plato. As we have seen, Plato was well aware of the phenomenon of socialization; hence his program of censorship. But while Plato saw the dangers of exposing future guardians to stories in which gods and heroes were cowardly or quarrelsome, he failed to recognize the special ways in which a society can stunt the development of reason in females. Enlightenment thinkers acknowledged that reason's development could be stunted. Indeed, one of their central tenets was that the ills of society derived not from the exercise of reason but from its stultification by existing social institutions, that if reason were allowed to rule, progress would be assured. Part of Wollstonecraft's originality lies in her perception that it is both formal institutions such as the church and the informal education society transmits that prevent reason from developing.

Confident in her insights into female socialization, Wollstonecraft proposes an experiment in living. Since women have been denied the very sort of education necessary for the development of reason and instead have been brought up to be Sophies, it is impossible, she says, to know if they are rational by nature. Instead of continuing to give girls an education designed to produce more Sophies, provide them with one sufficient to cultivate their understanding, she suggests, and then see if women are not rational creatures. The burden of proof thus shifts: those who would deny women's rationality must first give females an education similar to that given males and must then evaluate its results.

Wollstonecraft even tells her readers how to interpret these results. Should you find—and you well may, she says—that the reason of males is more highly developed than that of females, do not conclude that females are not rational; any differences in rationality that emerge between the sexes will be ones of degree, not kind, for reason is everywhere the same. Thus, to succeed, the experiment to prove that women do not by nature possess reason must show that *no* understanding is cultivated in females by a rationalistic education.[7]

Wollstonecraft's approach to her second task, to show that women's domestic duties do not suffer when the rights of man are extended to females, is as inspired as her approach to the first. One would expect her simply to assert that citizenship is compatible with the wife-mother role, but she goes well beyond this. By redefining the wife-mother role, she makes the performance of women's domestic duties and even domestic tranquility dependent on the extension of the rights of man to woman and also a natural consequence of it.

According to Wollstonecraft, to be a good mother a woman must be intelligent. How can a woman void of reflection be capable of educating her children? How can she discern what is proper for them? How can she incline them to those virtues she is unacquainted with or to that merit of which she has no idea? Thinking is not enough, however. Steadiness of purpose is also necessary to the maternal character, and this requires strength of mind, as opposed simply to an active mental life. Good mothers, Wollstonecraft insists, will often be obliged "to act contrary to the present impulse of tenderness or compassion," on the one hand, because they must exemplify order, "the soul of virtue," and, on the other, because to be useful they must have a plan of conduct and be resolute enough to persevere in carrying it out (p. 68). In effect, to mother well a woman must be precisely what Rousseau's ideal citizen must be: her own legislator.

This redefinition of mothering has clear implications for marriage. The sense and the independence of mind required of the good mother are possessed by few women "who are taught to depend entirely on their husbands" (p. 152); indeed, a woman with sufficient judgment to manage her children "will not submit, right or wrong, to her husband" (p. 177). Thus, Rousseau's conception of the wife who obeys even her husband's unjust commands is rejected once and for all. Wollstonecraft's daughters must be their own persons in their relations to their husbands as well as to their children. Whereas for Rousseau harmonious marriage is predicated on the subordination of women, Wollstonecraft makes the equality of husband and wife its central feature.

Upon the equality of the marriage relation rests the rational affection Wollstonecraft considers to be the only enduring attachment between a husband and a wife. Love, which she associates with instability, disappears quickly in marriage, Wollstonecraft repeatedly says. "To seek for a secret that would render it constant, would be as wild a search as for the philosopher's stone, or the grand panacea." The master and mistress of a family "ought not to continue to love each other with passion," for if love does not subside into friendship it will be succeeded by indifference (p. 30). In the rational affection that for Wollstonecraft constitutes the only satisfactory marriage bond, the fondness of a lordly protector has no place. Instead, there must be mutual regard and respect.

To realize how remarkable Wollstonecraft's account of mothering is, one need only consider that as recently as 1957 the noted British psychoanalyst D. W. Winnicott wrote:

> You do not have to be clever, and you do not even have to think if you do not want to. You may have been hopeless at arithmetic at school; or perhaps all your friends got scholarships but you couldn't stand the sight of a history book and so failed and left school early; or perhaps you would have done well if you hadn't had measles just before the exam. Or you may be really clever. But all this does not matter, and it hasn't anything to do with whether or not you are a good mother. If a child can play with a doll, you can be an ordinary devoted mother.[8]

Her account of marriage is also remarkable. Wollstonecraft places women in the home, but she makes the home a brand-new place by changing both its emotional atmosphere and its social relationships. For Wollstonecraft, equality and rational affection are the essence of the harmonious union Rousseau sought in *Emile,* book 5.

Wollstonecraft accomplishes her second task by incorporating the characteristics the Enlightenment associated with the good citizen into her redefinition of the wife-mother role. Rationality and personal autonomy in the sense of self-government: these are the traits thought to be required for citizenship, and these are the traits she attributes to good mothers and successful wives. Place Sophie in the polity—teach her to be her own legislator, let her exercise her reason in the interests of society as a whole—and she may be unwilling or unable to subordinate her judgment at home continually to Emile's. But Wollstonecraft's daughters are supposed to be their own legislators at home. Hence the personal autonomy and the rationality they must exercise as citizens will not incapacitate them for their domestic duties; indeed, their domestic pursuits will be enhanced once women are granted the rights of men. "We shall not see women affectionate till more equality be established in society," Wollstonecraft says (p. 191). And she appeals to "the history of all nations" in arguing that women will not fulfill their family duties if they are confined to domestic pursuits. "Unless their minds take a wider range," she warns (p. 174), the wife-mother role itself will suffer.

Just as Rousseau envisions a society in which males are both citizens and husband-fathers, Wollstonecraft posits one in which females do double duty. Her daughters are to be wife-mothers *and* citizens, their place in the polity providing essential nourishment for the performance of their domestic duties. A breathtaking conception of women's role, Wollstonecraft's vision stands in sharp contrast to Plato's as well as Rousseau's, for while the female guardians of the Just State are placed in the polity, they are taken out of the home. No motherhood for them, just childbearing. No marriage, just mating. It remains to be seen if the female education Wollstonecraft outlines is adequate to the dual role she assigns women and if her redefinition of the wife-mother role is itself tenable. But when we remember that Rousseau confines women to the home and Plato places the home out of bounds to them, whatever limitations her theory may have, we cannot doubt its power and depth.

The Education of Emily

It must be understood that in attributing rationality to female nature Wollstonecraft is assigning to it simply the *capacity* to be rational. Her daughters are no more born with reason full blown than are Plato's female guardians. Like the guardians, the women in the good society Wollstonecraft contemplates possess at birth a potential for rational thought that can be developed only through education. The knowledge, skills, and habits of mind that constitute the exercise of reason do not automatically emerge as a person matures but must be acquired, and their acquisition is not a wholly informal process but requires systematic teaching and learning.

According to Enlightenment thought, the rights Wollstonecraft wants to extend to women properly belong only to those who can, through their use of reason, grasp natural law and in so doing distinguish right from wrong. Thus her interest is in the actual exercise of female reason, not just in the female potential for rationality. Her daughters must display the highly developed powers of reasoning and possess the abstract ideas that are the prerequisites for the possession of rights; they must be self-legislating individuals whose thought and action are grounded in knowledge and governed by reason. No wonder the third task she sets herself is to provide an account of female education. The intellectual qualities women must possess to deserve the rights of men are the very ones the Sophies Wollstonecraft perceives in her world lack because of their misdirected training.

The account of female education developed in *A Vindication* constitutes a rejection of Sophie, but not of Rousseau. The most perfect education, Wollstonecraft says, "is such an exercise of the understanding as is best calculated to strengthen the body and form the heart. Or, in other words, to enable the individual to attain such habits of virtue as will render it independent. In fact, it is a farce to call any being virtuous whose virtues do not result from the exercise of reason. *This was Rousseau's opinion respecting men: I extend it to women*" (p. 21; emphasis added). And indeed she does, for the qualities Wollstonecraft wants females to possess in the society she envisions are precisely the ones Rousseau wants Emile to acquire. Female Emiles, or Emilys, as I will henceforth call them—these are the women Wollstonecraft would have rise out of the ashes of the Sophies she abhors.

Given Wollstonecraft's object of extending the rights of men to women, it is hardly surprising that she claims for her daughters the educational ideal Rousseau sets for Emile. If Emily can become the rational autonomous agent Emile is supposed to be, she argues, there will be no grounds for barring her from full-fledged citizenship.

Curiously enough, although Wollstonecraft appropriates the guiding ideal of Emile's education for her daughters, the educational program she prescribes for Emily differs from Emile's in important aspects. In the first place, Emily is not to live apart from society, as Emile is. "A man cannot retire into a desert with his child, and if he did he could not bring himself back to childhood, and become the proper friend and playfellow of an infant or youth," Wollstonecraft says (p. 157). She adds that children who are confined to the society of adults "very soon acquire that kind of premature manhood which stops the growth of every vigorous power of mind or body." If they are to think for themselves, children must mix with their fellows and jointly pursue the same objects. Otherwise, a child will rely on the answers elicited by his questions and will contract "a benumbing indolence of mind."

Wollstonecraft's wariness of what she calls "private education" also stems from her belief that in youth "the seeds of every affection should be sown, and the respectful regard which is felt for a parent, is very different from the social affections which are to constitute the happiness of life as it advances" (p. 157). Equality and "an intercourse of sentiments" unclogged by seriousness are the basis of the social affections, she suggests, and neither of these is to be found in the relation between parent—or, presumably, tutor—and child.

Wollstonecraft is as opposed to boarding schools as she is to a private education of the sort Rousseau prescribes for Emile. She finds these schools to be "hot-beds of vice and folly, and the knowledge of human nature supposed to be attained there merely cunning selfishness" (p. 158). Boys become gluttons and slovens in boarding schools; instead of cultivating domestic affections, they harden the heart. The way to avoid the equally injurious extremes of public (boarding school) education and private (home) education, in her view, is to send children to day schools, so that they can be educated both with the family and with other children.

The best education, she insists, is one in which both sexes in school, as in the family, are educated together (p. 247). "Were boys and girls permitted to pursue the same studies together," she says, "those graceful decencies might early be inculcated which produce modesty without those sexual distinctions that taint the mind" (p. 165). Thus she rejects not only Rousseau's doctrine of a different education for males and females but his doctrine of a separate education for the two sexes. Like Plato, she advocates coeducation, where this is understood to entail both identical education and the mixing together of the sexes, although she does advocate separate instruction in the afternoons for those girls and boys who are "intended for domestic employments, or mechanical trades" (p. 168).

Wollstonecraft wants her daughters and sons to be educated "after the same model" (p. 165), but if the ideal she holds up for them is derived

from Rousseau, the methods she proposes are not his. The early education Wollstonecraft would give Emily is a good deal more verbal and
abstract than the one Rousseau would give Emile. The elementary education Wollstonecraft's children are to pursue up to age nine includes
reading and writing as well as botany, mechanics, astronomy, arithmetic,
natural history, simple experiments in natural philosophy, and the elements of religion, history, and politics. Moreover, she conceives of Emily's
education in a way he does not conceive of Emile's—namely, as a list of
subjects to be studied.

Wollstonecraft acknowledges that young children "should not be
confined to any sedentary employment for more than an hour at a time"
(p. 168) and that relaxation and exercise can themselves be considered a
part of elementary education insofar as they "improve and amuse the
senses." Her very defense of relaxation, however, and her insistence that
the studies she lists should never encroach on gymnastic play in the open
air reveal her commitment to a form of education Rousseau vehemently
rejects for the young Emile. Emile's pursuits, too, are not sedentary. He
walks with his tutor, watches the sun rise, observes the stars, plants a
garden, attends a fair where he encounters a magician. But in the course
of his activities, he becomes educated. Since he learns at his own pace
while engaged in occupations that interest him, he needs no periods of
recess and recreation in which to let off steam and regain his powers of
concentration.

Plato takes education to be a pervasive feature of a society, and
Rousseau takes it to be a pervasive feature of a child's life. Of course, it
is the tutor's task to ensure that the education Emile receives from the
activities in which he engages is the right sort. If Emile is to become an
independent thinker, the tutor most pose questions that take genuine
thought for him to answer; if he is to acquire firsthand experience of the
world, he must be left on his own even to make mistakes; if he is to learn
from nature and things rather than from books, his attention must be
directed to particular phenomena such as night clouds passing between
him and the moon or a stick dropped into the water.

Once the form Emile's education is to take becomes clear, it is easy
to understand why manipulation is a part of it. Since Emile's learning is
to be a by-product of his activities without his realizing it, his environment must be controlled so that he will undertake activities that will
yield the desired learning, his attention must be directed to phenomena

that will arouse his curiosity, and his thought processes must be engaged through conversation and dialogue. But it should not be supposed that Wollstonecraft's reason for rejecting the portion of Rousseau's philosophy that so delights progressive educators is that it is manipulative. Without reference to those books of *Emile* containing Rousseau's most creative educational ideas, she simply espouses a model of education for both sexes that in structure and content resembles the very education for boys that was anathema to Rousseau.

The education Wollstonecraft claims for Emily is relatively traditional in form and it is intellectualistic in content. In these important aspects it resembles that of Plato's guardians rather than of Emile. But while Plato initiates the guardians of his Just State into abstract studies at a relatively late age after a long regimen of music and gymnastics, Wollstonecraft does so from the beginning. She does stress Emily's physical education. The gymnastic play in the open air she prescribes is not meant simply to curb Emily's restlessness and boredom. The infancy of all children should be passed "in harmless gambols" (p. 41), and we would hear of no "infantine" airs, she says, "if girls were allowed to take sufficient exercise, and not confined in close rooms till their muscles are relaxed, and their powers of digestion destroyed" (p. 62). For Wollstonecraft, as for Plato, physical education is no frill. Yet if she makes it an integral component of female education, like Plato she ultimately justifies it by its contribution not simply to good health but to reason and virtue.

A False Dilemma

Since, from Wollstonecraft's point of view, the primary object of Emily's education is to develop her reason sufficiently for her to become a self-governing agent, in her eyes the worst thing one could say about a woman is that she is a slave to her passions. That is the trouble with Sophie: it is the reason she does not deserve the rights accorded men; it is the reason she can attain neither virtue nor immortality. " 'Educate women like men,' " Wollstonecraft quotes Rousseau as saying, " 'and the more they resemble our sex the less power will they have over us.' This is the very point I aim at. I do not wish them to have power over men; but over themselves" (p. 62).

For Wollstonecraft, power over oneself is attained when not merely the passions but the senses are subdued by reason. Otherwise, with the understanding neglected and the senses "inflamed," a person will be "blown about by every momentary gust of feeling" (p. 60). Called "sensibility," this condition of being the prey of one's senses is the one in which civilized women find themselves. Wollstonecraft's whole object in educating Emily is to ensure that her intellect acquires "that sovereignty which it ought to attain to render a rational creature useful to others, and content with its own station" (p. 61). Above all, her daughters must avoid that "over exercised sensibility" that

> not only renders them uncomfortable themselves, but troublesome, to use a soft phrase, to others. All their thoughts turn on things circulated to excite emotion; and feeling, when they should reason, their conduct is unstable, and their opinions are wavering—not the wavering produced by deliberation or progressive views, but by contradictory emotions. By fits and starts they are warm in many pursuits; yet this warmth, never concentrated into perseverance, soon exhausts itself; exhaled by its own heat, or meeting with some other fleeting passion, to which reason has never given any specific gravity, neutrality ensues. Miserable, indeed, must be that being whose cultivation of mind has only tended to inflame its passions! (p. 61)

Wollstonecraft might be describing Jane Austen's Marianne Dashwood here rather than Lily Bart. Although unstable in conduct and wavering in opinion, Lily is not so much blown about by gusts of passion as she is rendered helpless by her enormous capacity for self-deception and her inability to adapt to new circumstances. Marianne Dashwood, on the other hand, actively feeds her passions and prides herself on acting upon them, and miserable indeed does that protagonist of *Sense and Sensibility* become before the novel ends. Written in the same decade as *A Vindication,* although not published until 1811, Austen's novel satirizes the very vogue of sensibility Wollstonecraft considers so damaging to women. Representing an excess of sensibility as her sister, Elinor, represents the sovereignty of reason, Marianne insists on being guided by feeling and swept away by emotion. What is sensibility? Wollstonecraft records Dr. Johnson's definition as "quickness of sensation; quickness of perception; delicacy" (p. 63). But the "over exercised sensibility" to which Wollstonecraft and Austen object is much more than this. Marianne is portrayed as "sensible and clever; but eager in every thing; her sorrows, her joys, could have no moderation. She was generous, amiable, interesting; she was everything but prudent."[9] She is not merely imprudent; she suffers from both a dreadful self-indulgence and a thoughtlessness that only too frequently becomes a want of kindness.

"Elinor, in quitting Norland and Edward, cried not as I did. Even now her self-command is invariable. When is she dejected or melancholy? When does she try to avoid society, or appear restless and dissatisfied in it?" exclaims Marianne to the mother whose sensibility she has inherited (p. 63). When Marianne's turn comes to be parted from a lover, her behavior is as different as possible from Elinor's. Giving way to heartbreak and despair to the point of neglecting her health and courting death, she allows the self-indulgence brought on by sensibility to turn into self-destruction, as she herself finally admits. Thus Austen, like Wollstonecraft, diagnoses women's lack of rational self-government as a fatal disease, although she seems to attribute it to individual predilection rather than female socialization.

In *Sense and Sensibility* the only tenable alternative to Marianne presented by Austen is Elinor. No more intelligent or well read than Marianne, Elinor is, however, the sister who knows how to govern her feelings. Unhappy in love as is Marianne, Elinor is as serene in her conduct as Marianne is agitated—not, as she eventually tells her sister, because she is incapable of feeling but because of "the effect of constant and painful exertion" (p. 275). All the time Marianne has been feeding and encouraging sorrow almost as a duty, Elinor has been making self-control her business. Calm, cheerful, and composed, Elinor serves as adviser to her mother and support to her sister even as her own hopes for happiness appear to be dashed.

In contrasting the behavior of two sisters who have grown up together and whose intellectual and cultural attainments are roughly equivalent, Austen shows us that the difference between sense and sensibility does not lie in the simple possession of knowledge. Rather, it is the subjection of feeling and of sense experience to the claims of reason that distinguishes Elinor from Marianne. Marianne acts on impulse, Elinor on considered deliberation. No matter what the consequences, Marianne immediately says what she thinks; in contrast, Elinor takes the reactions of others and the dictates of propriety into account before speaking. Marianne judges people by their emotional responses to experience; Elinor distrusts those in whom feeling prevails. Above all, Marianne subordinates to feeling and emotion the very judgment that rules Elinor.

Austen never directs Elinor's attention to public concerns. Elinor's family and its affairs are her domain. But she is as self-governing as Rousseau could wish Emile to be, indeed as Plato could wish the guardians of his Just State to be, and she is quite as capable of guiding those who are swayed by their passions as they are. Thus, although the rights of men have not been extended to her and she is perhaps not quite as well versed in history, politics, and science as Wollstonecraft might wish, we are entitled to consider Elinor a fictional representation of Emily. As such, let us ask if the forecast for Emily made by one recent commentator on *A Vindication* seems warranted.

In her book *The Radical Future of Liberal Feminism* Zillah Eisenstein points out that while *A Vindication* opposes both women's economic dependency and their uneducated existence, it lays claim only to women's right to an education. She concludes that the economic dependency of Wollstonecraft's daughters stands in the way of their equality in part because it "relegates" them to the "emotional and passionate sphere of life."[10] If she is right about this—if Emily will ultimately suffer Sophie's fate of being a slave to her passions—Wollstonecraft's entire project flounders.

Is Eisenstein's prediction warranted? Once Elinor is married to Edward, the suitor she had mistakenly thought lost to her forever—once made responsible for running his household and rearing his children—will she dwell in "the emotional and passionate sphere of life" and be transformed into the twin of her sister? No reader of *Sense and Sensibility* could think so. The wives and mothers Austen has bequeathed us do not instill confidence that after her marriage Elinor will remain the paragon of sense she is at age nineteen. Yet if Austen found it easier to portray silly than sensible wives and vain rather than loving mothers, it would nonetheless be quite out of character for the Elinor she depicts to acquire either these defects or her own mother's overstretched sensibility.

Elinor's problem—and Emily's, too—is not that in being responsible for running the domestic sphere her life will be dominated by feeling and emotion but that by fulfilling Wollstonecraft's rationalistic redefinition of the wife-mother role feeling and emotion will be entirely suppressed. Until Elinor tells Marianne otherwise, readers of *Sense and Sensibility* may be pardoned for assuming, with her sister, that Elinor is scarcely capable of feeling. Austen reports that Elinor struggles in private to govern strong emotions, but since those struggles are never made visible to the reader it is difficult to believe in them. Still, supposing Elinor to be capable of full-fledged emotional response, she is certainly not the one to show her feelings, let alone allow them to be the wellsprings of action.

Nor is she the one to react directly and spontaneously to the people in her immediate environment.

Of her own experience as a mother, the British novelist Margaret Drabble reports: "I used to be a reasonably careless and adventurous person, before I had children; now I am morbidly obsessed by seat belts and constantly afraid that lowflying aircraft will drop on my children's school."[11] When her children were young, Adrienne Rich made the following entry in her journal:

> My children cause me the most exquisite suffering of which I have any experience. It is the suffering of ambivalence: the murderous alternation between bitter resentment and raw-edged nerves, and blissful gratification and tenderness. Sometimes I seem to myself, in my feelings toward these tiny guiltless beings, a monster of selfishness and intolerance. Their voices wear away at my nerves, their constant needs, above all their need for simplicity and patience, fill me with despair at my own failures, despair too at my fate, which is to serve a function for which I was not fitted. And I am weak sometimes from held-in rage. There are times when I feel only death will free us from one another, when I envy the barren woman who has the luxury of her regrets but lives a life of privacy and freedom. And yet at other times I am melted with the sense of their helpless, charming and quite irresistible beauty—their ability to go on loving and trusting—their staunchness and decency and unselfconsciousness. I *love them.* But it's in the enormity and inevitability of this love that the sufferings lie.[12]

Of course, Elinor was never carefree and adventurous—of that we can be sure. Thus the profound contrast between life before and after motherhood to which Drabble points will not be part of Elinor's experience. Neither will the fears and sufferings of motherhood nor the sudden joys and blissful tenderness to which these give way be hers. "From hours of irritation and hard work," Drabble says, "one can snatch a few good moments, and they appear to be both a right and a blessing. Two hours of sickening anxiety waiting for a late child to get home can be redeemed by the sight of its guilty face smiling nervously at the door, and one's own redemption can be as immediately lost again in the foul bad temper that usually follows on the initial relief" (p. 7). Be it annoyance or sheer delight, anger or engulfing love, the direct emotional response to a loved one's behavior will remain beyond Elinor's experience.

It must not be supposed that seeing oneself reflected in Drabble's or Rich's account of motherhood is necessarily a sign that one's reason is subject to the dictates of capricious passion, that one who finds Elinor too self-controlled has no recourse but to embrace Marianne. Whether or not in *Sense and Sensibility* Austen really considers Elinor an acceptable alternative to Marianne is not entirely clear.[13] As Marianne is meant to be a caricature of sensibility, so Elinor may be intended as a caricature of sense. Questions of literary interpretation aside, however, we need only look to Austen's later novel, *Persuasion,* to meet a heroine who manages to avoid both the excessive sensibility of the one sister and the excessive self-control of the other. At age twenty-nine Ann Eliot is able to speak from the heart—something Elinor scarcely knows how to do—without becoming reckless or thoughtless in the manner of Marianne. Not quite a Dorothea Brooke in either the acuteness of her intellect or the purity and strength of her feeling, she nonetheless displays toward others the "generous sympathy" for which the heroine of *Middlemarch* is known.

One cannot imagine Elinor, with heart full and breath oppressed, saying, as Ann Eliot does to Captain Harville, "All the privilege I claim for my own sex (it is not an enviable one; you need not covet it) is that of loving longest, when existence or when hope is gone!"[14] It is out of the question that in speaking to a person she scarcely knows but wants to help, Elinor would be, as Dorothea is with Rosamund Lydgate, "completely swayed by the feeling that she was uttering" and would forget everything "but that she was speaking from out of the heart of her own trial."[15] Yet Dorothea and Ann are not slaves to their passions but intelligent, conscientious, highly principled women.

Perhaps intentionally, perhaps not, in *Sense and Sensibility* Austen presents what the logicians call a false dilemma: reducing the number of possible choices to two, she implies that the only alternative to Marianne's overstretched sensibility is Elinor's all-controlling sense. Wollstonecraft succumbs to just this fallacy in *A Vindication*: assuming that a woman either must be a slave to her passions or must invariably keep them under the tight control of reason, she presents Emily as the only viable alternative to the Sophie she pities and despises. From a strategic point of view Wollstonecraft's partiality to Emily is understandable. If she is to convince her readers that women are rational and hence deserve to be awarded the rights of men, she is wise to opt for a female ideal that minimizes feeling and emotion, those supposed foes of reason. But the false dilemma into which Wollstonecraft draws her readers is not simply a function of her immediate political program. It is built into the very model of human nature she adopts.

A political imagery underlies Wollstonecraft's theory of the human personality as it does Plato's. She considers the human soul or psyche to be made up of parts that necessarily stand to one another in the relation of governor and governed.[16] Moreover, she assumes that some part or parts of the psyche must govern the others, and that the ruling element must be everywhere and eternally the same and must be the ultimate source of control. No give and take, no interaction, no sensitivity to context in this sovereignty model of personality. Either reason rules absolutely or passion does. The sovereignty model allows Wollstonecraft to construct an Emily who is a counter to Rousseau's Sophie: in Sophie the passions and senses will rule, in Emily reason will rule; in Sophie reason will forever be subordinate to feeling, in Emily feeling will always be suppressed by reason. The problem with this model, however, is that it forces one to choose between Sophie and Emile—Marianne and Elinor— for it does not accommodate personalities, such as Dorothea's, in which there is no one fixed source of authority.

To do Wollstonecraft justice, it must be pointed out that she mentions feeling and passion with approval in many passages of *A Vindication*. She speaks, for example, of "those nobler passions that open and enlarge the soul" (p. 10), says that God willed "that the passions should unfold our reason" (p. 14), calls passions "spurs to action" (p. 30). She also wants women to feel affection for their husbands; indeed, the friendship upon which marriage ought to be founded is, she says, "the most sublime of all affections" (p. 73). And she advocates an education that will "form the heart" (p. 21) and insists that she wants the heart, as well as the understanding, to be "opened by cultivation" (p. 66).

Yet Wollstonecraft gives Emily feelings and emotions only to take them away. After saying that the passions are spurs to action and open the mind, she adds, "but they sink into mere appetites, become a personal and momentary gratification, when the object is gained." Hence reason must "teach passion to submit to necessity" (p. 30). After insisting that education forms the heart, she describes this task as the development of virtues resulting from the exercise of reason (p. 21). In truth, the pages of *A Vindication* reveal Wollstonecraft's ambivalence about feeling and emotion. On the one hand, men have superior judgment and fortitude because "they give a freer scope to the grand passions" (p. 110). "It is not against strong, persevering passions; but romantic feelings that I wish to guard the female heart by exercising the understanding," she says (pp. 74–75). On the other hand, the passions are capricious "winds of life" (p. 109) and inherently dangerous.

Acknowledging that the most difficult task in the education of both sexes "is so to adjust instruction as not to narrow the understanding, whilst the heart is warmed by the generous juices of spring, just raised by the electric fermentation of the season; nor to dry up the feelings by employing the mind in investigations remote from life" (p. 66), Wollstonecraft is nonetheless required by her own ambivalence and by the sovereignty model of personality to educate Emily in Elinor's image. That model gives her only two choices: the absolute subjection of feeling and emotion to reason or the absolute subjection of reason to feeling and emotion. Having rejected the latter option, only the former is open to her.

Different Roles, Same Education

Wollstonecraft locates the precedent for Emily's education in rational self-control in Emile, but Rousseau would be the first to acknowledge that Emile himself is modeled after the guardians of the Just State, indeed, that Plato's *Republic* supplies a precedent for extending Emile's education to women. He and Plato would both remind Wollstonecraft, however, that Plato's educational program presupposes the abolition of institutions she wants to preserve—private home, family, marriage, and child rearing—and of the traditional female role itself. And he would question her assumption, as Plato no doubt would too, that it is coherent to embrace Plato's radicalism concerning women's education while adopting Rousseau's traditionalism concerning women's domestic functions.

Wollstonecraft might defend herself by claiming that in her philosophy education is not tied to social roles. A careful reading of *A Vindication* leaves no doubt, however, that Wollstonecraft embraces a version of Plato's production model of education. It is true that she says that education is viewed in a false light when it is not considered "as the first step to form a being advancing gradually towards perfection; but only as a preparation for life" (p. 53). The operative word in this passage is *only*. In her view, as in Plato's and Rousseau's, the function of education is to equip people to carry out the particular societal roles to which they are suited by nature. In other words, she accepts Plato's Functional Postulate and also his Postulate of Specialized Natures. Whereas Plato assumes that each person is born more apt for one task than another, Wollstonecraft assumes that women are born with an aptitude for two tasks corresponding to two societal roles, that of citizen and that of wife-mother. That she thinks education should not only prepare people for their pre-assigned roles in society does not, therefore, warrant detaching her account of female education from her theory of women's place.

Wollstonecraft might also defend herself by pointing out that she advocates citizenship for women and redefines both marriage and motherhood so as to make a place for reason in the wife-mother role. So she does. Yet in retaining the domestic sphere Plato abolishes, and in giving women responsibility for carrying on the activities and duties associated with it while advocating an education designed for those who have no such responsibility, Wollstonecraft leaves her theory of female education vulnerable to the criticism that Emily's education is not well suited to one of the societal roles for which it is supposed to prepare her.

Eisenstein's script for Emily turns on the assumption that the domestic sphere is necessarily emotional and passionate and that a woman who lives her life in it cannot be—or at least cannot remain—a rational, self-governing individual. Armed with her redefinition of the wife-mother role and an educational ideal designed originally for Plato's guardians and for Emile, Wollstonecraft might well scoff at this. Anyone acquainted with Elinor would also find this fate an unlikely one for Emily. Even Rousseau might say that Eisenstein goes too far, that women relegated to the home *can* be rational and self-governing; it is just that they *should not* possess these qualities. One need not agree with Rousseau on this last point to wonder if, in the kind of society Wollstonecraft envisions— one in which child rearing is private and is primarily in the hands of mothers—Emily will display sufficient feelings and emotions to be a good wife and mother, not if she will be overwhelmed by passion. In particular, one must ask if a woman whose feelings are always subdued by reason will show her children enough affection, if she will possess the requisite nurturing capacities, if she will provide the warmth and the physical affection they need, if she will delight in their company.

It is scarcely an exaggeration to say that an ideal of the educated woman lies at the very center of A Vindication. Since Wollstonecraft's concern is women, we should not be surprised that historians of education have ignored this book. However, recent scholarship on A Vindication also tends to overlook the fact that Wollstonecraft presents us with an educational ideal. Concentrating on her defense of female rationality and her arguments for extending the rights of men to women, this body of work acknowledges Wollstonecraft's critique of Sophie's education and her insights into female socialization.[17] Her positive philosophy of women's education is scarcely examined, however. This scholarship notes that she claims for her daughters the education of men as well as their rights. But it accepts without question the appropriateness for women of an education whose guiding ideal resembles the one constructed for Plato's guardians and for Emile.

As we know, the family that will be Emily's is not supposed to be patriarchal. Still, Emily is the one destined to bear primary responsibility for carrying on its domestic and nurturant tasks. In Wollstonecraft's social vision, Emily's husband is as dependent on Emily in domestic affairs as Emile is on Sophie. Her decision to give Emily Emile's education cannot therefore be viewed as unproblematic and leads to obvious questions about the adequacy of Emily's preparation for running a household. I will leave these for Catharine Beecher to raise since her philosophy of female education addresses this topic directly. Here let us confine ourselves to the issue of whether, in holding up for Emily an ideal of rational self-control, Wollstonecraft does not neglect her education in nurturing capacities and in the care, concern, and connection so essential for Emily's family functions in general and for her mothering responsibilities in particular.

Many people in Wollstonecraft's time would have argued that the attitudes, skills, behavior, and traits of character needed by mothers are inborn in women and emerge automatically as they mature and so would maintain that there is no reason to take these into account in a theory of female education. Even today there are those who view human mothering as instinctual and agree with Helen Andelin, the author of *Fascinating Womanhood,* that "a quality of the Domestic Goddess is her love for children and her joy in bearing them and nurturing them. This is a natural instinct of the feminine woman. You do not have to teach her to be this way—it is inborn." She goes on to assert that the "Feminine Woman"

> also has a natural instinct to care for her little ones. She has an instinctive concern for their physical welfare, to see that they are properly fed and bathed, and would never allow them to go hungry, cold or unprotected if within her power to prevent it. She takes pride in their appearance, is gentle and loving, teaches them how to be happy, and offers them praise and understanding, giving them bread for their souls as well as their bodies.[18]

Despite her assertion that motherhood is woman's duty by nature, however, Wollstonecraft is no instinctualist: indeed, *A Vindication* can be read as an attack on instinctual theories of woman's nature. It is possible, nevertheless, that although she dismisses instinctualism, Wollstonecraft assumes that the feelings and emotions she herself believes are required for good maternal practice develop automatically in females. In the context of chastising mothers who do not suckle their young, she asserts that "a mutual care produces a new mutual sympathy" between mother and child and that affections "must grow out of the habitual exercise of a mutual sympathy" (p. 152). Perhaps, then, she believes that the deliberate cultivation of the feelings, emotions, and passions associated with good mothering is not necessary because these can be learned in the course of doing.

Wollstonecraft's insistence that mothers nurse their infants and her claim that this will produce a mutual sympathy between mother and child must be understood in the light of child-rearing practices of her time. Elizabeth Badinter has shown that in eighteenth-century France the mortality rate for children under one year was consistently above 25 percent.[19] The rate varied from region to region according to climate and local health conditions, but also according to who nursed the child. The death rate for infants kept at home and nursed by their mothers was half that for children sent out to nurse. The wet-nurse system so prominant in that period was, according to Badinter, "a disguised form of infanticide" (p. 112).

It should be noted that the practice of sending infants out to be nursed was by no means restricted to women too poor to stay home with their children but was widespread among women of all classes: of twenty-one thousand babies born in Paris in 1780, approximately a thousand were nursed in the home, many of these not by their mothers (p. 92). It has sometimes been said that the high infant mortality rate of that period caused mothers to harden their hearts and become indifferent to the death of their child. Badinter argues, however, that children died *because* of maternal indifference. Children were sent out to wet nurses who operated under the most shocking conditions because women were bored by nursing or thought it unseemly and disgusting, because they already had a child at home, or because they had other ways of spending their time.

When Wollstonecraft was writing, mother love as we tend to think of it was not a given, and neither was suckling one's young. She recognized that the two phenomena are related, but she oversimplified the connections between them. Nursing cannot be counted on to produce enduring maternal affection in those who do not want a child in the first place, in those who want children but do not want to be bothered with them, or in those who are experiencing great economic, social, or psychological stress. That it can be counted on in the case of women who are educated to be Emiles is also doubtful. But assuming for the sake of argument that it can be, we must remember that, given the structure of society Wollstonecraft posits, a good mother will tend to exhibit, besides affection, awareness of and sensitivity to her child's feelings and situation, protective love and a desire to foster her child's growth, and a sense of connection with her child.[20] Surely the many cases we see today of child abuse, neglect, and abandonment; failure to protect children from incest; and inability to enter into one's children's plans and projects cannot all be attributed to a failure to nurse.

Wollstonecraft's suggestion—and that is all it is—that the nurturant and caring aspects of mothering, although not instinctual, emerge automatically in females who nurse their young finds its counterpart in contemporary feminist theory. Nancy Chodorow argues that nurturing capacities and the desire to mother "are built into and grow out of the mother-daughter relationship itself."[21] She argues not that women learn to mother by mothering, as Wollstonecraft seems to do but that they learn to mother by being mothered by women. Toward the end of her book Chodorow sums up her theory as follows: "Because women are themselves mothered by women, they grow up with the relational capacities and needs, and psychological definition of self-in-relationship, which commits them to mothering. Men, because they are mothered by women, do not. Women mother daughters who, when they become women, mother" (p. 209).

Although Wollstonecraft's theory of mothering, such as it is, differs from Chodorow's, we must nonetheless ask if, in the world Chodorow describes, education in the feelings, emotions, and passions of mothering is necessary. Supposing for the sake of argument that Chodorow's theory is valid, if it denies the relevance of education to the acquisition of nurturing capacities, then Wollstonecraft's theory of female education cannot be faulted on the ground that it does not constitute adequate preparation for the mother role.

One might think that in the tightly determined world of Chodorow's theory educators need not apply, but appearances are deceptive. Whatever the specific content of the nurturing capacities Chodorow attributes to women, the point to remember is that mothering—at least, good mothering—involves not merely the possession of certain capacities but a certain standard of performance: for instance, acting in nurturant ways and doing and saying nurturant things, not just having the potential to become a nurturant person.

Chodorow looks forward to a society in which both males and females mother. Thus she believes that both sexes have the necessary potential to develop empathy and other nurturing traits. Otherwise how could men ever be mothers? But if men as well as women possess a potential for nurturance, what makes females so distinctive? Chodorow occasionally speaks of the greater potential of girls, but whether the differences between the sexes she perceives is a matter of degree of potential or whether she thinks that daughters automatically acquire the ability to nurture from their mothers—as opposed simply to the potential to become nurturant—there is still room in her theory for education. This is because in either interpretation there is a gap between capacity and performance.

Like Wollstonecraft, Chodorow makes frequent reference to mothers whose practice has gone awry. Thus she recognizes the gap between possessing nurturing capacities and being a good mother. But then the question arises of how to fill the gap. This is a question Wollstonecraft needs to address, even if we give her the benefit of the doubt by granting the truth of Chodorow's psychoanalytically based theory.[22] It is especially important for Wollstonecraft to be able to answer it because the nurturing capacities and ethics of care Emily must acquire and exercise to be a good mother are nowhere to be found in the ideal of the educated woman she holds up for Emily.

Needless to say, education cannot by itself solve large-scale social problems. Neither child abuse nor incest will disappear just because an effort is made to help people become nurturant and caring. But that education is not a social panacea does not mean that it can do no good at all. In individual instances an education for nurturance and care may improve the quality of mothering; in some cases it may even prevent harm from being done to children. Moreover, the point to keep in mind here is that whatever efficacy education for mothering may have, the internal logic of Wollstonecraft's philosophy requires that Emily be provided such education. Given Wollstonecraft's acceptance of Plato's Functional Postulate that the task of education is to prepare people to fill necessary societal roles, given her rejection of the instinctualist position, and given her insistence that women have primary responsibility for child rearing, her theory of female education must include education for mothering.

We have already seen that Wollstonecraft embraces Plato's Functional Postulate as well as a version of his Postulate of Specialized Natures. In view of her coeducational scheme it should be clear that she also accepts the Identity Postulate of same role, same education. In contrast to Plato, however, Wollstonecraft believes that a person can be suited by nature for more than one societal role and that at least some roles can be shared by people whose natures are not identical. Thus her daughters are destined to be citizens and wife-mothers and her sons to be citizens and husband-fathers. In effect, then, she embraces a modified Postulate of Specialized Natures and also a modified Correspondence Postulate, which maintains that societal roles and human nature correspond to one another although not necessarily in one-to-one relation. Wollstonecraft denies the Difference Postulate altogether, however, for her daughters must perform two societal roles, one of which differs from that of her sons; yet the education the two sexes are to receive is to be identical.

Both of these deviations from Plato's production model of education can be traced back to Rousseau. Just as Wollstonecraft intends Emily to be a citizen and a wife-mother, Rousseau wants Emile to be a citizen and a husband-father; just as Emily is to receive an education designed specifically to fit her for the one role of citizen, so is Emile. Rousseau would, of course, defend his prescription of an identical education for Emile's two societal roles by pointing out their essential oneness: in the small fatherland that is the family, as in the large one, Emile is to be sovereign. Likewise, Wollstonecraft would remind us how similar the wife-mother and citizen roles are in her social vision. That there can be considerable overlap between social roles is undeniable. Still, if the overlapping characteristic of some roles gives the lie to the assumption that totally different educations are required to fit people for different roles, the assumption that different roles require no differences in training is questionable. Certainly, for Wollstonecraft's daughters there are significant differences between their two roles, which their education ignores at its peril.

As we know, Emile is not adequately educated to be a good husband and father. How unlikely, then, that his education will help Emily become a good wife-mother! In truth, in her understandable outrage at the education Rousseau proposes for Sophie, Wollstonecraft fails to notice that whatever plausibility his account of Emile's education may have is due to Sophie's existence. Rousseau knows this. He recognizes that the Platonic ideal of a self-governing individual in whom reason rules is incomplete and that a well-constructed philosophy of education must include both an account of education for citizenship and an account of education for carrying on the reproductive processes of society. Rousseau's mistake is to insist that these two kinds of education be assigned on the basis of sex. Furthermore, in constructing Emile's education he forgets that, according to his own social vision, Emile is to live his life in the family he and Sophie are to establish.

Rousseau's fundamental insight that Emile's education is partial is overlooked by Wollstonecraft, in part, perhaps, because, in her concern to reveal Rousseau's misogyny, she ignores Sophie's positive qualities. On balance, Sophie is definitely not a person to admire. Nevertheless, although she is passive and manipulative, she is also the one with the patience and gentleness, zeal and affection necessary for rearing children, the one with the tenderness and care "required to maintain the union of the whole family" (p. 361), and the one who is willing and able to make the lives of her loved ones "agreeable and sweet" (p. 365). Because Sophie acquires through her education the attributes so necessary for carrying on the reproductive processes of society, it makes a certain amount of sense that Emile does not. But not a great deal of sense, for as Sophie's husband, father of her children, and head of family, one would hope that he too would be tender and caring and disposed to make the lives of his loved ones agreeable and sweet. Be that as it may, it makes no sense at all to advocate Emile's and *only* Emile's education for both sexes—no sense, that is, if one cares about the quality of child rearing and family living.

Wollstonecraft does care about the quality of domestic life, indeed, she cares about it passionately, but her rationalistic philosophical framework does not permit her to claim for her daughters the education in Sophie's virtues that those with responsibility for carrying on the reproductive processes of society must have. Wollstonecraft's rationalism is thus the source of both her strength and her weakness. It allows her to extend the rights of men to women, thereby bringing women into the domain of citizenship. As we know, this in itself is no guarantee of political equality, but at least it puts women in a position from which to begin to pursue that elusive goal. At the same time, her rationalism allows Wollstonecraft to demonstrate the compatibility of the citizen and the wife-mother role, something neither Plato nor Rousseau attempts. Wollstonecraft accomplishes this by the revolutionary strategy of altering the patriarchal family structure. This is no guarantee of sex equality either, but if the total abolition of patriarchy requires women's economic independence, Wollstonecraft's conception of the relationship of husband and wife at least sets the stage for egalitarian marriage.

Wollstonecraft's rationalism serves also to illuminate aspects of mothering that even today are too often ignored. Intelligence and a certain stability of character are seldom considered maternal qualities, yet they are as important to child rearing as to other activities, and it is to Wollstonecraft's credit that she brings this out so clearly. In particular, she highlights the parts reason and self-control play in the educative aspects of mothering. Arguing that Sophie will not have "sufficient character to manage a family or educate children" (p. 35), she makes it very clear that the duty of forming her child's character cannot be successfully fulfilled by a mother who herself is ruled by whim and caprice.

Finally, Wollstonecraft's rationalism inspires her to claim for women the academic education historically reserved for men and, like Plato, to recommend a system of coeducation. Unfortunately, these proposals pose the same problems of male-based methods, male-biased disciplines, and genderized traits for her daughters as they do for Plato's guardians. Wollstonecraft is sensitive, as Plato is not, to the differential socialization of girls and boys. Yet she extends to her daughters the education of men without addressing the question of whether Emily will be at a serious disadvantage in an educational scheme that takes Emile as its norm. Wollstonecraft is sensitive also to the fact that a woman whose intelligence is cultivated is considered masculine, and yet she appropriates Emile's image for Emily without addressing the questions of what education can do to ensure that Emily will not be considered abnormal by others and ultimately by herself or of how she is to receive the respect and esteem Wollstonecraft considers to be prerequisites of equality.

Despite these problems, Emily's education is such an improvement on Sophie's that it seems almost churlish to criticize it. Yet even if the academic education that is to make her own reason sovereign will spare Emily the fate of a Lily Bart, it must still be criticized not only for the harm its male-based methods, curriculum, and mold do to Emily but for the one-sidedness that is itself, of course, a function of its genderized origins. As the example of Emile makes clear, Emily's rationalistic education will not equip her for the citizenship Wollstonecraft would give her. Bonds of sympathy and an affection for the state are as important for Wollstonecraft as for Plato and Rousseau, but one can have little confidence that Emily's education will foster them. Like Rousseau, Wollstonecraft thinks that the seeds of civic sympathy and affection must be planted in the home: "If you wish to make good citizens, you must first exercise the affections of a son and a brother. This is the only way to expand the heart; for public affections, as well as public virtues, must ever grow out of the private character, or they are merely meteors that shoot athwart a dark sky, and disappear as they are gazed at and admired" (p. 162). Yet the rationalism of the domestic environment Emily will create makes one wonder if her family, any more than Sophie's, can succeed in performing its patriotic duty.

The one-sided female education Wollstonecraft proposes is in part a function of a definition of the wife-mother role that makes Sophie's virtues of nurturance and care all but invisible. We can appreciate the theoretical and practical considerations that lead Wollstonecraft to define marriage and mothering in strict rationalistic terms. Still, in making her case for the rights of women, this great feminist philosopher presents us with an ideal of female education that gives pride of place to traits traditionally associated with males at the expense of others traditionally associated with females.

Wollstonecraft denies not only Sophie's coquettishness but her concern for detail, not only her guile but her quickness of perception. She disparages women for thinking more about the incidental occurrences on a journey than the end in view, as men would. And she scorns women's sensibility. Just as she constructs a false dichotomy between the self-control represented by Elinor and the chaos represented by Marianne, so too the only alternative Wollstonecraft posits to the life of abstract reason extolled by Plato is one of intellectual poverty. Yet Wollstonecraft gives us no good reason to believe that delicacy and quickness of perception are inferior qualities, that the ongoing details of a journey are necessarily of less importance than the end in view, that in all contexts it is better to suppress than to act upon one's immediate feelings.

In her talk to teachers of women, Adrienne Rich warned against training women students to "think like men." Men in general, she said, think

> in disjuncture from their personal lives, claiming objectivity where the most irrational passions seethe, losing, as Virginia Woolf observed, their senses in the pursuit of professionalism. It is not easy to think like a woman in a man's world, in the world of the professions; yet the capacity to do that is a strength which we can try to help our students develop. To think like a woman in a man's world means thinking critically, refusing to accept the givens, making connections between facts and ideas which men have left unconnected. It means remembering that every mind resides in a body; remaining accountable to the female bodies in which we live; constantly retesting given hypotheses against lived experience.[23]

Wollstonecraft is not to be faulted for embracing a rationalism that enabled her to write a classic work on the rights of women. She is not to be faulted for claiming an intellectually demanding education for her daughters. But those of us today who want to claim an education for women should recognize the limitations of her philosophical framework even as we echo Emma Goldman's praise:

> It has been said that nature uses a vast amount of human material to create one genius. Mary was born and not made through this or that individual incident in her surroundings. The treasure of her soul, the wisdom of her life's philosophy, the depth of her World of thought, the intensity of her battle for human emancipation and especially her indomitable struggle for the liberation of her own sex, are even today so far ahead of the average grasp that we may indeed claim for her the rare exception which nature has created but once in a century.[24]

And those of us who want to claim the best possible education for both sexes should remember that a society that does not abolish the institutions of private marriage, home, family, and child rearing cannot afford to take as its model the education Plato devised for his guardian class.

As rationalistic, in her own way, as Wollstonecraft, Catharine Beecher seeks not to liberate her own sex but to gain it the respect it deserves. Although Emily's reasoning powers will presumably be adequate to the task of running her household and raising her children, it is open to question if her education will give her the requisite knowledge and skill to do the job on which her husband depends and at the same time command his respect. Beecher certainly doubts its efficacy in this regard. Indeed, her entrance into this conversation will initiate us into the complexities of the role Wollstonecraft assigns to Emily but does not prepare her for and into a form of education constructed specifically with that role in mind. In attending to Beecher's ideas about the education of girls and women, we will also discover something that Wollstonecraft did not fully realize: the dependency of male on female, which in Rousseau's philosophy results in Sophie's exploitation, can instead be made the cornerstone of a theory of female autonomy and of a sophisticated female education that represents the analogue in domestic affairs of Rousseau's theory of Autonomous Man.

5 Beecher's Homemakers

In *A Treatise on Domestic Economy,* published in the United States just fifty years after *A Vindication* was published in England, Catharine Beecher extols the wife-mother role for which her daughters, like Wollstonecraft's, are destined.[1] The first text to systematize American domestic practice, this work sets forth the details of household maintenance, gardening, cooking, sewing, child rearing, caring for the sick, and other tasks carried out in the home. According to Kathryn Kish Sklar, Beecher's biographer, *A Treatise* established Beecher as a national authority on the American home, and its rigorous descriptions of household functions set the stage for the household automation movement that was to come later. But it is a mistake to regard *A Treatise* simply as a description of domestic work. Sklar says that it "defines a new role for women within the household,"[2] that although Beecher was by no means the first to write about domestic life, her predecessors assumed male control of the domestic environment, whereas she does not. Sklar's point of reference is nineteenth-century America. In eighteenth-century England Wollstonecraft had already defined a domestic role for women in which they were to be rational, autonomous agents. Nevertheless, if the female role Beecher defines is not entirely new, her elaboration and defense of it are of great interest.

Unlike Wollstonecraft, Beecher presents a detailed account of female education tied directly to the wife-mother role. No discrepancy between education and societal tasks and functions exists for Beecher's women; destined to be homemakers, they are to acquire the knowledge and skill they need to manage a home and rear children. Will this domestic education prepare them to be the citizens Wollstonecraft intends Emily to be? For Beecher the question is irrelevant since she does not want her homemakers to play the dual female role Wollstonecraft posited in 1792.

Beecher's philosophy of female education, like Rousseau's, is a mirror image of Plato's. Whereas Plato is able to design an education in ruling for females because he has detached them from family and children, Beecher is able to design a domestic education for her daughters because she has detached them from the responsibilities and duties of citizenship. On the face of it, Beecher's philosophy appears to represent a return to Rousseau; yet she would surely tell Rousseau that her homemakers are not creatures of guile, that they share Sophie's duties but not her character. Beecher's wife-mothers are to possess Emily's sense, not Sophie's sensibility; Emily's steadfastness, not Sophie's instability; Emily's independence, not Sophie's docility. In sum, although denied the full rights of men, they are to be educated to be rational, autonomous beings—revised Sophies, or Sarahs, as I will call them.

Subordinate Women

The three parties to our conversation thus far would doubtless ask Beecher how she can reconcile a view of women as rational creatures with a theory of society that denies women direct political participation. In particular, Wollstonecraft would remind Beecher that the fundamental strategy of *A Vindication* is to argue from women's rationality to women's citizenship; Plato would point out that he relies on essentially this same strategy in the *Republic* when he insists that with respect to ruling the Just State, the possession of reason—not being male or female—is the difference that makes all the difference; and Rousseau would say that in denying Sophie the kind of education that would allow her to participate in the General Will, he too associates rationality with the right to rule. Rousseau and Plato would also warn Beecher that the wife-mother role she envisions for Sarah does not call for rational judgment and autonomous action. Thus, they would argue—and here Wollstonecraft would part company with them—that Sarah is doomed to failure in the very role Beecher assigns her, even as Beecher denies her the role for which her reason would seem to suit her.

How does Beecher resolve the problems to which a theory combining Emily's reason with Sophie's place gives rise? To answer this question we must take seriously both the social and political philosophies contained in *A Treatise* and its philosophy of female education.

For Catharine Beecher the "great maxim" that all men are created equal and are equally entitled to life, liberty, and the pursuit of happiness is another mode of expressing the Golden Rule. To love one's neighbor as oneself requires "that each individual of our race shall regard the happiness of others, as of the same value as his own" and forbids "any institution, in private or civil life, which secures advantages to one class, by sacrificing the interests of another" (p. 2). Thus the principles of American democracy are for her identical to those of Christianity. If Beecher were certain that each individual would obey the Golden Rule, she might have seen no need for laws and government. She recognizes, however, that Scripture will not always conquer greed, and so she deems a system of laws necessary to ensure that each individual may pursue happiness "unimpeded by the selfish interests of others." In Beecher's eyes, then, the state rests on the fundamental principle established by the "Great Ruler of the Universe," which implies that government and laws be designed with reference not to the wishes of the few but to "the general good of all."

Monarchical and aristocratic rule are incompatible with Christianity, Beecher says, because they secure advantages to the few by sacrificing the interests of the many. Democratic rule, on the other hand, meets her requirement that the state take into account the "great mass of the people." It should not be supposed, however, that in approving a democratic form of government, Beecher espouses a nonhierarchical society. The system of laws she considers necessary to secure the good of all must sustain certain relations in social and civil life involving "duties of subordination." Society could not go forward harmoniously, she says, if "superior and subordinate relations" were not instituted and maintained. Distinctions of rank or station thus constitute the social fabric out of which her ideal democratic polity is cut.

Exactly what relations involving the duties of subordination does Beecher have in mind? She lists magistrate and subject, employer and employed, teacher and pupil, parent and child, husband and wife. In each of these the superior "is to direct, and the inferior is to yield obedience." And who is to fill the higher and the lower stations in social and civil life? In the case of parents and children the Creator has decided, for He has given children into the control of their parents until they reach a certain age, or as long as they remain members of the household. In other relations, however, Beecher claims that in a democracy the superior or subordinate station is a matter of individual choice. Every domestic, artisan, or laborer can choose "the employer to whom he is to accord obedience or, if he prefers to relinquish certain advantages, he can remain without taking a subordinate place to any employer" (p. 3).³ Every subject has equal power to choose his ruler. No woman "is forced to obey any husband but the one she chooses for herself; nor is she obliged to take a husband, if she prefers to remain single."

Now, relations of inequality are certainly compatible with political democracy; indeed, they can scarcely be avoided in society. Although even an infant can possess capacities its parents lack—for example, sight or hearing—on a great many measures a small child will be inferior to its parents. A pupil, in turn, will not necessarily be inferior to a teacher with respect to size or any number of other qualities, yet except in very unusual circumstances pupils are not their teachers' equals in their mastery of the area under study. Similarly, in knowledge of medicine patients will often—although by no means always—be the inferiors of their physicians as in knowledge of the law clients will be the inferiors of their attorneys.⁴

Note, however, that Beecher uses the language of subordination, not inequality, in speaking of social relationships and that she characterizes the relation of subordination as one of obedience. One member of the parent-child or teacher-pupil dyad directs; the other obeys. Relations of inequality do not have to be characterized in this fashion. Teachers can be viewed as the guides, advisers, facilitators, helpers of their pupils, and parents as the caretakers or guardians of their children. In these cases, an emphasis on obedience to directives appears misplaced. And the husband-wife relation does not have to be viewed as one of inequality at all, let alone as a relation involving female obedience to male commands. In weaving the social fabric for the democratic state, however, Beecher rejects one of Wollstonecraft's central teachings: her Sarahs are to obey their husbands as willingly as Rousseau expected Sophie to obey Emile.

Beecher's daughters owe obedience to men not only in the marriage relation: whether or not they are married, their social and civil interests are to be entrusted to men. "Women have an equal interest in all social and civil concerns," Beecher says. But while denouncing any "domestic, civil, or political institution" that sacrifices women's interests in order to promote those of men, she denies her daughters the rights and duties of citizenship. Neither voting, making, nor administering laws is to be their concern. The result of a political order which secures women's interests without their participation "has been fairly tested," she claims. Quoting Tocqueville's *Democracy in America* with approval, she portrays a country in which "women never manage the outward concerns of the family, or conduct a business, or take a part in political life" (p. 5).

Given the Christian underpinnings of Beecher's political philosophy, one might have expected her justification of the subordination of women to rely on an appeal to the Supreme Lawgiver, but it does not. Nor does it rest solely on an appeal to distinct male and female natures. Although Beecher cites Tocqueville's reference to the "wide differences between the physical and moral constitutions of man and woman" nature has appointed, in placing her daughters in a position of obedience to their husbands and barring them from full citizenship, she looks to tradition and efficiency. "The Americans," Beecher quotes Tocqueville as saying, "have applied to the sexes the great principle of political economy, which governs the manufactories of our age, by carefully dividing the duties of man from those of woman, in order that the great work of society may be the better carried on" (p. 5). Efficiency thus constitutes the test Beecher says tradition has passed.[5] Shades of Plato, this, for he too makes efficiency a prime social value. In its name, however, he does not exclude women from direct political participation as Beecher does.

Rousseau also excludes women from direct political participation, but there is a significant difference in political status between his Sophie and Beecher's Sarah. Like Sophie, in obeying the law Sarah will be following the commands of others. But at least in Beecher's polity a husband is expected to represent his wife's interests. Thus, although Sarah lacks the political freedom Rousseau assumes to be a good for males, she has a political standing Rousseau denies Sophie. Beecher's daughters are not full citizens, but in requiring their husbands to represent them, Beecher gives women an indirect voice in the laws they must obey. Moreover, in maintaining that women have an equal interest in social, civil, and political concerns and institutions, she acknowledges that although they are not exactly citizens of the state, they are nonetheless to be counted among its members. As much cannot be said for Sophie. Although she is a member of what in *The Social Contract* Rousseau calls the earliest and only natural society, the family, she is not included in the "moral and collective body" that is the state. The "public person" formed by the union "of all other persons" is "composed of as many members as there are votes in the assembly."[6] Sophie has no vote; hence, she does not even belong to that civil state into which the state of nature is transformed by the social compact.

As a participant in the General Will, Emile will be his own legislator even as he obeys the laws of the state. Imagining the duty of obedience to be Sophie's by nature, Rousseau sees no loss of freedom resulting from her subjection to the commands of Emile or the state. Thus, although Rousseau might have required Citizen Emile to represent Sophie's interests when he participates in the General Will, he did not. Instead, Emile must set aside all special interests, including hers.

It may not have occurred to Rousseau, but it did to Beecher that to require a woman to obey her husband's commands seems to conflict with the demands of individual liberty. How else are we to explain her insistence that in a democracy no woman is obliged to take a husband and that every woman who does marry chooses her husband? For a person to *have* a choice there must *be* alternative courses of action from which to pick, and for one to *make* a choice he or she must *recognize* alternative courses of action as *real options*. In our own day the pressures to marry are so intense that many women do not entertain alternative life-styles as possibilities for themselves. Even supposing that the pressures were less intense in Beecher's time than they are now, for every independent woman like Beecher, who deliberated at great length before becoming engaged and remained single after her fiancé's untimely death, how many more there must have been who either never saw "spinsterhood" as an option or let others select their mates for them.

Beecher is driven to her assumption of marital choice by her need to reconcile the subordinate place she assigns women in marriage with the demands of liberty. Choice is relevant to this problem: it is often maintained that to the extent that one chooses one's rulers, liberty is preserved. Yet choice of a ruler accompanied by a requirement of obedience to that ruler is scarcely a formula for freedom. It is just this formula that seems to represent the plight of her daughters. For supposing that they do choose their husbands, the doctrine of wifely subordination apparently dooms them forever to a life of conformity to another's orders.

Beecher's appeal to marital choice may not preserve women's freedom, but it marks a very real difference between her theory of women's subordination and Rousseau's. Let us not forget that Sophie does not choose Emile, she is "given" to him. That Beecher's daughters in principle have a choice regarding marriage suggests that they are capable of at least a degree of self-determination. This, in turn, implies that, despite women's subordinate place in marriage and the polity, Beecher attributes to them the capacity for rational self-legislation.

In fact, in the world Beecher envisions women *must* be capable of reasoning for themselves and acting on their own, for as wives, mothers, homemakers, and "members of a social community" they have grave responsibilities. It is true that they are required to obey their husbands, yet the responsibilities Beecher assigns women are theirs alone. Moreover, she makes it clear that to carry them out well women must attain a high degree of skill and intellectual achievement and must be prepared to exercise judgment and take independent action. The duties belonging to Sarah could not possibly be fulfilled adequately by Sophie. It is not merely that Sophie's education would not provide her with the necessary knowledge to carry out the tasks Beecher describes. It would make Sophie too dependent on Emile's commands to be her own legislator even in the role that is peculiarly hers.

Sarah's Education

The title of Beecher's book is as misleading as Rousseau says Plato's title is. Just as the *Republic* is an educational treatise as well as a political one, so *A Treatise on Domestic Economy* sets forth not only a theory of domestic management but a theory of female education. In Beecher's presentation the two are interwined, since, in her view, female education constitutes a preparation for carrying out the domestic role. Nonetheless, it is possible—and important—to disentangle these two elements in her thought, for while Beecher delineates the tasks and functions belonging to the domestic role, her views on education clarify both the way the tasks are to be done and the character of the women who are to perform them. Recent commentary on Beecher has tended to pass over the educational aspects of her work; yet it is only when her proposals for female education are taken seriously that the innovative and perhaps even radical nature of her philosophy can be appreciated. It is only then that Sarah can be distinguished from the women portrayed in the magazines and religious tracts of the period.[7]

Historian Barbara Welter has summed up the mid-nineteenth century's ideal woman, saying that "the attributes of True Womanhood, by which a woman judged herself and was judged by her husband, her neighbors, and society, could be divided into four cardinal virtues—piety, purity, submissiveness, and domesticity. Put them all together and they spelled mother, daughter, sister, wife—woman. Without them, no matter whether there was fame, achievement or wealth, all was ashes. With them she was promised happiness and power."[8] Welter does not herself cite Beecher's writings, but the four cardinal virtues will be familiar to readers of *A Treatise,* for they are as essential to Beecher's Sarah as to the True Womanhood Welter describes. Because they are, it has been easy for historians to view Beecher's work as simply providing the theoretical underpinnings for an ideology that confined women to the home and reinforced their political subjection.[9] Yet to do this is to lose sight of the fact that the four cardinal virtues do not spell Sarah, as Welter says they spell True Womanhood.

That they do not becomes clear when one compares Sarah to Meg March, Louisa M. Alcott's example of True Womanhood. The oldest of Alcott's "little women," Meg possesses piety, purity, and submissiveness in an abundance surpassed only by her younger sister Beth. But although Beth takes pleasure in doing small domestic tasks, she wants only to play the piano and stay home with father and mother. It is Meg who exemplifies the kind of domesticity that is the concern of the cult of True Womanhood. "Why don't you say you'd have a splendid, wise, good husband, and some angelic little children? You know your castle wouldn't be perfect without," says Jo, whose own castle in the air consists of a stable full of Arabian horses, rooms piled with books, and a magic inkstand for writing the novel that will bring her fame and fortune.[10]

In disposition and temperament Meg is as domestic as the proponents of the Cult of True Womanhood could wish, but when she marries John Brooke, she does not possess the domestic skills she needs to keep his house. The catastrophe of the currant jelly testifies to her ineptitude: Meg spends a long, miserable day picking, boiling, straining, reboiling, resugaring, and re-straining jelly that never jells while racking her brain to remember what she has left undone. Thus Meg falls short of Beecher's ideal homemaker. Such a catastrophe could never happen in Sarah's home. Long before she marries she will have undergone an apprenticeship in domestic tasks, something Meg apparently never had to do. More important, in the unlikely event that the jelly fiasco occurred in Sarah's household, she would not give way to the tears, petulance, and anger

Meg displays when, surrounded by the mess she has created, she discovers that John has brought a friend home to dinner. In Beecher's vision of women, rational self-control joins piety, purity, submissiveness, and domesticity as a fifth cardinal virtue. Deriving from a kind of education Meg is never given, Sarah's self-control distinguishes her from the True Woman of Beecher's day, even if her early mastery of domestic skills and arts does not.

An understanding of Beecher's views on education allows us to perceive the great gulf between Sarah and Welter's True Woman; it also makes possible an interpretation of the two apparently conflicting theses in Beecher's rather complex philosophy: her thesis of women's subordination and her thesis of female control of the domestic environment. It is only when we grasp Sarah's mastery of the theoretical knowledge underlying the True Woman's domestic skills that we can be sure of Beecher's sincerity in asserting her second thesis. Furthermore, it is only when the educational dimension of *A Treatise* is probed that we can begin to appreciate her claims for the societal importance of the domestic role and hence for the equality of women.

In the first pages of *A Treatise* Beecher affirms the subordination of wives to their husbands, yet she ultimately leaves no doubt that her daughters are to be in charge of the domestic environment. Emily is to be in charge of this environment, too, but Sarah's position is different from Emily's, for Beecher's social vision greatly magnifies the importance of home and family. Beecher does not simply show how many and varied are women's tasks. By setting the domestic environment within the larger societal context, she reveals both its social and its political significance. Sklar's interpretation is helpful here.[11] Beecher, she says, points to domestic experience "as a focus around which a new and unified national identity could be built." Thus, the domestic sphere is for Beecher "not so much removed from as central to the national life." Beecher considers the home "an oasis of noncommercial values in an otherwise acquisitive society," but at the same time domestic activities and processes are directed toward the improvement of that society.

Given the strict limits she places on female participation in the larger society, one might expect Beecher to have prescribed a course of study designed simply to enable women to carry out narrow, specific household tasks in rote fashion. To the contrary, the education she would give Sarah is to be both broad and deep: Sarah is to undertake the kind of liberal course of study Wollstonecraft seeks for Emily plus a specialized curriculum in domestic economy. Moreover, this is to be accompanied by a vigorous program of physical education, for, like Plato, Beecher is certain that a strong mind in a weak "casket" is of little use.

"As a general rule," Beecher says, "daughters should not be sent to school before they are six years old; and when they go, far more attention should be paid to their physical development" (p. 26). They should never be confined for more than an hour at a time, she adds, and any such confinement should be followed by sports in the open air "at all seasons, and in all weathers." Until a girl is fourteen or fifteen the principal object of her education should be "to secure a strong and healthy constitution"—something Beecher perceived to be sadly lacking in the women of her day—"and a thorough practical knowledge of all kinds of domestic employments." During this time, "intellectual culture" should not be totally ignored, but it should be of secondary importance: "Such a measure of study and intellectual excitement, as is now demanded in our best female seminaries, ought never to be allowed, until a young lady has passed the most critical period of her youth, and has a vigorous and healthful constitution fully established" (p. 27).

Beecher gives mothers primary responsibility for the early physical and domestic education of girls. "Less time should be given to school," she says, "and much more to domestic employments" (p. 26). A child of five or six can assist her mother in household tasks, and "if properly trained, by the time she is ten, she can render essential aid." Even in the wealthy classes "all the sweeping, dusting, care of furniture and beds, and clear starching and the nice cooking, should be done by the daughters of a family, not by hired service" (p. 27). For this domestic apprenticeship Beecher provides a twofold justification: the daughters will acquire essential skills, and, since their time will be spent in active employments, "a strong and healthful constitution" will be secured.

If for Beecher a sound constitution is the major aim of early female education, mental discipline is the main objective of the systematic three-year course of study she then prescribes. After condemning the influence of the ordinary boarding school "on health, manners, disposition, intellect, and morals," she presents an account of her ideal institution in the form of a detailed sketch of the Monticello Female Seminary in Alton, Illinois. There is no need, Beecher says, to propose "a theory, which may, or may not, be approved by experience," for an institution already exists that "will give an idea of what can be done, by showing what has actually been accomplished" (p. 31). Needless to say, this model institution makes ample provision "to secure adequate exercise for its pupils." It requires that two hours a day be spent in domestic employments and introduces a system of calisthenic exercises combined with music. Its main feature, however, is its liberal curriculum, which includes mathematics, language, philosophy, chemistry, astronomy, botany, geology and minerology, intellectual and moral philosophy, political economy, the evidences of Christianity, geography, and history.

The liberal studies Beecher recommends for Sarah are to be rigorous as well as extensive. "The same textbooks are used as are required at our best colleges," she notes with approval. Moreover, in history "a more complete knowledge is secured, by means of charts and textbooks, than most of our colleges offer," while in geography "the largest work, and most thorough course, is adopted." To this demanding curriculum, adapted from male colleges—mathematics, for example, is to include "the whole of Arithmetic contained in the larger works used in schools, the whole of Euclid, and such portions from Day's Mathematics as are requisite to enable the pupils to demonstrate the various problems in Olmsted's larger work on Natural Philosophy" (p. 35)—is to be added the study of vocal music and linear drawing, as well as of certain texts in physiology, technology, and archaeology.

The first object of this education, which ranges across the intellectual disciplines, is not the amassing of information but the development of what today would be called the skills and attitudes of critical thinking and problem solving. "Many persons seem to suppose, that the chief object of an intellectual education is the acquisition of knowledge," Beecher says, "but it will be found, that this is only a secondary object." Rather, she says, "it is the formation of habits of investigation, of correct reasoning, of persevering attention, of regular system, of accurate analysis, and of vigorous mental acts, that are the primary objects to be sought" (p. 34).

Why, since she denies the duties and responsibilities of citizenship to women, does Beecher claim for Sarah the very education aimed at the development of reason and rational self-discipline that Wollstonecraft claims for Emily? She offers two responses. The first is that women's arduous domestic duties "demand not only quickness of perception, but steadiness of purpose, regularity of system and perseverance in action"

(p. 34). The second emerges from a close examination of the branch of study she calls "Domestic Economy." This subject was not a part of the curriculum of Beecher's model institution nor of other schools. Indeed, her object in writing *A Treatise* was to show the need "for introducing Domestic Economy as a branch of female education to be studied at school" (p. 41). Thus as she justified its inclusion in a female education, she was constructing a new field.[12] Chapters 5 to 40 of *A Treatise* set forth the content of the new subject under chapter headings such as "On Clothing," "On Healthful Food," "On Whitening, Cleansing, and Dyeing," "On Social Duties," and "On Management of Young Children."

Why should this subject be incorporated into female education? The first reason Beecher gives is its usefulness: at some time or other every female will be called upon to perform the duties to which domestic economy is directed. Furthermore, it cannot be assumed that young ladies will master this body of content in any other way. "What proportion of mothers are qualified to teach a *proper* and *complete* system of Domestic Economy?" she asks. "What proportion of those who are qualified have that sense of the importance of such instructions and that energy and perseverance which would enable them actually to teach their daughters in all the branches of Domestic Economy presented in this work?" And she asks, "How many mothers *actually do* give their daughters instruction in the various branches of Domestic Economy?" (p. 43).

To the objection that domestic economy cannot be taught through books, Beecher replies that young ladies learn chemistry this way and asks, "Why, then, should not that science and art, which a woman is to practice during her whole life, be studied and recited?" To the further objection that, if studied, domestic economy will be forgotten, she replies that much of everything studied in school will be forgotten; "Why should that knowledge, most needful for daily comfort, most liable to be in demand, be the only study omitted, because it may be forgotten?" (p. 44). To still another objection that young ladies could learn domestic economy simply by reading the books on their own, she replies, "And so they can get books on Chemistry and Philosophy, and study them out of school; but *will* they do it? And why ought we not to make sure the most necessary knowledge, and let the less needful be omitted?" (p. 45).

An education in domestic economy is not merely claimed for Sarah in *A Treatise,* it is created for her, and it is not reducible to simple skill training. Sarah is expected to acquire her domestic skills during long apprenticeship to her mother. Her formal study of domestic economy is designed to build upon that apprenticeship by providing her with a set of rules or principles of action to guide domestic practice and, more important, with a grasp of the theoretical knowledge upon which those principles rest. Thus, for example, Beecher says at the beginning of her chapter on the care of health: "There is no really efficacious mode of preparing a woman to take a *rational* care of the health of a family, except by communicating that knowledge, in regard to the construction of the body, and the laws of health, which is the first principle of the medical profession" (p. 48). There follow detailed descriptions of bones, muscles, nerves, blood vessels, and organs of digestion and respiration, accompanied by illustrations. Chapter 6, on healthful food, contains an even more elaborate account of the digestive organs, and chapter 8, on clothing, discusses details of circulation. Throughout *A Treatise* principles and technical knowledge are intermixed.

Although *A Treatise* was a best-seller in its day, it is not a superficial how-to manual—a purveyor of skill without understanding. Beecher believes that the principles governing the domestic environment can be applied properly only by one who understands the reasons for them. In the matter of health care, for example, a woman need not have a physician's training, "but she should gain a general knowledge of first principles as a guide to her judgment in emergencies when she can rely on no other aid" (p. 48). In the matter of healthful food, a woman should know that at least five hours should elapse between meals because the stomach requires three hours for labor and two for rest. Once she understands this she can take into account unusual circumstances such as the need very young, healthy, and active children may have for "a more frequent supply of food." In the matter of infant care, a woman should have "a knowledge of the wonderful and delicate construction of the several organs of life, and of the causes which operate to produce their diseased action" (p. 218), on the one hand, because physicians are rarely consulted until some damage is done, and on the other, because intelligence and information is required to obey physicians' directions.

Besides the principles of domestic practice, Beecher's subject of domestic economy includes a body of knowledge drawn from sources ranging from anatomy, chemistry, and botany to architecture, child development, and moral philosophy. A grasp of both practical and theoretical elements is necessary if Sarah is to carry out her domestic duties. If she acquires only the background knowledge upon which the principles rest, she will not know *what* to do; if she simply learns the principles of action, she will not know *how* to apply them wisely.

Beecher, then, prescribes a curriculum in domestic economy that will give Sarah the expertise to carry out the complex wife-mother role successfully. But the question remains: if this specialized study will make Sarah an expert homemaker, what grounds are there for claiming Emily's liberal education for her? Beecher's answer, that a liberal education has "transfer" value, should be familiar to those today who seek to justify liberal studies. What interests Beecher are the qualities of mind and character that Sarah will presumably derive from her liberal studies. In her view, Sarah will need these if she is to combine theory and practice intelligently in both the learning and the performance of her domestic duties.

Professional Homemakers

The ability to exercise independent judgment in practical matters, which Beecher wants Sarah to have, is precisely the mark of a professional, and it is to Beecher's credit to have realized that it results from a combination of theoretical and practical training. The knowledge of theory and fact that the study of domestic economy is supposed to yield will give women the expertise to make up their own minds about what to do in domestic matters. Lacking it, they will be "mere" technicians who carry out in robotlike fashion the procedures learned during their apprenticeships to their mothers.

The concept of professionalism is central to an understanding of Beecher's philosophy. Of course, if a professional is defined as one who exercises a skill for pay, Beecher's application of the term to women's domestic role cannot be taken literally. But there is a sense of the term *professional* that turns not on the issue of pay but on issues of knowledge and education, and a careful reading of the educational philosophy embedded in *A Treatise* suggests that, so interpreted, Beecher's conception of women as professionals in domestic matters should be taken literally.

In an article on Beecher, historian Joan N. Burstyn points out that "an occupation becomes professionalized when people systematize the knowledge needed to perform it. They draw generalizations from the specific knowledge of individual practitioners, and publish these generalizations so that those wishing to become practitioners may learn them and become qualified for the occupation."[13] She goes on to say that "Beecher's prescience on the need for women to professionalize their work was astounding"; she saw that men were professionalizing *their* work and sensed that women must do the same.

Burstyn makes clear how difficult it is for readers in the late twentieth century to comprehend Beecher's achievements. In an era of fast foods and miracle fabrics, we can scarcely grasp the nature of everyday life for most women in the 1840s. The sewing, ironing, washing; the making of hard and soft soap, starch, spot removers, dye; the cultivation of gardens and orchards; the care of domestic animals and barns: those who had servants and did not have to do all these things themselves still had to oversee and manage an enormous range of tasks. Moreover, because architecture has become a predominantly male profession, we assign little importance to Beecher's efforts to keep the design of houses and schools within women's sphere of influence. Perceiving teaching to be an underpaid and undervalued profession, we forget that in training the women who would teach domestic economy to Sarah, Beecher "was staking out a new territory for women: they were to be trained for their work, as men were trained for theirs" (p. 396). Knowing all too well that the professionalization Beecher espoused has not ensured women's control of work traditionally considered to be female, we fail to appreciate the remarkable vision at the center of her philosophy.

Burstyn describes Beecher's mission as teaching mothers how to care for their families and preparing teachers to educate children "from unfortunate homes." *A Treatise* bridges the gap between these two aims, for in constructing the subject the teachers are to transmit, the book specifies what mothers must know and do. Burstyn would acknowledge, however, that it is an underestimation of Beecher's philosophy to suppose that it is directed simply to the education of mothers and their teachers. In introducing the concept of professionalism into women's education and women's work, Beecher is trying to transform both the traditional female role and the education intended for it.

If Beecher were equating Sarah's expertise simply with being skilled, we would not be justified in taking her vision of professional homemakers seriously. The mark of a professional goes far beyond skilled performance.

But Beecher proposes that in the domestic domain Sarah should function as a physician or architect is expected to today.¹⁴ This conclusion is compelling when we contrast Beecher's analysis of domestic economy with a skill-oriented one.

In a book subtitled "Some Philosophical Problems with Feminism," Carol McMillan has said that "the assumption that reasoning is a characteristic peculiar only to those pursuits that have traditionally been confined to men—and that traditionally feminine roles such as child-rearing and home-making involve little or no use of the reasoning or intellectual faculty—is taken to be axiomatic on both sides of the debate between feminists and sexists."¹⁵ Wanting to convince her readers of the importance of domestic activities, and convinced herself that both feminists and sexists deny them value because they deny that they involve reason, McMillan argues that domestic activities involve foresight, preparation, and training.

McMillan does not acknowledge that Wollstonecraft and Beecher wanted to persuade their readers of the same thing. Ignoring Wollstonecraft's redefinition of the wife-mother role in terms of rational understanding and self-control and Beecher's attempts to show that a good homemaker must combine theoretical knowledge, skilled performance, and practical judgment, McMillan looks instead to the crafts of the Trukese navigator and the nineteenth-century British wheelwright for illumination of women's traditional activities. Describing these crafts as involving what philosophers call "tacit" and she calls "intuitive" knowledge—knowledge derived from years of practical experience and apprenticeship—McMillan concludes that domestic activities do require knowledge and reason, but of a sort neither feminists nor sexists admire. These groups take scientific knowledge as their model and thus value only theoretical reason, says McMillan; indeed, they often define reason as necessarily theoretical. But once reason is construed broadly to include nontheoretical, nonscientific thought, she believes that the domestic form of life—a form that she, like Beecher, seems to think is peculiarly appropriate for women—can be seen to be as significant as any other.

In reading McMillan, one is reminded of George Eliot's Mrs. Poyser. In knitting and spinning, cleaning and ironing, making butter and cheese, this wonderful minor character in *Adam Bede* displays the very kind of intuitive knowledge and practical judgment McMillan attributes to the navigator and the wheelwright. Coincidentally, in an introduction to some of Beecher's writings on education, Barbara Cross cites Mrs. Poyser as a fictional representation of Beecher's ideal homemaker.[16] Yet her assumption that Eliot's warm, friendly, strong-minded woman embodies Sarah's image is mistaken.

In the first place, although its absence takes different forms in the two women, Mrs. Poyser, like Meg March, noticeably lacks Sarah's rational self-control. Were Sarah to have a landlord, she would never talk to him as Mrs. Poyser does to Captain Donnithorne. "Mrs. Poyser, once launched into conversation," comments Eliot, "always sailed along, without any check from her preliminary awe of the gentry. The confidence she felt in her own powers of exposition was a motive force that overcame all resistance."[17] Nor would Sarah scream at her children as Mrs. Poyser screams at Totty for emptying the starch bowl over the ironing sheet or become agitated and tremble with anger as Mrs. Poyser does.

Highly excitable and garrulous, Mrs. Poyser lacks the command over her feelings that Sarah is supposed to derive from her liberal education. Nor does she have the theoretical background Sarah will gain from her formal study of domestic economy. Thus, despite Mrs. Poyser's demonstrable domestic skills—in this she is unlike Meg—and the fact that her dairy is prosperous, Beecher would undoubtedly judge her to be an inefficient homemaker, a poor role model for her daughter, an incompetent manager of her servant, and a hopeless educator of her nieces.

Indeed, it is not just the Meg Marches but also the Mrs. Poysers of her world whom Beecher's Sarah is meant to replace. Thus, McMillan's thesis about the kind of rationality required by the domestic form of life are precisely what Beecher rejects. In her philosophy, the domestic environment is a domain not of mere skilled performance but of theory and practice joined together.

Her professional status distinguishes Sarah from Mrs. Poyser and also provides Beecher with a way to escape the problem of conflicting theses her philosophy seems to present. We have seen that Beecher makes wives subordinate to their husbands and that subordination, in her view, entails obedience. We have also seen that she posits female control of the domestic sphere. How is this possible? How can women be their own legislators in domestic matters if in all things they must obey their husbands? One tempting way to solve this problem is to deny that Beecher advocates the thesis of female control. However, the education she would give Sarah is so clearly conceived as preparation for managing domestic affairs—as opposed merely to carrying out the commands of another—that to deny Beecher's acceptance of the thesis of female control would be an act of sheer desperation. Why would Beecher prescribe professional training in domestic economy if Sarah were to be a "mere technician"? Why would she insist on a liberal education if Sarah were destined to exercise the domestic skills she had learned during her apprenticeship to her mother only under the commands of another?

That in Beecher's view women are supposed to control the domestic environment cannot be denied once her theory of female education is taken into account. Given the extent to which Sarah's reason is to be developed and her judgment trained and enlarged by her education, Beecher clearly means it when she says that "she, who is the mother and housekeeper in a large family, is the *sovereign* of an empire" (p. 144). How different is Rousseau's notion of women's "empire" as one

> of gentleness, skills, and obligingness; her orders are caresses, her threats are tears. She ought to reign in the home as a minister does in a state—by getting herself commanded to do what she wants to do. In this sense, the best households are invariably those where the woman has the most authority. But when she fails to recognize the voice of the head of the house, when she wants to usurp his rights and be in command herself, the result of this disorder is never anything but misery, scandal, and dishonor. (p. 408)

Beecher's thesis of female control cannot be wished away, then, but her thesis of subordination can be interpreted so that contradiction is avoided. One way would be to construe it as having application only in nondomestic affairs. The trouble with this solution, however, is that it does not fit comfortably with the passage from Tocqueville, quoted approvingly by Beecher, that states "that every association must have a head, in order to accomplish its object; and that the natural head of the conjugal association is man" (p. 6). Moreover, one wonders why, if the subordination thesis is meant to apply only in nondomestic matters, Beecher says that women are subordinate in the domestic relation.

A more plausible interpretation of the subordination thesis may derive from a distinction between having the right to command another and exercising this right. Let us grant that Sarah's husband has the right to issue commands about housekeeping and child rearing and that she has a duty to obey all his commands. The question of the contexts in which he ought to exercise that right remains. In view of Sarah's professional education in domestic economy—an education Beecher does not extend to Sarah's husband—it makes no sense for him to tell her what to do in domestic affairs. Sarah is the one with the expertise. The rational thing for her husband to do, therefore, is to acquiesce to her judgment in domestic matters. The relationship of husband to wife in Beecher's philosophy can be understood as analogous to that of a king to his physician. The king, having the right to command all his subjects, has the right to order his physician to prescribe one medication rather than another, and the physician's duty is to do what the king tells him. Yet, if the physician is well trained, is not suffering from amnesia, and does not belong to an opposing faction and the king himself has not studied medicine, it would be irrational for a king to demand obedience from his physician, since the doctor's professional competence gives him an authority in medical matters the king lacks.[18]

Sarah's education in domestic economy is intended to transform her into a professional in domestic matters, to provide the grounding for her control of the domestic environment or, to put this in another way, to provide the warrant for her husband's accepting her autonomous judgment in domestic matters. It would be as unreasonable for Sarah's husband to direct her activities as it would be for a king to direct his physician's. By virtue of her education Sarah thus becomes a self-governing agent in her own household even as in civil and political matters she is prevented from being her own legislator.

It is helpful here to compare the position in the home Beecher envisions for Sarah to Meg's position in John Brooke's home. Were Meg to possess Sarah's professional knowledge and skill, she would not look to John to bail her out of her difficulties in the kitchen. Nor would she have to show him her accounts each month. The kindest and gentlest of husbands, John Brooke has no desire to run his household; on the contrary, he wants and expects Meg to do so. But it is *his* household; at the time of the novel's action, both legally and economically, it is *his* responsibility. Upon discovering that Meg cannot run it, John has little choice but to give her whatever guidance he can, if not actually to issue commands.

Married to Sarah, John's pride in his wife's skills would be vindicated, and he could leave to her the management of his home. One surmises that he might miss Meg's childlike dependency on him, for he does seem to derive enjoyment from acting as his wife's superior in domestic matters. In exchange for a pleasure that Beecher, like Wollstonecraft, would doubtless consider suspect, however, he would have what both philosophers would consider the greater happiness of being able to respect his wife's opinions about her own realm. Unfortunately, we do not know what John would do if his wife's autonomous judgment in domestic matters came into conflict with his own judgment in nondomestic matters. Suppose Sarah decides that a child of theirs requires a form of education that John deems too costly. It is difficult to say whether Beecher would have the two "experts" in their respective spheres work out a compromise in every instance of conflict, or would have Sarah give way to John in all cases on the ground that her husband has ultimate authority over her, or would have John give way to Sarah on the ground that her professional judgment always takes precedence in domestic affairs. But it is possible to understand how, in practice, Sarah can be sovereign in the home even as she is theoretically subordinate to her husband.

This interpretation of the subordination thesis allows Beecher to maintain both her thesis of female control and the subordination thesis without contradiction. Moreover, this reading accords with her commentary on Tocqueville: "In civil and political affairs," she says, "American women take no interest or concern, except so far as they sympathize with their family and personal friends; but in all cases, in which they do feel a concern, their opinions and feelings have a consideration, equal, or even superior, to that of the other sex." She continues, "In matters pertaining to the education of their children, in the selection and support of a clergyman, in all benevolent enterprises, and in all questions relating to morals or manners, they have a superior influence. In all such concerns, it would be impossible to carry a point, contrary to their judgement and feelings; while an enterprise, sustained by them, will seldom fail of success" (p. 9).

Beecher is not content merely to assert female control of the domestic environment. After appealing to Tocqueville's description of American men and women in order to convince her readers that "equal" does not necessarily mean "identical," she quotes him as saying: "There are people in Europe who, confounding together the different characteristics of the sexes, would make of man and woman, beings not only equal, but alike. . . . It is not thus that the Americans understand the species of democratic equality, which may be established between the sexes" (p. 5). And she sums up his position: "It appears, then, that it is in America, alone, that women are raised to an equality with the other sex, and that, both in theory and practice, their interests are regarded as of equal value" (p. 9).

Beecher's acceptance of Tocqueville's different-but-equal thesis makes it dubious to ascribe to her an explicit assumption of female inequality. Perhaps her philosophy does not succeed in making women's role equal to men's, but there can be no doubt that she puts forth a claim of equality in *A Treatise*. Nor is there any doubt that her adherence to the different-but-equal thesis raises new questions about the internal consistency of her theory. How are we to reconcile her different-but-equal thesis with the thesis of subordination? How can women and men be thought to be equal when one sex has the right to command and the other the duty to obey?

Women as Educators

It must be emphasized that the different-but-equal thesis rests ultimately not on an assumption of differences per se but on the assumption that different tasks and functions are equally important or valuable and hence deserve equal respect. How is the importance or value of a task or function to be determined? Beecher answers this question, as Plato might, by reference to the contribution it makes to the development and maintenance of the good society. She is thus able to consider the roles of her daughters and sons to be equal, even though the females are denied the rights of full citizenship, because she thinks their domestic activities contribute to the good society no less than men's political activities. "The builders of a temple are of equal importance," Beecher says, "whether they labor on the foundations, or toil upon the dome" (p. 14).

That the tasks Beecher assigns women are important scarcely needs to be said. In any society infants must be cared for, food must be prepared, clothing made, laundry washed, the sick nursed, gardens tended, houses cleaned. Beecher's case for her different-but-equal thesis does not rest, however, on this obvious point but rather on her claim for the overriding social significance of the educative function of women. "Are not the most responsible of all duties committed to the care of women?" she asks. "Is it not her profession to take care of mind, body, and soul? and that, too, at the most critical of all periods of existence?" (p. 30). The happiness of the race, she insists, depends "on the formation of habits of self-denying benevolence"; therefore, "this ought to be the prominent object, in the minds of those who have control of young children" (p. 225).

To Beecher, control of young children is the sphere of women, especially mothers. Her philosophy may give men *ultimate* control over their children. But *A Treatise* specifies the kind of competence in child rearing women must have to guarantee that their husbands, if rational, will neither undermine nor overrule what their wives do. In several of her chapters—for instance "On Domestic Manners," "On the Management of Young Children," and "On Domestic Amusements"—Beecher spells out the details of the female educative task. Submission of the will, self-denial, and benevolence "are the three most important habits to form in early life," she says (p. 225), and she recommends also that children be taught at an early age that lying and stealing are wrong and that both sexes be trained to "modesty and purity of mind" (p. 233). She charges mothers with the cultivation of benevolent and social feelings by "influencing children to share their fruits and flowers with friends and neighbors, as well as to distribute roots and seeds to those who have not the means of procuring them" (p. 259); she suggests that mothers enter the sports of childhood to make them more entertaining and to exert "a healthful moral influence over their minds" (p. 262). She charges them also with remedying a serious defect in the manners of the American people: namely, "a deficiency in the free expression of kindly feelings and sympathetic emotions, and a want of courtesy in deportment" (p. 121).

Beecher is not the first philosopher to notice that mothers are educators of their young. According to Wollstonecraft, one reason Sophie is destined to fail as a mother is that she would not have "sufficient character to manage a family or educate children" (p. 69). Indeed, the education of children is one of the two duties Wollstonecraft associates with mothering—the other being suckling one's infants—and the concern of that education is nothing less than the formation of character. A good mother, she says, will live "to see the virtues which she endeavored to plant on principles, fixed into habits, to see her children attain strength of character sufficient to enable them to endure adversity without forgetting their mother's example" (p. 91). One of the first and most important steps in this process, as any reader of *Little Women* will know, is "the management of temper." But the teaching done by a good mother will include instruction and the fostering of domestic affections as well as the inculcation of virtue. Thus Wollstonecraft recognized that mothers are teachers and, further, that the teaching mothers do is directed not just to the transmission of discrete skills such as tying shoelaces but to the development of values, principles, and habits.

As the following excerpts from his pedagogical novel *Leonard and Gertrude* (1781–87) makes clear, the philosopher of education Johann Heinrich Pestalozzi recognized this, too:

> "Well, my dears, how has it been about doing right this week?" The children looked at each other, and were silent. "Annie, have you been good this week?"
>
> Casting down her eyes in shame, the child replied: "No, mother; you know how it was with my little brother"——
>
> "Annie, something might have happened to the child,—and just think how *you* would like it, if you should be shut up in a room all alone without food or amusement! Little children who are left alone in that way sometimes scream so that they injure themselves for life. Why, Annie, I could never feel easy about going away from home, if I thought you would not take good care of the child."
>
> "Indeed, mother, I will never leave him alone again!"
>
> "And Nicholas," said Gertrude, turning to her oldest son: "How is it with you this week?"[19]

That mothers are educators is scarcely acknowledged today; social scientists and educational researchers say that mothers "socialize" their young, but the term *educator* is reserved for what teachers do, and in their view teachers and mothers stand "worlds apart."[20] Still, although lost to us, Beecher's fundamental insight into the mothering role was shared by Wollstonecraft and Pestalozzi, both of whom wrote in the late eighteenth century, and is implicit—albeit undeveloped—in Rousseau's claims for the necessity of the traditional family. Nevertheless, if a perception of mothers as educators is not original with Beecher, she is the one who elaborates women's educative function and derives the strongest possible implications from it. For Wollstonecraft, educating her children is a woman's duty. For Pestalozzi, that education provides a model for schoolteachers to emulate. For Beecher, the educative function of women provides an essential grounding for her claim to sex equality, if not actual superiority.

Beecher could not look to women's educative function to support her different-but-equal thesis if she imagined it to consist simply of skill training. In a chapter entitled "To Mother Is to Teach," contained in a book on motherhood published in 1978, Elaine Heffner says, "Child rearing is essentially education." Yet the picture she paints of mothers teaching their children to drink from a cup, eat with a spoon and fork, and put away their toys scarcely does justice to the insight of Wollstonecraft and Pestalozzi, let alone that of Beecher.[21] In the brief dialogue from Pestalozzi quoted above we see the mother not merely transmitting values—something social scientists have repeatedly told us that families do—but actively attempting to form her child's character. Beecher assigns just this task to Sarah when she says, "The formation of the moral and intellectual character of the young is committed mainly to the female hand" (p. 13).

Beecher could not look to women's educative function if the larger culture of her day contributed to the formation of character in the way ours does. In *Family Politics,* Letty Cottin Pogrebin makes claims for families in 1983 rather like those Beecher made for mothers in 1841. The family, says Pogrebin, "is where we learn love, communication, trust, sharing, a sense of humor, a value system, and the control and expression of anger and of sexuality. It is where we experience the consequences of our actions, the limits of egoism, and the pleasures of pleasing others."[22]

Pogrebin is right that the family is an educative institution, and one would like to think it promotes at least some of the virtues she lists. But in the late twentieth century our characters are surely not formed solely or even primarily by the family. It is simply not true that in America today the family is "almost omni-powerful," as Pogrebin suggests. Whether we like it or not, schools, libraries, peer groups, and above all the mass media contribute enormously to the moral and intellectual character of our young. In Beecher's day, however, the home had relatively little competition in forming the character of the young. For this reason Beecher could deny women direct participation in politics and still make her case for their equality. Even as she charges Sarah as a mother with forming the character of her own children, she charges her as a sister and a wife with forming the character and destiny of the nation: "The mother writes the character of the future man; the sister bends the fibres that hereafter are the forest tree; the wife sways the heart, whose energies may turn for good or for evil the destinies of a nation" (p. 13).

Compare Beecher's vision of a wife as her husband's teacher with the picture Alcott paints in *Little Women.* In the novel we twice encounter the reverse of the educative relation Beecher prescribes. In an early scene Marmee tells her rebellious daughter Jo about her own struggles to conquer her temper. "How did you learn to keep still?" Jo asks. Marmee replies that first her mother helped her and then, after she married, Jo's father did:

> "He never loses patience,—never doubts or complains,—but always hopes, and works and waits so cheerfully, that one is ashamed to do otherwise before him. He helped and comforted me, and showed me that I must try to practice all the virtues I would have my little girls possess, for I was their example."
>
> "I used to see father sometimes put his finger on his lips, and look at you with a very kind, but sober face, and you always folded your lips tight or went away: was he reminding you then?" asked Jo softly.
>
> "Yes; I asked him to help me so, and he never forgot it, but saved me from many a sharp word by that little gesture and kind look."[23]

Meg also finds herself her husband's pupil, not his teacher. "Poor little thing!" John exclaims to himself after the currant jelly episode. "It was hard upon her when she tried so heartily to please me. She was wrong, of course, but then she was young. I must be patient and teach her" (p. 225). And so he does, by praising her when the bills are paid and the books are all in order, and by returning the new overcoat he needs when vanity and extravagance—these, not anger, are Meg's "bosom enemies"—get the best of her.

Granted, in Beecher's philosophy a woman's educative effect on the nation is mediated by a man—her husband or perhaps her brother—in that she will educate him and he then will go on and take political action. Nevertheless, Beecher would have us see Sarah as the decisive link in the causal chain. A professional by virtue of her study of domestic economy, she is not only an educated but an educative being, and for Beecher, education is a moving force—indeed, *the* moving force—in society.

Beecher's thesis of the significance of women's role rests, then, on a conception of women's educative function that extends beyond skill training to character formation, and beyond the formation of the character of individuals to the formation of the character of the nation itself. This thesis in turn supports her different-but-equal thesis, for in making women determinants of the national character, it gives them a profoundly important societal role. Moreover, when it is understood that this role is to be carried out by rational, self-governing women, the apparent incompatibility of the different-but-equal thesis and the subordination thesis disappears. Her sons do have the right of command over her daughters, but in light of women's de facto control of domestic affairs and the social and political significance of those affairs for society as a whole, their role can plausibly be seen as equal to that of men.

The domestic tasks Beecher assigns to Sarah have such a significant contribution to make to the larger society that one is left wondering if, in Beecher's social vision, Sarah's role does not actually outweigh her husband's. We are so accustomed to according the highest social significance to political activity it is difficult for us to imagine how a role that does not encompass direct political participation could possibly be considered equal to—let alone more important than—one in which political action is central. Yet this is precisely what Beecher asks us to do in *A Treatise*. She is challenging both the hierarchy of values that places the political above the domestic and the assumption that the domestic is not also the political. Granted, direct participation in politics is forbidden Sarah. But in Beecher's philosophy this does not detract from the importance of Sarah's domestic role, nor does it mean that her educative function is not itself political. Sarah may not be allowed to act *in* the political realm, but she is expected to act *on* it.

It will be recalled that for Rousseau the educational is the political. So it is for Beecher too. Actually, for Beecher the educational is doubly political in that domestic education is supposed to produce a person who not only exerts a causal influence on politics but does so through education. Beecher's daughters are to provide her sons with a political education: not, of course, with a vocationally oriented one that transmits skills of governing, nor with a professionally conceived one that provides rules or principles to guide political practice and a body of fact and theory to support them, nor even with one designed to instill patriotism; but rather with an education of the heart that will guarantee that political action, when taken, will be moral.[24] Women, she says, have "the exalted privilege of extending over the world those blessed influences, that are to renovate degraded man, and 'clothe all climes with beauty!' " (p. 13).

Is Sarah's education adequate to this task? Sophie's is not, and neither is Emily's. If Beecher has her way, in carrying out her domestic duties Sarah will be using the considerable intellectual powers she derives from her education. Thus she will presumably be spared Emily's frustration at having been educated for a life of reason but not in the application of reason to the societal functions she must carry out. Sarah will also be spared Emily's dissatisfaction with having to manage the domestic environment, for, as a professional homemaker, she will have been educated to see the complexity and believe in the overriding importance of domestic functions, whereas Emily's education will have taught her to look down on them, if not actually to despise them. Moreover, the realization that she holds the fate of a nation in her hands will no doubt give her the desire to maintain a proper home atmosphere for husband as well as children.

Nevertheless, although Sarah may have the intelligence and desire Sophie lacks to create a proper domestic environment and none of Emily's misgivings, it is far from clear that her education will develop in her the nurturing capacities and the care, concern, and compassion required of one who is to be the educator of her children and who is to sway her husband's heart toward moral political purposes. *A Treatise* contains a remarkable section in which Beecher criticizes Americans for "a deficiency in the free expression of kindly feelings and sympathetic emotions," which she attributes to the harsh conditions under which the new country was settled: "The sufferings they were called to endure, the subduing of those gentler feelings which bind us to country, kindred, and home, and the constant subordination of the passions to stern principle, induced characters of great firmness and self-control" (p. 121). It thus became custom and habit, she says, "to repress, rather than to encourage, the expression of feeling." But if she attempts to understand the reasons people "are predisposed to conceal the gentler emotions" (p. 122), she does not approve this tendency. Rather, she argues that when kindness is tendered in a cold, unsympathetic manner or is accepted with nonchalance its value is diminished.

This defect in the expression of the "gentler emotions" falls to mothers to correct, Beecher tells us. Yet instead of proposing that mothers must therefore instill an ethics of care in their children, she discusses the rules of good breeding: who takes precedence over whom, the proper mode of address between child and adult, suitable table manners. Beecher may not quite see, as Adrienne Rich does, that as both mothers and daughters, women above all need trust and tenderness,[25] but she does recognize the importance of the free flow of gentle emotions in human relationships. She then pulls back from this genuine insight and so does not actually build it into the educative function. Since there is no place for it in the liberal and professional education she prescribes for her daughters, the education they must have in order to sustain a home life permeated by these gentler emotions and to pass them on to their children can only be gotten from their mothers. However, this is exactly the point at which Beecher fails. Having designed an education for Sarah to ensure the health of her "casket," the powers of her intellect, and her self-control, she gives short shrift to the very feelings and emotions she believes Sarah needs to have and to pass on to her own young.

In the final analysis, then, Sarah's liberal education, her professional education, and the moral education she receives at home do not make adequate provision for the development of the "kindly feelings" and "sympathetic emotions" Beecher herself says Sarah must have to be a good wife and mother. It is tempting, of course, to suppose that Sarah's home will be so filled with the gentler emotions that no specific provisions are needed in Beecher's philosophy. Yet her own comments that Americans are deficient in them make it impossible for us to adopt this easy answer.

Domesticity and Reason

It is understandable that Sarah's education, like Emily's, stresses the acquisition of knowledge, reasoning power, self-discipline, and independent judgment at the expense of the development of the gentler emotions. These emotions were genderized in favor of females in Wollstonecraft's and Beecher's society, as they are in ours. Historically, traits associated with females have been considered to be inferior virtues at best. Wollstonecraft dare not include the development of the gentler emotions in Emily's education lest Emily be denigrated for possessing qualities that are thought to detract from her rationality and hence from her capacity to carry out the duties of citizenship. Nor does Beecher dare to include it, lest Sarah fail to be respected in her capacity of homemaker. After all, Beecher's position is not just that women's role is at least as important to the good society as men's but that it deserves equal respect.

Actually, Beecher's position is that the domestic role deserves equal respect provided that, in carrying it out, women do not behave as "mere technicians" acting under the direction of men. Beecher is assuming that were their husbands to make the difficult domestic decisions, they and not their wives would be the ones to merit respect. The argument sounds plausible, but in view of McMillan's praise of nontheoretical expertise and of Mrs. Poyser's sovereignty in her kitchen and dairy, we must ask if, like Wollstonecraft in another context, Beecher has not committed the fallacy of false dilemma. Is Beecher wrongly assuming that the only alternative to Sarah is Meg March, a person of superficial skill and uncertain judgment? Does not Mrs. Poyser, a highly successful, skilled practitioner, represent another alternative?

There is no doubt that for all her noise and inefficiency, Mrs. Poyser, not her husband, has control over her family's domestic environment— or at least over those aspects of it considered the province of women. Moreover, she commands not only her husband's respect but her community's as well. Thus, insofar as Beecher thinks that to manage a domestic environment and be respected for it a woman must necessarily have theoretical learning, she is mistaken. In domesticity, as in navigation, authority can derive from an expertise gained through apprentice learning and firsthand experience.

However, while Mrs. Poyser's skills are such as to earn her respect and give her autonomy in her sphere of activity, they will not make her a better domestic practitioner than her predecessors or allow her to improve upon their practice. Like the Trukese navigator and the British wheelwright, Mrs. Poyser works within a tradition. Her training is essentially conservative—or, perhaps one should say, preservative: its object is to equip her to do exactly as her forebears did and, eventually, to teach her successors to do as she does. Beecher, however, is critical of traditional domestic practice. Her aim is that it be done better in the future than it has been in the past. Thus she would persist in denying that Mrs. Poyser represents a viable alternative to Sarah even while having to acknowledge Mrs. Poyser's domestic sovereignty at the Hall Farm.

Of course, one need not agree with Beecher's poor opinion of mid-nineteenth-century domestic practice. However, her emphasis on the theoretical intelligence required by good domestic practice is motivated only in part by her interest in improving it. The primary reason lies in her larger project of challenging a value hierarchy that places political above domestic activity. Although she rejects the most central features of Wollstonecraft's philosophy—the citizen role for women and egalitarian marriage—in her own way Beecher is as much a rationalist as Wollstonecraft is. Thus, while McMillan may be satisfied to discern a different but equal kind of intelligence at work in domestic affairs, Beecher is not. Just as Wollstonecraft believes that in order to extend to women the rights of men she must show that females possess the same kind of rationality as males, so Beecher believes that in order to extend to the female role the value attributed to the male role, she must show that domestic activity requires the same kind of rationality as political activity. Beecher may believe in different but equal roles, but in her philosophy, role equality is premised on the unity of reason.

Recognizing that the Western tradition values abstract, theoretical, deliberative reason over concrete, practical, intuitive judgment, and perceiving only the latter in domestic practice, McMillan proposes that if we are to acknowledge the value of domestic activity, we must change our attitudes toward reason itself. In contrast, Beecher would have us realize that domestic practice rests on a scientific base and thus requires the exercise of the abstract, theoretical, deliberative reason we value most. No wonder she claims for her daughters the liberal education her sons are to have. The assumption that their different roles require the same kind of intelligence is central to her philosophy, and she, like Wollstonecraft—and ultimately like Plato—assumes that the way to develop this kind of intelligence is through a liberal education.

In claiming this education specifically in relation to the wife-mother role, Beecher accomplishes something that neither Plato nor Wollstonecraft does and something Rousseau certainly does not do. Plato does not need to reconcile female reason with the domestic role, for those women who possess reason will not marry, maintain a household, or engage in child rearing. Rousseau does not need to do this either since his women are not meant to be rational beings. Wollstonecraft, on the other hand, does need to provide an account of female education that acknowledges reason in domestic affairs, but it is Beecher, not Wollstonecraft, who succeeds in this task. By ignoring Plato's Difference Postulate Wollstonecraft more or less by default extends the education she designs for citizenship to the domestic role. Beecher takes this postulate seriously, however, and develops an education for domestic affairs founded on the application of reason.[26]

Thus Beecher goes well beyond Wollstonecraft's initial insight that rationality is important to the proper disposition of domestic matters. She has a richer conception of the way reason functions in domestic affairs. In Wollstonecraft's philosophy one can know one's duties only through the use of one's reason; in relation to domestic affairs, however, rationality plays essentially a preventive role: it provides the self-control and self-discipline a woman needs to hold onto her husband, run her household, and bring up her children. By keeping women from being slaves to their senses, reason will keep mothers from being lost in the coquette, domestic servants from being tyrannized, children from being spoiled. Given Wollstonecraft's project of rejecting Sophie, this account is appropriate. But in Beecher's account of domestic affairs reason has a positive role to play in that domestic activities themselves require the application of theoretical knowledge to practical judgment.

Many modern readers of *A Treatise* would no doubt accuse Beecher of mystifying the domestic role, thereby making it more palatable to the women she confines in it. It is important, however, to distinguish the effect her theory of domestic economy may have had on her readers from the internal logic of her philosophy. In elaborating her thesis of female control, her thesis of the significance of women's role, and the different-but-equal thesis, Beecher's book may have served in its day to "pacify" women. Nonetheless, *A Treatise* is a remarkable philosophical achievement. In making clear that women are to be as much their own legislators in domestic affairs as men are in political matters, and that the domestic environment poses problems so difficult and challenging that both a liberal and a professional education are required of its practitioners, Beecher is able to conclude that women's tasks and functions ought to command the respect that men's do. Rich maintains that if women are to learn to love themselves they need not only trust and tenderness but a strong sense of "self-nurture," by which she means a sense of respect and affection for their bodies and a feeling of pride in being female.[27] Beecher's social and educational philosophy is designed to instill this pride.

Of course, since for all her professional competence, Sarah is just as dependent economically on her husband as Meg is on John Brooke and as Wollstonecraft's Emily is on hers, it is possible—perhaps even highly likely—that it will be difficult for him to respect Sarah's domestic activities. Even if he does, Sarah's economic dependence ultimately must place her at the mercy of his whims. Similarly, her political dependence on her husband may also serve to create a gap between the respect she deserves for her activities and that which she is actually given. In addition, Beecher may be unrealistic in attributing so much causal efficacy to people to whom she denies full political rights, people she places in a subordinate station. She may be unrealistic in supposing that the rougher emotions she discerns in the world outside the home will have less effect on the domestic environment than that environment has on the outside world.

Even so, in forging a causal chain in which women constitute the decisive link in the creation and maintenance of the good life and the good society, Beecher explicitly gives both women and the domestic form of life an importance few philosophers ever have. I say "explicitly" because it can be argued that Beecher's causal chain was forged earlier by Rousseau. But what is implicit in his account of Sophie and Emile and certainly not intentional becomes explicit in Beecher's social philosophy as reason and domesticity are consciously joined together. Furthermore, if Beecher has her way, Sarah's economic and political dependence on a man will no more prevent her from being perceived as his equal than will his domestic dependence on her. Indeed, Beecher's whole point is that men and women are dependent on one another. This is Rousseau's point, too, although in his paeans to Emile's autonomy he often loses sight of it, but whereas Rousseau deprives Sophie's role of the rationality the Western tradition values so highly, Beecher makes that rationality its most striking feature.

A *Treatise* is all the more remarkable because Beecher claims a liberal education for Sarah even though she wants to deny her the rights and duties of citizenship. Plato justifies a liberal education for women on the ground that it develops the rational mind people need to be rulers of his Just State, and Wollstonecraft also bases the case for women's liberal education on the citizen role. Beecher, however, realizes that another justification is possible. Construing liberal education very much as Plato and Wollstonecraft do and embracing Plato's Functional Postulate, she extends what has traditionally been men's education to women so that they will carry out well the societal role that has traditionally been theirs, not men's. This is an important switch, for if Beecher's daughters are to be teachers of the young and the continuing educators of their husbands, they must have not only the rational powers of mind she sees as the outcome of a liberal education but also the knowledge and breadth of vision such an education can yield. Recall our fear that Sophie will manipulate Citizen Emile to her own private ends. In view of Sarah's education in intellectual and moral philosophy, history, and political economy, this fear is unjustified. Sarah's domain may be domestic, but her education is liberal in both scope and purpose.

But Sarah's education is specialized as well as liberal, and therein lies whatever substance the charge of mystification has. Does the exercise of good judgment in domestic matters really require a detailed knowledge of anatomy, physics, chemistry, and the like? In view of the complex decisions even those who simply shop in a supermarket must make today, the answer to this question is not self-evident. Obviously, in the last years of the twentieth century both the principles of action and the background knowledge contained in *A Treatise* are outmoded, although readers of such publications as *Nutrition Action* and the *Tufts University Diet and Nutrition Letter* as well as members of the home economics profession will be sympathetic toward Beecher's endeavor. The question remains if those who, for instance, plan meals must possess all the knowledge these publications bring to bear on this single domestic task. And if this question receives an affirmative answer, the question then arises whether an adequate practical grasp of this material requires formal study.

In any case, it must nonetheless be acknowledged that in stressing the relevance of the various theoretical disciplines to domestic practice, Beecher shows us that domestic activity, which has traditionally been considered to belong to women, and theoretical learning, which has traditionally been considered to belong to men, do not after all stand worlds apart. This insight eluded both Plato and Rousseau, and McMillan's book testifies to the fact that even now Beecher's point is far from being our commonplace.

Both the philosophy of education and the social philosophy Beecher develops in *A Treatise* contain numerous insights. This is not to say that we should embrace a vision of the social order in which women are denied direct political participation or are required to be homemakers. But there is more to Beecher's social and political theorizing than might at first be realized. If her sex-based division of tasks and functions is to be rejected—as it surely should be—there is still a great deal to be learned from her philosophy. When Sklar says that by the end of *A Treatise* the domestic sphere is central to the national life she is correct. Beecher's ideal is not a stereotypical two-sphere society in which one distinctly inferior sphere, the domestic, supports the other, the public or political, which is then taken to constitute the whole of civil society. In Beecher's vision the domestic and the public spheres *together* constitute civil society, and there is *interaction* between them. It is taken for granted, of course, that men's economic and political activities will affect home and family, but for Beecher the primary flow of influence between spheres moves from the domestic to the public, and hence from women to men.

We have seen that this flow of influence from women to men may be impeded because Beecher neglects Sarah's education in the gentle emotions. Like Wollstonecraft, Beecher claims a one-sided intellectualistic education for women and for the same reason. True, Beecher rejects for her daughters the citizen role Wollstonecraft demands. Yet, she wants the wife-mother role to be as valuable as any societal role; and while her philosophy makes her daughters subordinate to their husbands, she wants them to be respected for being wives and mothers. Thus, even as Wollstonecraft feels that she must stress female rationality to show that women deserve to be citizens, Beecher feels that she must do so to show that their traditional duties are valuable and deserve respect. Beecher, then, has a twofold task: she has to show that women's reason can be developed through education; she must also show what McMillan claims is not acknowledged even today—namely that homemakers need reason.[28]

Beecher's educational philosophy deserves criticism for being one-sided and also because it makes no provision for the special ways in which males must be educated to be husbands and citizens. In the context of Beecher's thought, what good will it do to give women a professional education in domestic economy if men are not educated to be rational husbands? Why should men be expected to promote the civil interests of their wives and daughters if they are not educated to take women's concerns seriously? Can the diffusion of the gentle emotions through the population—if that is what Beecher really wants—be accomplished if men are not educated to reject their culture's identification of softness and femininity, toughness and masculinity? We can assume that Beecher's sons will receive a liberal education: after all, Sarah's liberal education follows the course of study used in the male colleges of Beecher's day. But that liberal education cannot be depended upon to foster a recognition of their wives' claims to autonomy in domestic matters, to respect for their domestic activities, or to an equal interest in all social and civil matters, let alone an appreciation of traits genderized in favor of females.

The gaps in Beecher's theorizing are very real, but we must not allow them to blind us to her remarkable achievement. Focusing on Emile's dependency on Sophie, rather than on Sophie's dependency on Emile, she carves out for her daughters a realm of theoretical and practical reason in which women are self-governing agents and claims for them an education to match. In so doing, she accomplishes for domestic affairs what Rousseau has long been acclaimed for accomplishing for politics. Rejecting Plato's program of assigning all but the rational few to a life of obedience to the guardians of the Just State, Rousseau develops an egalitarian theory of politics—at least for males—in which every man is his own legislator. Reconciling individual freedom and the obligation a citizen has to obey the law by means of the concepts of personal autonomy and the General Will, he then constructs a theory of citizenship education whose purpose is to foster the development of independent reason and with it the capacity of self-government in affairs of state. Rejecting Rousseau's assumption that only half the population is capable of the kind of rationality required for self-governance, Beecher develops an egalitarian theory of domestic life in which every woman is assumed to possess the capacity for reason and hence to be capable of being her own legislator. Reconciling female autonomy in the home and woman's obligation to obey her husband's commands by means of the concept of professional expertise, Beecher then constructs a theory of domestic education whose purpose is to foster the development of professionalism in domestic affairs.

Unless we decide to follow Plato's lead and abolish the reproductive processes of society from women's lives, we would do well to take seriously the spirit, if not the details, of the education Beecher constructs for Sarah. Even if women do not finally opt for Sarah's professional preparation in domestic economy, we should at least entertain the possibility that for those who must share, if not shoulder, responsibility for carrying on society's reproductive processes there might be subject matter to be claimed that does not fall within the boundaries of a traditional liberal education, and also that Sarah's self-legislation in domestic affairs might have value for women even today.

We tend to take it for granted that although liberal education is defective in its portrayal of women, it is nevertheless the only place for them to look in claiming their education. If we learn nothing else from Beecher's participation in this conversation, she at least teaches us to broaden our sights so as to contemplate including within the education women claim what she would call domestic economy. But there are more lessons to be learned than just this one. One of the most important is that the domestic role traditionally assigned women is of overriding significance, particularly in its educative aspect, and demands as much intelligence as any other societal function. If this role is to be carried out well and if those performing it—be they women or men—are to be able to think and act intelligently and independently, a preparation combining theory and practice is as important for it as for the role of citizen.

This lesson leads to one more: namely, that so long as social philosophy assumes that men and women live together in society, it must take into account the education of both sexes and for the two kinds of societal processes. Of the parties to our conversation whose voices have already been heard, perhaps Rousseau understands this best. It is because Charlotte Perkins Gilman understands this too that her utopian novel, *Herland,* is so instructive. Given the single-sex society Gilman posits, we are free to contemplate a theory of female education without having to worry about the complications of gender. In *Herland* there is no sex-based division of roles, and neither tasks nor traits are genderized. Thus, while Sarah's intelligence and independence in domestic affairs may create problems for her and her husband unless he is reeducated, in *Herland* women's rationality and autonomy make no such demands on educational theory. As we shall see, while *Herland*'s philosophy of education is fascinating to ponder, it is ultimately illusory, for when we leave Gilman's single-sex society behind, the problems generated for education by a two-sex society reappear. If the fundamental lesson to be learned from listening to Gilman's story about a land without men is that in a society like ours problems relating to gender do not vanish upon command, its vision of women's place and women's education will still repay our close attention.

6 Gilman's Mothers

Herland was originally published in 1915 in serialized form in Charlotte Perkins Gilman's magazine, the *Forerunner.* Historian Ann J. Lane, who had the serial published as a book in 1979, wrote in an introduction: "Gilman appealed to an assortment of our comic sensibilities—the satiric, the whimsical, the sardonic, the rousing belly laugh—all in the interest of exposing the absurdities of accepted pieties, particularly as they applied to women's 'eternal place' or 'eternal nature.' "[1] *Herland* may indeed represent "Gilman's playful best," but as Lane makes clear, it contains far more than a critique of accepted pieties, for in this utopian novel Gilman presents us with an alternative social and educational vision.

Herland's plot is simple. Three male adventurers discover a country inhabited solely by female adults, children, and infants. Captured by a band of healthy, serene, sure-footed citizens, the men report on the outside world to the Herlanders, particularly the social organization and mores of American society; they in turn are educated about Herland. They learn that there has not been a man in Herland for two thousand years; that all this time babies have been born by asexual reproduction; and that in this country of women, where the land is in a perfect state of cultivation, there is neither strife nor war, poverty nor disease. The three adventurers fall in love with three young women of Herland. Although these women have no understanding of sexual passion, no conception of marriage, and no sympathy for the institution of private home and nuclear family, they ultimately marry their American suitors. One husband is immediately expelled from the country for trying to "master" his wife, but the other two couples work out their difficulties, the one deciding to stay in Herland and the other to live in the outside world.

The moral of *Herland* is more complex than its plot. The three males who arrive in Herland are encrusted with layers of stereotypical beliefs about masculinity and femininity, male superiority, and sex roles. One of the first comments Van, the narrator, makes upon landing in Herland sums up their prejudices: "Why, this is a civilized country. . . . There must be men," he says (p. 11). Gilman's purpose is to show the falsity and absurdity of these beliefs. The women of Herland are fleet, fearless, agile, calm, wise, self-assured, healthy, and reasonable. They do not flirt, adorn themselves, or want to be mastered, as Terry expects. Nor do they want to be worshiped and protected, as Jeff would do. They are capable of carrying out whatever activity has to be done on their own or with one another; indeed, they are capable of performing these tasks *better* than men perform them in early twentieth-century America.

Herland thus has several lessons to teach. The first is that male dominance, a sex-based division of labor, and traditional notions of masculinity and femininity are presuppositions of the American society of Gilman's day. The second echoes Wollstonecraft's thesis that to the extent that women are in fact physically weak, emotionally unstable, and intellectually childish, these traits are theirs by socialization and expectation, not by nature. The third lesson diverges significantly from Wollstonecraft's philosophy: if women were allowed to develop their potential fully, Gilman is saying, the world would be a better place. Wollstonecraft argues that society would benefit from cultivation of women's minds, but she makes man her model: "Let woman share the rights and she will emulate the virtues of man," she says in the penultimate paragraph of her book. She does not contemplate, as Gilman does, a society in which competence is a derivative of mother love, nor does she entertain a social vision in which cooperation and united action replace competition and individual achievement.

Make no mistake. Herland's inhabitants possess reason in abundance. These women have great intellectual curiosity, profound powers of observation, a fund of theoretical knowledge, and a highly developed practical intelligence that has enabled them to rid their country of disease and danger and to make their land productive. However, Herland is a happier, healthier, safer, and saner society than Gilman's America not simply because reason has been applied to the problems of society but because its shared ideal is "to make the best kind of people" (p. 59). The Herland Dream is neither the accumulation of private wealth nor an increase in the gross national product; rather, it is the growth and development of children. Gilman and Wollstonecraft share a belief in the continuing progress of humankind; but Gilman considers the nurturant capacities traditionally associated with mothers to be fundamental elements of an improved social order, whereas Wollstonecraft locates improvement simply in a wider distribution of knowledge and rational self-discipline.

Gilman is not alone in stressing motherhood in her philosophy. Rousseau, Wollstonecraft, and Beecher do so, too. But whereas for Rousseau and Wollstonecraft motherhood is women's duty and for Beecher it is their profession, for Gilman it is a cultural ideal. And whereas Rousseau, Wollstonecraft, and Beecher take the indissolubility of the links among motherhood, marriage, and home for granted, Gilman does not. In Herland all adult women are mothers, no women are wives, and although some women perform traditional domestic functions, such as cooking, they are not carried out in the context of a private home or family, for these do not exist.

From earliest childhood each inhabitant of Herland occupies a room of her own, and when she comes of age she acquires two rooms and a bath; but food is prepared and eaten elsewhere, and we can safely assume that the numerous tasks that Beecher's Sarah must either do or oversee at home are removed from the dwelling:

> "Tell us—what is the work of the world, that men do—which we have not here?"
> "Oh, everything," Terry said grandly. "The men do everything, with us." He squared his broad shoulders and lifted his chest. "We do not allow our women to work. Women are loved—idolized—honored—kept in the home to care for the children."
> "What is 'the home'?" asked Somel a little wistfully. (pp. 60–61)

For everyone in Herland, then, there are living quarters in which to enjoy privacy and solitude, but these are not places in which families live or in which traditional household functions are carried on.

Ellador's Education

Motherhood in Herland must be understood in its internal historical context. When two thousand years earlier, an earthquake prevented the entire male population of Herland, then away at war, from returning home, the women left behind suffered a period of despair and then proceeded to live as best they could. They worked together "growing stronger and wiser and more and more mutually attached, and then the miracle happened—one of these young women bore a child" (p. 56). Eventually this "wonder woman" bore five daughters. Reared by a nation of women who surrounded them with loving service, each of these girls herself bore five daughters who grew up "as a holy sisterhood" with the devoted love and care of the entire population. Thus a new race of women was born and with it a culture whose dominant note was motherhood.

At the beginning, when the continued existence of Herland was in question, biological motherhood was the country's highest value. Once overpopulation threatened and the majority was allowed to undertake biological motherhood only once and those deemed unfit were not allowed even that, Herland's concept of motherhood changed. In explaining to Van that young women could voluntarily defer childbearing by engaging in active physical and mental work and could find solace for their longing to give birth by caring for and serving others' babies, Somel says, "We soon grew to see that mother-love has more than one channel of expression. I think the reason our children are so—so fully loved, by all of us, is that we never—any of us—have enough of our own." When Van tells her that "a whole nation of starving mothers" seems "piteous beyond words," she assures him that he has misunderstood. "We each go without a certain range of personal joy," she says, "but remember— we each have a million children to love and serve—*our* children" (p. 71).

In Herland, then, motherhood is not simply a biological category but a social one. It is a social category for us, too, but Gilman gives it social content without tying it to the wife and homemaker role. Nor does she tie it to specific tasks of child rearing, such as feeding and diapering, or to the social expectations surrounding them. For Gilman, motherhood has a social content because it constitutes a particular relation of love in which an adult stands to a child—a love whose overriding concern is the child's welfare and development. Thus the ideal of motherhood in Herland has two aspects: on the one hand, it makes a sacrament of biological processes essential for the continuation of the race; on the other, it makes love of and service to children the highest possible calling for everyone.

Motherhood is a social category for Herlanders because it involves an interpersonal relationship, and it is a universal category because this relationship is one in which every adult is expected to stand to all children. In an essay on maternal thinking the feminist philosopher Sara

Ruddick urges her readers to work "to bring a *transformed* maternal thought into the public realm, to make the preservation and growth of *all* children a work of public conscience and legislation."² In Herland, as in Plato's Just State, there is little if any necessity for laws of any kind, let alone ones concerning children. In both utopias the control of human behavior derives from a system of socialization and education of the young rather than from a system of laws and punishment. But if Ruddick's goal of making the protection of children a work of public legislation has no counterpart in Herland, her goal of making the preservation and growth of children a work of public conscience is Herland's goal:

> "Motherhood means to us something which I cannot yet discover in any of the countries of which you tell us. You have spoken"—she turned to Jeff, "of Human Brotherhood as a great idea among you, but even that I judge is far from a practical expression?"
>
> Jeff nodded rather sadly. "Very far"—he said.
>
> "Here we have Human Motherhood—in full working use," she went on. "Nothing else except the literal sisterhood of our origin, and the far higher and deeper union of our social growth."
>
> "The children in this country are the one center and focus of all our thoughts. Every step of our advance is always considered in its effect on them—on the race. You see, we are *Mothers,*" she repeated, as if in that she had said it all. (p. 66)

The adults of Herland, all of them, are surrogate mothers, not in the modern sense of putting their wombs in the service of another, but in the old-fashioned sense of loving and serving children to whom they have not given birth: the sense in which Pestalozzi's Gertrude was a mother to the neighbor children she took into her home and in which the mature Jo March of *Jo's Boys* was a mother to all the boys who lived at Plumfield, the school she and her husband ran. The children of Herland, in turn, are the private property of no one. Ruddick notes that in our society mothers' "misguided efforts on behalf of the success and purity of our children [often] frighten them and everyone else around them," and she anticipates the establishment of "a creative tension between our inevitable and fierce desire to foster our own children and the less compulsive desire that children grow and flourish" (p. 361). In Herland no such creative tension can exist since the concept of one's *own* child that Ruddick takes as a given is not operative. Information about the biological mother of each infant is recorded, but a child does not take her mother's name. "As to everyone knowing which child belongs to which mother—why should she?" asks Somel. It is not that Herlanders take no pride in their children, she hastens to explain; on the contrary, "We're magnificently proud of them." It is rather that children in Herland are considered to be public, not private, "products" (pp. 75–76).

In Gilman's utopia biological mothers nurse their infants, but from the very beginning child care is undertaken by specialists. "Education is our highest art, only allowed to our highest artists," Somel tells Van (p. 82). "The care of babies involves education, and is entrusted only to the most fit," she continues; "Childrearing has come to be with us a culture so profoundly studied, practiced with such subtlety and skill, that the more we love our children the less we are willing to trust that process to unskilled hands . . . even our own." In response to his protests that to put a child in the care of someone other than its biological mother is a denial of mother love, Somel invokes an analogy:

> "You told us about your dentists," she said, at length, "those quaintly specialized persons who spend their lives filling little holes in other persons' teeth—even in children's teeth sometimes."
> "Yes?" I said, not getting her drift.
> "Does mother-love urge mothers—with you—to fill their own children's teeth? Or to wish to?"
> "Why no—of course not," I protested. "But that is a highly specialized craft. Surely the care of babies is open to any woman—any mother!"
> "We do not think so," she gently replied. "Those of us who are the most highly competent fulfill that office; and a majority of our girls eagerly try for it—I assure you we have the very best." (p. 83)

Thus, to describe the women of Herland as surrogate mothers is not to say that they are the rearers of children whose biological parents they are not, but that they love and serve those children. Since all adults in Herland are surrogate mothers, those who qualify to be child rearers do, of course, love and serve children, too. But filling the office of child rearer is not what makes a Herlander a surrogate mother; quite the reverse is true. It is because all women are surrogate mothers, because motherhood is universal, that some—called "co-mothers"—are given the special responsibility of rearing and educating children. The women of Herland care too much for their country's children, and understand too well how easily the growth and development of a child can be stunted, to allow them to be reared by incompetents. Furthermore, it is because each woman loves and serves all children—and because the gulf between "mothers" and "nonmothers" to which Adrienne Rich calls attention in

Of Woman Born[3] is closed in Herland—that no woman is possessive toward any. The fierce desire to foster one's own children to which Ruddick refers is translated in Herland into a desire to foster all children, and this desire, in turn, translates into both a policy of specialized child rearing and a child-centered educational philosophy.

> "It was a butterfly that made me a forester," said Ellador. "I was about eleven years old, and I found a big purple-and-green butterfly on a low flower. I caught it, very carefully, by the closed wings, as I had been told to do, and carried it to the nearest insect teacher . . . to ask her its name. She took it from me with a little cry of delight. 'Oh, you blessed child,' she said. 'Do you like obernuts?' Of course I like obernuts, and said so. It is our best food-nut, you know. 'This is a female of the obernut moth,' she told me. 'They are almost gone. We have been trying to exterminate them for centuries. If you had not caught this one, it might have laid eggs enough to raise worms enough to destroy thousands of our nut trees—thousands of bushels of nuts—and make years and years of trouble for us.'
> "Everybody congratulated me. The children all over the country were told to watch for that moth, if there were any more. I was shown the history of the creature, and an account of the damage it used to do and of how long and hard our foremothers had worked to save that tree for us. I grew a foot, it seemed to me, and determined then and there to be a forester." (pp. 100–01)

Ellador's story is typical. Adults in Herland are expected to specialize, although they are not confined to a single activity as are the inhabitants of Plato's Just State. Indeed, in striking contrast to Plato's female guardians, the women of Herland can take up as many specialties as they wish—some for work, and "some to grow with" (p. 105)—the lines they pursue resulting from personal choice rather than being imposed by nature; a wide range of interests and associations is open to each woman for life. Specialized training begins in Herland when a girl is half grown: "Then the eager young minds fairly flung themselves on their chosen subjects, and acquired with ease, a breadth, a grasp, at which I never ceased to wonder," Van notes (p. 95). The major part of a girl's education, however, is concerned neither with specialized knowledge nor with narrow, vocational goals but with the development of the two powers deemed "basically necessary for all noble life: a clear, far-reaching judgment, and a strong well-used will" (p. 106).

"We spend our best efforts, all through childhood and youth, in developing these faculties, individual judgment and will," explains Somel. With the babies, an environment is provided "which feeds the mind without tiring it." As early as possible, and going very carefully so as not to tax the mind, she adds, "We provide choices, simple choices, with very obvious causes and consequences." The vehicle for these choices is games. Never bored, never tempted by lack of occupation into doing mischief, the children of Herland forever play games or else engage in "peaceful researches of their own" (p. 106). Born into a carefully prepared world "full of the most fascinating materials and opportunities to learn" and into a society "of plentiful numbers of teachers" (p. 107), Herlanders are educated to be intelligent, strong-minded, independent people who are able to use and control their own bodies.

From infancy Herland's children are taught to be surefooted and steady-handed. Learning to swim before they learn to walk, these babies grow up "just as young fawns might grow up in dewy forest glades and brookfed meadows" (p. 100). Physical play in houses, gardens, and fields having in them "nothing to hurt" provides at one and the same time an inexhaustible form of amusement and a rigorous physical education. Physical training and activity are not, however, limited to the early years. Women of all ages go to gymnasiums to do acrobatics and "posture dancing" and to participate in "processional performances." They also play games there, ones Terry and Van find lacking in fight and hence uninteresting. All three men, however, are impressed with the speed with which Herland women run, the agility with which they climb trees, and the grace with which they leap. Although Terry is strong, Van wiry, and Jeff a great sprinter, the physical accomplishments of even the fifty-year-old Herlanders gain their reluctant admiration.

One key to understanding education in Herland is to be found in the principle that mental and physical capacities develop best when they develop together. Another lies in the principle that people are educated best when they do not know they are being educated at all, and in its corollary that the best way to do this is to provide an agreeable and interesting environment in which children are encouraged to pursue whatever activities they enjoy. Formal instruction is thus limited to the short period of specialized training every girl undertakes. The forced exercise of a girl's mind and the requirement that she run an obstacle-course curriculum are unknown. "We seek to nourish, to stimulate, to exercise the mind of a child as we do the body," Somel says, but she makes it very clear that forced feeding does not occur. Rather, information is efficiently transmitted to healthy youngsters passionately eager to acquire it, while graduated series of exercises intended to develop mental faculties are arranged for each child in a way that will be welcomed by her.

From the standpoint of the children of Herland, most learning is an unintended, unanticipated by-product of what is considered to be natural activity. But that fascinating materials and countless opportunities for action exist in the child's environment is no accident. Her environment is a deliberate construction built not just by the highly skilled teachers whose business it is to accompany the children along what Van calls "that, to us, impossible thing—the royal road to learning" (p. 107) but by the whole community. Thus, from the earliest age children are provided with an environment offering them "all manner of simple and interesting things to do" (p. 106) that engage their mental as well as their physical "faculties."

In its fundamental opposition to compulsion and its emphasis on activity and on the importance of a rich environment for learning, the philosophy of education Gilman set forth in *Herland* in 1915 resembles that of the open classroom movement emerging in Britain and North America some fifty years later. But in Herland, where it is "all education but no schooling," the world is the classroom. "It's an everlasting parlor and nursery," Terry grumbles. "And workshop," Van adds. "And school, and office, and laboratory, and studio, and theater" (p. 98). Thus, babies are reared in the warmer part of the country, and older children become acclimated to the cooler heights, making continuous excursions from one part of the land to another, during which they learn from "the rich experience of living" (p. 100). The open classrooms developed a half century after the publication of *Herland* brought the world—or at least selected parts of it, such as water and sand, birds' nests and grasses, old tires and wallpaper samples—into schools. In Herland the school-world dichotomy has no meaning. In this country devoted to the making of people, no distinction is drawn between education and life or between world and school.

Because education in Herland occurs in the context of living, there is no sharp compartmentalization of subjects: an exquisite literature "unfailing in appeal to the child-mind, but *true*, true to the living world about them" (p. 103) permeates the atmosphere; the sciences—anatomy, physiology, nutrition, botany, chemistry—are linked everywhere to practice; history and psychology are closely bound up with each other; physical and mental development are expected to take place together. Van reports that the earthquake occurred at a time when drama, dance, music, religion, and education were all conjoined and that instead of developing in "detached lines," in Herland they had been kept as one. Although he does not pursue the matter, we can assume that detached lines did not develop because in Herland a premium is placed on interconnection and wholeness. "The things they learned were *related*, from the first; related to one another, and to the national prosperity," Van comments (p. 100). Ellador's story of the butterfly is a case in point. She was not simply told what kind of butterfly she had caught; rather, she was introduced through the butterfly to a whole range of scientific information, to a piece of natural history, and to a vital strand of the human past. And, moreover, she was encouraged to see her simple act of catching a butterfly as contributing to the welfare of all and thus as having the widest possible social significance.

The Ideal of Mother Love

The methods employed in Ellador's education are the very ones Rousseau prescribes for Emile. While implicitly rejecting the progressive manner in which Emile is educated, Wollstonecraft appropriates for her daughters the ideal Rousseau holds up for males, but Gilman appropriates the manner while rejecting the ideal. Activity, experience, discovery, concrete manipulation of the environment: these are fundamental elements of Emile's education and of Ellador's, too. Yet Gilman's object is not to produce a female Robinson Crusoe. Ellador is educated to be neither Sophie nor Emile but instead a woman who stands in the relation of mother to the children of Herland and of sister to its adults.

For Gilman, the disappearance of the private family heralds the birth of a public one. Although it is never put in quite this way in *Herland,* the image running through that work is of the private family writ large. This image is not grounded simply in the fact that the mothers and daughters of Herland can all trace their ancestry back to the same woman. Their shared heritage is no doubt an important factor in their lives, but it is primarily from the principle of universal motherhood that the image of Herland as a family emerges. In making every adult in Herland a mother to all children, Gilman makes mother love Herland's overarching cultural and educational ideal.

Concern for the growth and development of children exhibited through the application of reason to the task of making Herland a better place to live: this is what mother love means in Gilman's philosophy. Neither the passionate delight that characterizes the unmarried Rosamund's response to her infant daughter's smiles in Margaret Drabble's *Thank You Very Much* nor the uncertain temper Jane Austen's Mrs. Bennet exhibits while seeking husbands for her daughters in *Pride and Prejudice* is captured by Gilman's notion of mother love. The women of Herland are not victims of sensibility as Wollstonecraft fears Sophie will be and as she might well judge Drabble's Rosamund to be. They do not display Mrs. Bennet's frivolity and lack of understanding. They are not, as Rich reports that she was, driven by maternal guilt to ask, "daily, nightly, hourly, Am I doing what is right? Am I doing enough? Am I doing too much?"[4] On the other hand, they are not mere replicas of Emily or Sarah, for while they are as rational as Wollstonecraft and Beecher could wish—as rational, indeed, as Austen's Elinor—their reason is at all times harnessed to the practical goal of making the best kind of people. This is one of Emily's goals too, as, of course, it is Sarah's: both women are supposed to form their children's values and shape their characters. But it must be remembered that in Wollstonecraft's and Beecher's philosophies mothers are concerned only with the growth and development of their own children, whereas in Herland each woman is concerned with the growth and development of every child. This makes all the difference, because a concern for the growth and development of children entails a concern that their environment be conducive to that end, and while the environment of both Emily's and Sarah's children is their private home, the environment of all the children of Herland is Herland itself.

In Herland, where there are few, if any, schools, and where no line is drawn between education and life, mother love thus requires that not only all children but the whole land be nurtured. It should not be surprising, therefore, that Van describes Herland as in "a state of perfect cultivation: where even the forests looked as if they were cared for, a land that looked like an enormous park, only it was even more, evidently an enormous garden" (p. 11). Not merely the physical environment of children but the social and economic environment is cultivated to such an extent that Herland is a country with no sickness, poverty, social stratification, violence, punishment. "All the surrendering devotion our women put into their private families," Van observes, "these women put into their country and race" (p. 95). And for the good reason that Herland is their home, the race is their family.

Lane notes that while "most utopias neglect the central role of education in reconstructing their worlds," education in Gilman's novel "evolves as a natural device in the creation of new people, especially the young" (p. xxiii). Gilman understands, as of course Plato also does, that a vision of the good society must be supplemented by a well-developed theory of education. Plato has Socrates say to Adeimantus that the orders the guardians are to be given "are not, as one might think, either numerous or important; they are all secondary, provided that they guard the one great thing, as people say, though rather than great I would call it sufficient." "What is that?" asks Adeimantus. "Their education and their upbringing," Socrates replies (423e). Gilman, in turn, has Somel tell Van that education is allowed only to "our highest artists" (p. 82). But although she embraces Plato's Functional Postulate that the task of education is to equip people to take their place in the state, Gilman makes teaching Herland's highest art because she has created a utopia in which the growth and development of children is everyone's primary concern.

Gilman's ideal of mother love thus translates into a desire to perfect the environment of children—including that of future generations—and a desire to perfect their education. It is not surprising that young children in Herland "planned, freely and gaily with much happy chattering, of what they would do for the country when they were grown" (p. 103). Their whole education is designed with this end in mind. Once this is understood, it is easy to see why Ellador decided to become a forester. The motive of mother love—that is, a desire to promote the welfare of the country as a whole—having been instilled in her from earliest childhood, on the day she caught the butterfly she was wondering not what her country could do for her but what she could do for her country. The piece of natural history the insect teacher related to Ellador enabled her to perceive a real societal need, while the teacher's praise, combined with the enthusiasm of the other children, sparked a desire to be the person to meet that need.

On that fateful day Ellador lacked both the competence she required to nurture Herland and a clear perception of Herland's needs. As we know, she ultimately acquired competence by undergoing a specialized training in forestry. What must be noted is that this competence had its source in mother love. In Herland a concern for the growth and development of children translates into a drive to acquire the expertise necessary to ensure the best environment possible. Hence the emphasis in the educational system on the development of "a clear, far-reaching judgment and a strong, well-used will" (p. 106).

It will be recalled that Wollstonecraft would educate Emily solely for citizenship yet would have her be both a citizen and a good wife-mother. In redefining the wife-mother role so that the traits central to it—rationality and self-control—are the very ones she takes to be central to the role of citizen, Wollstonecraft goes some way toward eliminating the discrepancy between Emily's single-role education and her two-role destiny. Still, Emily's two roles do not overlap completely, and she will suffer the consequences. That is, she will suffer them unless she moves to Herland, for in that utopian community in which, admittedly, there is no wife role for Emily to play, there is no gap at all between the role of citizen and that of mother. To be a good citizen in Herland is to be a good mother, even though a surrogate one. And conversely, to be a good surrogate mother is to be a good citizen. Of course, the education for the sovereignty of reason Wollstonecraft prescribes for Emily will not prepare her to be a mother-citizen in Herland. To nurture her children and Herland itself, Emily must be able not to suppress emotion but to join it with reason. In Gilman's utopian vision the interests of women, children, and the state become one, so that an education for citizens is an education for mothers, just as an education for motherhood is an education for citizenship.

The identity Gilman sees in women's interests and the state's makes her utopian vision very special. She is by no means the only social philosopher to construct the state on the model of a family, but she brings to this conceptualization a particular image of family relationships. In *Republic,* book 5, Socrates says that when one guardian meets another "he will think he is meeting a brother or a sister, a father or a mother, a son or a daughter" (463c). Thus for Plato, as well as Gilman, the disappearance of the private family heralds the birth of a public one. To be sure, in Plato's case, only one part of society is considered to constitute a family, whereas for Gilman the whole society constitutes one. "If there is no discord among the guardians there is no danger that the rest of the city will start factions against them or among themselves," Socrates maintains (465b). In other words, the unity of the state is a function of the unity of the guardians, and so it is they alone who must think of themselves as mothers and fathers, brothers and sisters, sons and daughters. Nonetheless, Plato's use of the family image provides an interesting contrast to Gilman's because it reveals an underlying theory of human relationships so very different from hers.

According to Socrates, "common feelings of pleasure and pain bind the city together" (426). One finds such feelings, he says, in the city that most closely resembles the individual:

> When one of us hurts his finger, the whole organism which binds body and soul together into the unitary system managed by the ruling part of it shares the pain at once throughout when one part suffers. This is why we say that the man has a pain in his finger, and the same can be said of any part of the man, both about the pain which any part suffers, and its pleasure when it finds relief. (462d)

Predicated as it is on the analogy between justice in the individual and justice in the state, the *Republic* cannot do without the metaphor of the state as a human individual writ large. Yet this metaphor of the individual does not support Socrates' thesis. There is no doubt that if your finger has a pain in it, you may be in pain. By analogy, then, if one member of society suffers or rejoices, society itself may suffer or rejoice. However, if you are in pain, it does not follow that all the various parts of you are suffering; moreover, if your finger is in pain, there is no reason at all to suppose that your foot or heart is in pain. But then, by analogy, there is no reason to suppose that when one member of a society suffers or rejoices, most of the individual members, let alone all do. Yet this is the point Socrates wants to make.

Does his image of the guardian class as a family writ large accomplish what his image of the individual writ large does not? The parts of a human organism do not suffer and rejoice with one another—how can they when they are not the sorts of things that experience emotion?—but family members do. Not always, of course, but the family is certainly the place in which we have come to expect this phenomenon. Perhaps nowhere are both the presence and the absence of this mutuality so movingly depicted as in *Middlemarch*. In the hour of Mr. Bulstrode's humiliation, his wife dons plain bonnet and black dress, not to signify that she has lost a husband, but to make it clear that she has "espoused" his sorrow. In stark contrast to Rosamond, who never acknowledges Lydgate's pain and certainly does not make it her own as he wants her to, and to Dorothea, who wants to take on Mr. Casaubon's mental anguish but is not allowed to, Mrs. Bulstrode shares her husband's dishonor as in happier hours she shared his prosperity. Similarly, in her parents' time of need, occasioned by Fred Vincy's failure to honor a debt, Mary Garth suffers their pain with them just as, several years later, her father rejoices in her happiness at being able to respect and marry a reformed Fred Vincy.[5]

The common feelings of pleasure and pain Plato attributes to members of the Just State by no means find their analogue in all the families Eliot portrays. But in some of them, loving children suffer when their parents do, devoted parents rejoice in their children's happiness, caring spouses share each other's pains and pleasures. Yet if the family metaphor is in principle capable of illuminating the communal aspects of Plato's social philosophy, there is reason to believe that he does not really envision his Just State as one in which the family relationship exemplified by the Garths and the Bulstrodes flourishes.

Having said that when one guardian meets another he will think he is meeting a family member, Socrates insists that these guardian family relationships will exist not simply in name but also in action; thus a man must show to his fathers "the respect, solicitude, and obedience to parents required by law" (463d). If he acts differently, Socrates continues, "he will fare worse at the hands of gods and men as one whose actions are neither pious nor just" (463d). Will a younger man, except by orders of the rulers, apply violence to an older one? "There are two adequate guardians to prevent this," says Socrates, "namely shame and fear; shame will prevent him laying hands on his parents, fear because the others will come to the rescue of the victim, some as his sons, some as his brothers, and some as his fathers" (465b).

The family relationships Plato depicts in these passages bear no resemblance to the relationships of Mrs. Bulstrode to her husband or Mary Garth to her parents. When in *Middlemarch* old Mr. Featherstone says to Mary, "I suppose your father wanted your earnings. . . . You're of age now; you ought to be saving for yourself," she replies: "I consider my father and mother the best part of myself, sir."[6] Assuming, as Mr. Featherstone does, that a child and its parents lead separate lives and have separate interests, Plato prescribes the proper treatment of fathers by sons in terms of obedience and respect. Starting from an assumption of separation, these attitudes are designed to preserve distance between people.[7] Indeed, for all its apparent overlay of mutual caring and concern, even the solicitude Socrates expects sons to show fathers presupposes distance rather than intimacy, separation rather than connection. When Mary Garth learns that her father must, to pay a debt that is not his, use money her mother has saved for her youngest boy's schooling, it is not solicitude she exhibits but grief. "Oh, poor mother, poor father!" Mary says as her eyes fill with tears and a sob rises.[8] Nor does Mrs. Bulstrode's response to her husband's plight suggest anything so remote as solicitude: "After an instant of searching shame in which she felt only the eyes of the world," reports George Eliot, "with one leap of her heart she was at his side in mournful but unreproaching fellowship with shame and isolation" (p. 549).

Plato wants the members of his guardian family—and ultimately all members of the Just State—to suffer and rejoice with one another, and yet he never notices that the relationships in which common feelings of pain and pleasure occur are based on shared interests, positive feelings of love and sympathy, and a denial of distance. Gilman knows this, and, through her principle of universal motherhood, builds these conditions into her utopia.

As a consequence, the question Plato asks about sons and fathers in the Just State does not—could not—arise in Herland: that a young Herlander would apply violence to an older one is simply unthinkable. Furthermore, supposing for the sake of argument that one of Gilman's daughters were tempted to strike one of her elders, the motives preventing her would surely not be shame and fear. It is because Plato's account of family relationships rests on an assumption of individual aggression and competition that it is necessary for him to invoke essentially coercive sanctions. Since Gilman rests her account of the family on an assumption of peaceful cooperation and shared interests, no such measures are required. Indeed, in the mother-daughter relationships of Herland, even obedience, solicitude, and respect play no role. It is not that children are *dis*obedient, *dis*respectful, *un*solicitous. Rather, the opposition of interests so necessary for these attitudes is missing. Just as Mary Garth has her money ready for her father before he asks for it and, indeed, would have him take more than he needs; just as Mrs. Bulstrode of her own accord places her hand on her husband's shoulder; so, Gilman wants us to believe, the daughters of Herland will help and comfort their mothers when needed, not because they are coerced into doing so, but because they care so deeply for those who have taken care of them.

In an interesting essay on John Dewey's philosophy of education, Eamonn Callan has pointed out that Dewey uses the family to exemplify the nature of democracy[9] and that the concept of fraternity, in particular, provides the key to understanding Dewey's political and educational thought. Cooperation, common interests and beliefs, altruism, social solidarity: these constitute the foundation of Dewey's philosophy, according to Callan, and they are "specifically fraternal" values.

Callan makes it clear that the word *fraternity* plays a minor role in Dewey's writings, but we have no reason to suppose that in identifying the family with one specific kind of relationship, and in choosing the fraternal relationship in particular, Callan does violence to Dewey's thought. If Dewey's vision of the family is selective, so is Plato's. If in his selectivity women drop out of his family portrait, so too they drop out of Plato's portrait. And if sons and fathers are implicitly taken by Plato to be the focal figures in the family—as they certainly were by those later philosophers who attempted to use the concept of patriarchy to illuminate political authority—why should not Dewey, an heir to the French Revolution's ideals of liberty, equality, and fraternity, take brotherhood as his point of focus?

Let us leave it to the metaphysicians to decide whether Plato and Dewey introduce different metaphors of the family into their respective philosophies or simply different versions of the same one. We need only recognize how selective metaphorical thought is. In using the notion of the family, rather than something else, to elucidate the nature of democracy, Dewey is already making choices. In conceptualizing the family in terms of the fraternal relationship, he further restricts his vision. But the fraternal relationship itself covers a host of phenomena: sibling rivalry as well as cooperation, acts of egotism as well as ones of altruism, private as well as common interests. Thus, even his portrayal of fraternity is selective in that it preserves only those aspects he approves of, the others dropping out of the picture as surely as mothers and wives, daughters and sisters, have dropped out of the family portrait itself.

The family metaphor Gilman employs in *Herland* is, of course, as selective as Dewey's and Plato's. What makes her philosophy so distinctive and her social vision so radical in comparison to theirs is not that her picture of the family is more accurate, more faithful to the totality of family reality, but that she chooses to portray the very family members they and the other social philosophers who invoke the family ignore:

mothers and daughters, particularly mothers. And Gilman's selectivity does not stop here. Of the many aspects of maternal practice she could focus on, she chooses mother love; furthermore, just as Dewey in his portrait of the family highlights what he takes to be the virtues of brotherhood and ignores its problematic features, she highlights what she takes to be the virtues of motherhood and only them.

Love of Family, Love of Country

Recall now Rousseau's criticism of Plato's proposals to abolish private marriage, home, family, and child rearing in the Just State. The question that must be addressed is whether in a society so organized the heart will be attached to the "public" family. Would he not tell Gilman that his statement that the heart attaches itself to the large fatherland by means of the small one holds for her land of mothers? Certainly, the similarities between Plato's social vision and Gilman's are so striking that one might readily assume that they are equally vulnerable to Rousseau's criticism.

In the value it places on specialization, as in its abolition of the institutions of marriage, home, and private family, *Herland* resembles Plato's *Republic*. For the guardian class in Plato's Just State, the domestic sphere of society, whose worth Beecher tries so hard to enhance and whose existence Rousseau and Wollstonecraft believe to be a prerequisite of the ideal polity, disappears. In Herland the domestic sphere disappears for everyone. This is not to say that the reproductive processes of society do not take place in Herland. Gilman understands, however, as does Plato, that these processes are detachable from their traditional location in the home. Thus, even as she abolishes private home and family, she preserves what she perceives to be the vital processes associated with them, making them the responsibility of society as a whole and taking it for granted that those best suited to these tasks will perform them for all.

The removal of the domestic realm from a society does not entail the disappearance of its reproductive processes. Nor does it require that a program of eugenics be established or that private property, and especially private "ownership" of children, be abolished. Yet Gilman follows Plato's lead in adopting just these policies for Herland.

The details of Plato's system of breeding need not detain us long.

Suffice it to say that Socrates holds that "the best men must have intercourse with the best women as frequently as possible, and the opposite
is true of the very inferior men and women; the offspring of the former
must be reared, but not the offspring of the latter, if our herd is to be
of the highest possible quality" (459e). What will happen to the offspring
of these matings? The children of good parents will be taken by officials
"to a rearing pen in the care of nurses living apart in a certain section
of the city; the children of inferior parents, or any child of others born
defective, they will hide, as is fitting, in a secret and unknown place"
(460c). Gilman's faith in the powers of education makes it unnecessary
for her to devise such plans for the children of inferior inhabitants of
Herland, but she has no doubt that there are inferior women in Herland
and that for the good of the race they ought to renounce biological
motherhood:

> "We have, of course, made it our first business to train out, to breed
> out, when possible, the lowest types."
> "Breed out?" I asked. "How could you—with parthenogenesis?"
> "If the girl showing the bad qualities had still the power to appreciate
> social duty, we appealed to her, by that, to renounce motherhood. Some of
> the few worst types were, fortunately, unable to reproduce. But if the fault
> was in a disproportionate egotism—then the girl was sure she had the right
> to have children, even that hers would be better than others."
> "I can see that," I said. "And then she would be likely to rear them
> in the same spirit."
> "That we never allowed," answered Somel quietly. (p. 82)

In both Herland and the Just State biological motherhood becomes
the legitimate concern of the society as a whole and for the same reason,
namely the improvement of the species. And if childbearing is thus no
longer a purely personal matter, child rearing is an entirely societal one.
No woman in either Herland or the guardian class of Plato's Just State
rears her own child. Concerning children there is no "mine" and "thine"
in either Plato's vision of the guardians or Gilman's vision of Herland
as a whole. "No mother shall know her own child" even when nursing,
says Socrates (460d). Gilman allows women to nurse their biological
daughters, but she too rejects private "ownership" of children:

> "When they are babies, we do speak of them, at times, as 'Essa's Lato,'
> or 'Novine's Amel'; but that is merely descriptive and conversational. In
> the records, of course, the child stands in her own line of mothers; but in

dealing with it personally it is Lato, or Amel, without dragging in its ancestors." (p. 76)

Lane has suggested that utopias tend to follow one of three models— Plato's *Republic,* Thomas More's *Utopia,* or Francis Bacon's *New Atlantis*—but that *Herland* does not fit comfortably into any of these categories. There are some very significant differences between Herland and Plato's Just State. Besides being a single-sex society, Herland is a classless one. Furthermore, although she is an advocate of specialization, Gilman rejects Plato's Postulate of Specialized Natures and his Correspondence Postulate: the destiny of the inhabitants of Herland is not fixed by nature but is a matter of happenstance, interest, and choice. Moreover, identifying change with deterioration, Plato takes geometry to be the model of all knowledge and insists that the Just State, once established, must remain exactly as it is. Identifying change with progress, Gilman takes experimental science as the proper mode of acquiring knowledge and makes the growth and development of Herland a primary concern of its inhabitants.

In spite of these differences, the resemblances between the social policies of Herland and Plato's Just State are so marked as to lead one to wonder what fundamental assumptions the two thinkers must share. In Plato's case the programs and policies that resemble the ones Gilman adopts for Herland have their source in his overriding concern for social cohesiveness. In *Republic,* book 5, Socrates argues that the institutions of private home, marriage, family, and child rearing pose a clear threat to the state because they are likely to cause dissension and discord. Common ownership, he says, will allow the guardians to escape the petty evils men must endure in the course of bringing up children and maintaining a household. Were the guardians to make distinctions of "mine" and "not mine," "one man would then drag into his own house whatever he could get hold of away from the others; another drag things into his different house to another wife and other children" (464d).

Plato's object in abolishing private home, property, and family for his guardians is to prevent them from placing their personal interests and desires ahead of the good of the state. Gilman's object is twofold. She might not have agreed completely with Ann Oakley who, writing in 1974, maintained that "the abolition of the housewife role requires the abolition of the family,"[10] but her proposal for the abolition of private home and family is certainly motivated above all by her desire to demonstrate what women can achieve if they are not confined by society to the domestic sphere. Yet while Gilman's perception of the historical plight of women informs the social programs of Herland, she too is concerned with unity. Plato's ideal for the city is that all its citizens rejoice equally or feel equal pain at the same successes and failures; Gilman holds the same ideal for Herland. She rejects the practice of giving children surnames on the ground that the inhabitants of Herland are "all one 'family' in reality" (p. 75). "To them," says Van, "the country was a unit—it was theirs. They themselves were a unit, a conscious group; they thought in terms of the community" (p. 79).

In their pursuit of unity, Plato and Gilman make such similar recommendations that Rousseau's doubts that citizens of the Just State would attach themselves to the large fatherland cannot be ignored in considering Herland. From Rousseau's remarks it can be inferred that he takes one's ties to the family to be natural and one's ties to the state to be conventional or artificial: "I speak of that subversion of the sweetest sentiments of nature, sacrificed to an artificial sentiment which can only be maintained by them—as though there were no need for a natural base on which to form conventional ties" (p. 363). Nature, in other words, provides the base upon which artifice rests, and, Rousseau is saying to Plato, this base has to be in place before artificial sentiment can develop.

Rousseau's thesis can be viewed as a type of developmental theory according to which one who has achieved the stage of conventional sentiment will necessarily have gone through the stage of natural sentiment. Clearly, he does not hold the position that everyone who reaches the stage of natural sentiment is guaranteed entry into the conventional stage. After all, by virtue of both her nature and her education, Sophie is much more likely than Emile to feel attached to her family; yet, according to Rousseau, she is much less likely than Emile to become attached to the polity. For Rousseau love of private family is a necessary condition for love of country.

We have already glimpsed the problems Sophie's children will confront in attaining love of private family. The question readers of *Herland* must ask is whether this love is really necessary in all possible worlds. Herland is a society dominated by motherliness; children are its raison d'être. In Herland, everyone grows up in a wide, friendly world and knows it for theirs. In Herland, from the very first memory every child knows "Peace, Beauty, Order, Safety, Love, Wisdom, Justice, Patience, and Plenty" (p. 100), not because they have been experienced in a private home, but because they characterize the society itself. Given this setting and given that from the earliest age children are taught to think of their elders as mothers and their peers as sisters, would it not be "natural" for them to become attached to the nation? Is not love of country as "natural" in Herland as Rousseau believes love of family is in Sophie's and Emile's land?

For the children of Sophie and Emile their country is a distant, incomprehensible abstraction while their private family is an immediate, familiar, "natural" fact. In effect, their family is their world and their country an unknown, barely glimpsed region beyond. For the children of Herland, however, a private family is a foreign, incomprehensible abstraction and their country is an immediate, familiar, "natural" fact: their country is their world as surely as Sophie's home is her children's world, and the Herlanders love it as readily as Sophie's children love her home. In Rousseau's philosophy the family may be classified as a natural institution and the state as a conventional one, but even if one grants Rousseau this problematic distinction, one need not grant his classification of sentiments. Nothing follows about the nature of the sentiments people have toward an institution from whether it is natural or conventional: thus, for example, one can hate a "natural" institution and love a "conventional" one.

There is no reason to believe that love of country is weakened in those modern societies that have established communal child-rearing practices.[11] Even though the bonds of attachment Rousseau has in mind are the communal feelings Plato envisioned for his Just State, not simply a mindless patriotism, the example of Herland suggests that love of homeland could in the proper circumstances develop directly, and common sense suggests that if mediation is required, alternative structures to that of the private family could be devised.

None of this, however, suggests that Rousseau is mistaken about Plato's guardians. That they will acquire the sentiments toward one another and the state Plato envisions is, indeed, doubtful. No overarching educational ideal binding people to one another and to the land itself is presented in the *Republic*. On the contrary, the Platonic ideal of an educated person is individualistic. Stressing harmonious relationships between parts of the individual human soul rather than between and among human beings, this ideal acts, ironically enough, as a centrifugal force in a society whose goal is unity. Needless to say, the educational program

Plato prescribes for the citizens of his Just State does not compensate for the inherent individualism of his ideal. How can it when the program is devised with the ideal in mind? Gymnastics to develop the strong body needed to house a strong mind; deductive studies to strengthen the rational part of the soul; encounters with temptation to secure the submission of spirit and passion to reason: none of these is designed to teach people to respond directly to others in the manner of a Mary Garth or a Mrs. Bulstrode; none is designed to foster love or sympathy, care or concern. Of course, the stories told in the Just State are supposed to dispose their listeners to virtue, and it might be thought that they would be sufficient to foster the other-directed sentiments Plato wants to see flourish. Yet the virtues Socrates and his friends seem concerned about in determining which stories ought to be censored are not positive ones that serve to bind people together but negative ones such as the absence of crime, fighting, harsh punishment of fathers, hatred of friends and kin, which serve simply to prevent conflict.

Thus the educational program of the Just State is not conducive to the communal feelings Plato's theory of unity requires, nor is there great likelihood that these feelings will spring up spontaneously. Rousseau perceives a serious problem in Plato's social philosophy and correctly senses that it is intimately bound up with the issue of the family. But he misdiagnoses its cause. He assumes that attachment to country is impossible without prior attachment to private family, because he is unable to envision a land in which mother love is the central fact of family life.

Why this failure of imagination in one who knows that Plato would make a family of his guardian class, one who tells us that Sophie must teach Emile to love his children? Rousseau is also the one who calls the private family a small *fatherland,* as he is the one who bars Sophie from citizenship. He may glimpse her virtues but he does not begin to understand their value. It is thus left to Gilman to show that Plato's problem can be solved without restoring to the Just State the potentially divisive institutions of private home, marriage, family, and child rearing. It is left to her to show that mother love, just as surely as father rule or brotherhood, can be writ large.

The Most Radical Vision

In the afterword to *For Her Own Good,* Barbara Ehrenreich and Deirdre English say:

We refuse to remain on the margins of society, and we refuse to enter that society on its terms. If we reject these alternatives, then the challenge is to frame a moral outlook which proceeds from women's needs and experiences but which cannot be trivialized, sentimentalized, or domesticated. A synthesis which transcends both the rationalist and romanticist poles must necessarily challenge the masculinist social order itself. It must insist that the human values that women were assigned to preserve expand out of the confines of private lives and become the organizing principles of society. This is the vision that is implicit in feminism—a society that is organized around human needs: a society in which child raising is not dismissed as each woman's individual problem, but in which the nurturance and well-being of all children is a transcendent public priority . . . a society in which healing is not a commodity distributed according to the dictates of profit but is integral to the network of community life . . . in which wisdom about daily life is not hoarded by 'experts' or doled out as a commodity but is drawn from the experience of all people and freely shared among them.[12]

"This," they continue, is "the most radical vision," and it is the very one Gilman develops in *Herland*.[13]

In her major theoretical writings, Gilman does not reject the institution of private home altogether. "Is the home so light a thing as to be blown away by a breath of criticism? Are we so loosely attached to our homes as to give them up when some defects are pointed out?" she asks in *The Home*. "So long as life lasts," she continues, "we shall have homes; but we need not always have the same kind."[14] As William O'Neill points out in his introduction to the modern edition of this 1903 work, Gilman's "exposé of 'domestic mythology' has never been bettered" (p. xiv). He might have added that the changes in the home she demanded would inevitably reverberate throughout society as a whole.

In her own land, as in Herland, Gilman wanted such domestic functions as cookery, cleaning, and child rearing to be detached from their traditional site and carried on outside the home by trained specialists. In *The Home*, she makes it clear that this is necessary if women are to develop their potential as well as for reasons of efficiency, economy, and the improvement of the species. She fully anticipates that her program, if put into effect, would radically change the home, but she does not propose simply to take reproductive processes out of the home. In making the whole society responsible for carrying these processes on she sows the seeds of a social revolution whose dominant theme is mother love.

Perhaps because it has tended to focus on her analysis of women's economic dependency on men,[15] recent commentary on Gilman neglects the radical implications of her theoretical writings for society as a whole. Emphasizing that she wants to detach domestic tasks and functions from the home in order to effect fundamental changes in the traditional female role, this scholarship fosters the impression that Gilman would leave the traditional male role and, indeed, the entire "public sphere" untouched.[16] But a reading that places Gilman in the camp of those today who call for the assimilation of women into men's work and men's world without reconstructing that work or world does not do justice to the theory of education accompanying her proposals to remove child rearing from the home.

It must be understood that in Gilman's philosophy the objects of assimilation into the public sphere are not just women but also society's reproductive processes. Indeed, these processes can be considered the *primary* objects of assimilation for Gilman since, in her view, women can be assimilated into the public sphere only if such processes as cooking and child rearing are. Now, it may well be that in the course of history some processes have been removed from the home without society's having been changed radically. But Gilman is talking about the rearing of children, surely *the* most important reproductive process, and not just about washing clothes or even about cooking and eating. Nor is she asking the larger society simply to establish a holding operation such as day-care centers in which children are kept until parents get home from work. She is calling for something quite different: educational environments outside the home—"child gardens"—in which the "whole" child is cultivated.

As Gilman's book *The Man-Made World* (1911) makes very clear, she understands that men have defined the public sphere. Furthermore, her chapter on education reveals her unwillingness to send women out of the home into an unreconstructed world. The system will change, she says, and "will gradually establish an equal place in life for the feminine characteristics, so long belittled and derided."[17] She may be unduly optimistic about the future, but she certainly does not want it to be one in which women are assimilated into male roles in a male world.

In *The Man-Made World* Gilman says that education, even in its present state, "is the most important phase" (p. 143), and just as she does in *Herland*, she connects education to motherhood in very significant ways. The difference between *Herland* and her earlier account of education is that in the latter she discusses the education of boys as well as girls. Maintaining in her first sentence that the origin of education is maternal, she concludes that the ideal education would begin "at birth, yes, far before it, in the standards of conscious human motherhood" (p. 162).

The major point Gilman makes about education in *The Man-Made World* is that masculinity has so far predominated:

> There is the first spur, Desire, the base of the reward system, the incentive of self-interest, the attitude which says, "Why should I make an effort unless it will give me pleasure?" with its concomitant laziness, unwillingness to work without payment. There is the second spur, Combat, the competitive system, which sets one against another, and finds pleasure not in learning, not exercising the mind, but in getting ahead on one's fellows. Under these two wholly masculine influences we have made the educational process a joy to the few who successfully attain, and a weary effort, with failure and contumely attached, to all the others. This may be a good method in sex-competition, but is wholly out of place and mischievous in education. (p. 151)

In what would a feminine influence consist? she asks. Feminine characteristics, she replies, are maternal ones:

> To feminize education would be to make it more motherly. The mother does not rear her children by a system of prizes to be longed for and pursued; nor does she set them to compete with one another, giving to the conquering child what he needs, and to the vanquished, blame and deprivation. That would be "unfeminine." Motherhood does all it knows to give to each child what is most needed, to teach all to their fullest capacity, to affectionately and efficiently develop the whole of them. (p. 152)

It cannot be emphasized too strongly that Gilman is speaking here of the education of both sexes. With the exception of Rousseau, the parties to our conversation have not hesitated to extend to women traits the cultural stereotypes associate with males: it is women's right, Wollstonecraft protests; society will be better off for it, Beecher and Plato insist. Only Gilman reverses the process and argues for the extension to men of traits our stereotypes associate with females. No one else says that it is men's right; no one suggests that society will be the better for it. It is true that Plato requires the guardians of the Just State to be gentle to their own people, and is not gentleness genderized in favor of females? A close reading of the relevant passages in the *Republic* suggests, however, that his concern is not so much that the guardians be gentle in any positive sense of the term as that they not be savage. Once again, it is the absence of a negative quality often associated with males, rather than the presence of a positive quality associated with females, that he wants to foster in his male and female guardians. There is a hint of Gilman's reversal in Beecher, for Sarah is to teach her children the "gentler emotions." But this is the very part of her educational philosophy that Beecher leaves undeveloped, and so we cannot be sure that these emotions are to be taught to boys as well as to girls and whether, in touching her husband's heart, Sarah is, in effect, leading him to acquire the very emotions that are genderized against him.

When Gilman's proposals for detaching child rearing from the home and her ideas on education are read together, the reconstructive aspect of her philosophy becomes apparent. Then *Herland* no longer seems discontinuous with the rest of her work. Then her vision for her own society can be seen to be a particular working out of Ehrenreich and English's most radical vision. Then, too, we are able to perceive a flaw in Gilman's philosophy of female education, one that becomes particularly acute when the education is extended to males.

In Herland there are no sex stereotypes, hence no genderized traits. The women of that country do display characteristics genderized in favor of males in both our society and Gilman's. But since the ideology giving rise to trait genderization has long since been eradicated in Herland, such traits will not create the problems for its inhabitants that we anticipate for Plato's female guardians and Wollstonecraft's Emily.

Were our interest in Gilman's imagined society purely theoretical, the fact that her philosophy does not take trait genderization into account would be of no consequence. Our interest in Gilman's theory of female education is quite practical, however. On the one hand, we look to it for illumination as we claim an education for women today. Furthermore, in its general outlines, if not its specific details, the education she depicts in *Herland* is the kind she holds up for our two-sex society. But in our land, trait genderization is a fact of life that a theory of women's education and women's place cannot afford to ignore.

In *The Man-Made World* Gilman classifies traits as masculine, feminine, or human. The human category comprises those qualities she takes to be important. Undoubtedly, the motivation behind this threefold classification is to make it clear that the traits she believes people ought to possess can be acquired by both sexes. Yet in calling such traits as courage "human," Gilman only masks the fact that they are genderized. Misled by her own theoretical structure, she thus fails to make provisions in her educational theory for the problems that arise when both sexes are expected to acquire traits genderized in favor of one. In this respect Gilman is no different from our other philosophers; yet in her case the issue of genderized traits looms especially large because she is arguably the only one of our educational thinkers who wants males to acquire traits genderized in favor of females. It is one thing for girls to grow up to be fleet, fearless, agile, calm, wise, and self-assured in a society that considers these traits not so much human as masculine. It is another thing altogether for the ideal of mother love to be held up for boys in a society that considers nurturance and caring to be feminine traits.

Gilman's failure to address this issue is by no means an irremediable flaw. If she does not show us how to solve the problems posed by genderized traits, we can work this out for ourselves and graft our solution onto her theory of education. There is another apparent flaw in her vision, however, that is not so easily resolved. Like Wollstonecraft and Beecher before her, Gilman makes it clear that reason and rationality play a central role in mother love; that knowledge and competence are just as intimately bound up with child rearing as with politics and economics. And just as they seem loath to attribute to mothering the feeling and emotion typically associated with it, so Gilman too strips mother love of this dimension. No intense delight for the mothers of Herland, no shocks of joy, no sickening anxiety. And since mother love is the overriding ideal in Herland, that this dimension is missing from Gilman's definition of mother love means that it is absent from all human relationships there. Thus the emotion in Mary Garth's response to her parents' financial plight and in Mrs. Bulstrode's response to her husband's humiliation would seem to have no counterpart in Herland. Then the question arises whether the women and girls of Herland really will respond to one another as Gilman wants them to.

Gilman certainly assumes that they will; for example, she tells us of the general joy over the marriages of Ellador, Celis, and Alima to Van, Jeff, and Terry and of the shared sense of outrage over Terry's attempted rape of Alima. But is a theory of personality that denies the emotions, as Gilman's seems to do, adequate to her intentions? Moreover, Gilman's particular version of the ideal of mother love contains another apparent defect, for while her mothers have a definite sense of connection to others, they are not bound to their daughters, sisters, or own mothers by ties of intimacy. Thus, we must ask whether the intimate nature of Mary Garth's relationship to her parents is not a precondition of her response to their distress.

Toward the end of Ursala LeGuin's utopian novel *The Dispossessed,* there is a moving passage that speaks directly to the issue of intimacy, or rather the lack of it, in Herland:

> The child said, "Shevek, may I stay in the room tonight?"
> "Of course. But what's wrong?" Sadik's delicate, long face quivered and seemed to fragment.
> "They don't like me, in the dormitory," she said, her voice becoming shrill with tension, but even softer than before.
> "They don't like you? What do you mean?"
> They did not touch each other yet. She answered him with desperate courage. "Because they don't like—they don't like the Syndicate, and Bedap, and—and you. They call—The big sister in the dorm room, she said you—we were all tr—— She said we were traitors," and saying the word the child jerked as if she had been shot, and Shevek caught her and held her. She held to him with all her strength, weeping in great gasping sobs. She was too old, too tall for him to pick up. He stood holding her, stroking her hair. He looked over her dark head at Bedap. His own eyes were full of tears. He said, "It's all right, Dap. Go on."
> There was nothing for Bedap to do but leave them there, the man and the child, in that one intimacy which he could not share, the hardest and deepest, the intimacy of pain. It gave him no sense of relief or escape to go; rather he felt useless, diminished.[18]

This incident acquires its poignancy from the fact that the utopian society LeGuin describes in her book is far from perfect. In Herland, presumably, no one will be unkind to a child and no one will be called a traitor. Nevertheless, LeGuin's perception of the emptiness of a life without intimacy leads one to wonder if the women of Herland would not ultimately identify with Bedap:

> "I am thirty-nine years old," he thought as he walked on towards his domicile, the five-man room where he lived in perfect independence. "Forty in a few decades. What have I done? What have I been doing? Nothing. Meddling. Meddling in other people's lives because I don't have one. I never took the time. And the time's going to run out on me, all at once, and I will never have had . . . that." He looked back, down the long, quiet street, where the corner lamps made soft pools of light in the windy darkness, but he had gone too far to see the father and daughter, or they had gone. And what he meant by "that" he could not have said, good as he was with words; yet he felt that he understood it clearly, that all his hope was in that

understanding, and that if he would be saved he must change his life. (pp. 297–98)

Remarking on the total absence of sexuality and passion in Gilman's utopia, Evelyn Fox Keller points out that Gilman's vision of science is thereby diminished: "Nowhere in *Herland* do we hear about the role of intimacy and its identification with the acquisition of knowledge."[19] But it is not just science that may suffer because Gilman does not solve the problem of joining together reason, feeling, and emotion in her ideal of mother love. If what Marguerite Duras calls the "mad love" of maternity[20] and intimacy itself are excluded from the ideal guiding education in Herland, one cannot help but wonder whether Gilman's utopia can be a land of loving relationships in which people feel one another's pains and pleasures, joys and sorrows. On the other hand, there may be routes to unity and cohesiveness that do not require intimacy as we know it,[21] and there may even be intimacy that does not engage the emotions. Like the *Republic*, *Herland* is a thought experiment, and the possibility must be acknowledged that the flaw I attribute to it may be the result of my own failure of imagination, not Gilman's.

Herland is a brilliant experiment in thought. Because it depicts a one-sex society, Gilman is free to pursue to their radical conclusions the consequences for education and society of her ideal of mother love. Providing a vantage point from which to understand her theoretical writings, this utopian novel then allows us to see how her most radical vision might be worked out in a two-sex society.

Admittedly, it is difficult to tell if Gilman expects males as well as females to carry on the reproductive processes she detaches from the home. Will men be "child gardeners"? Will they cook and serve the meals at the communal dining centers? Or will these traditionally female occupations remain female when taken out of the home? And what will that home be like when stripped of its domestic functions? Moreover, it is difficult to know if she expects these processes, once detached from the home, to command respect and prestige. Will the specialization of child rearing place it on a par with, for example, medicine and law? Will it do so if child rearing remains a female occupation?

Gilman's version of the most radical vision gives rise to numerous questions, but we should not let these mar our appreciation of a social and educational philosophy in which the love women have for children is the central feature. Granted, in stripping feeling, emotion, and intimacy away from mother love, Gilman may have jeopardized her project. Granted, too, she does not acknowledge the full range of genderized traits and so does not realize that valuable traits as well as despicable ones are genderized, some in favor of males and some in favor of females. Thus, although Gilman realizes that some traits are associated in the culture with masculinity and some with femininity, she does not fully understand the implications of trait genderization for her own social and educational philosophy. Hence, while prescribing for those daughters and sons living in a two-sex society the acquisition of "human" traits, she makes no provisions for counteracting the gender-based assessments of courage and rationality, nurturance and compassion.

Despite these problems, as any of the other participants in our conversation would tell us, Gilman's project is an immensely powerful one. Its force lies not only in that it speaks directly to the issues of female education today but in that it speaks also to issues of the education of males as none of the other educational theories considered here has done. But her project does more, for in addressing the same issues of home, family, and child rearing that Plato considered in the *Republic,* it contributes to the solution of one of the classic dilemmas in the history of Western political thought.

Powerful as Gilman's vision may be, however, we must recognize that it is Wollstonecraft and Beecher who are the democrats with respect to the reproductive processes of society. Just as a comparison with Rousseau's political and educational philosophy reveals Plato's elitism concerning who is to be educated to be self-governing in matters of state, so a comparison with their philosophies—especially Beecher's—reveals Gilman's elitism concerning who is to be educated to be self-governing in matters of child rearing, nutrition, and the like. In Plato's Just State only those few individuals suited by nature to rule will be educated for the guardian role, whereas in Rousseau's ideal state all males will be educated to be Emiles. In Herland only those few talented and interested individuals will be educated for carrying on the reproductive processes of society, whereas in Beecher's ideal state all females will be educated to be Sarahs. Even as Rousseau, while adopting Plato's educational ideal for the self-legislating individual, extends it to all males, Gilman adopts Beecher's theory of professional domestic education and restricts it to the specially selected few.

Beecher, then, is as much a democrat in relation to domestic life and domestic education as Rousseau is in relation to political life and citizenship education. The political form Gilman espouses in *Herland* is not entirely clear, but in taking the reproductive processes of society out of the home and placing them in the hands of specialists, there can be no doubt that she rejects Beecher's egalitarianism, if not Rousseau's. Like Beecher, Gilman would have us believe that in claiming an education for those women who will carry on the reproductive processes of society we must cast a wide enough net to include domestic economy. Moreover, Gilman would claim for those responsible for feeding us and rearing our children the professional expertise and capacity for self-legislation Beecher claims for Sarah. But with Gilman's entrance into our conversation, Beecher's democratic assumption that all women should master Sarah's particular form of expertise and autonomy is challenged.

Just as the issue between Plato and Rousseau, and also between Wollstonecraft and Rousseau, is one of who should be educated for citizenship, the issue between Gilman and Beecher as well as between Gilman and Wollstonecraft is one of who should be educated for carrying on the reproductive processes of society. If on the first question we must side with Wollstonecraft rather than Rousseau, even as we prefer his egalitarianism to Plato's elitism, and even if we may doubt the adequacy of Emily's preparation for the citizen role, on the second question we need not side with any of the participants in our conversation, for options they may never have dreamed of are open to us—ones in which males share with females responsibility for carrying on society's reproductive processes. Yet if our five philosophers have not said the last word on women's place and women's education, especially in relation to the reproductive processes of society, it is evident from their work that we must consider both what would constitute a proper preparation for performing those processes and to whom such preparation should be extended. In particular, Gilman requires us to ask not only if the specialized and rather technical education in domestic economy constructed by Beecher is necessary for carrying on society's reproductive processes well but whether, like medical or legal training today, that education should be reserved for the expert few or, in the manner of citizenship education, should be extended to all.

7 Acquaintanceship and Conversation

In June 1955, Adlai Stevenson, twice Democratic nominee for president, told the graduating class of Smith College that commencement speakers across the United States were reminding seniors how important they were "as citizens in a free society, as educated, rational, privileged participants in a great historical crisis."[1] Making the Western struggle to preserve and perfect "the free society" the backdrop for his remarks, Stevenson said, "But for my part I want merely to tell you young ladies that I think there is much you can do about that crisis in the humble role of housewife—which, statistically, is what most of you are going to be whether you like the idea or not now— and you'll like it!"

Today, one can scarcely imagine a liberal public figure saying this to students at a prestigious women's college. That Stevenson's remarks forfeited his credibility with his audience is unlikely, however. In an era in which a rose was given to every Radcliffe College senior engaged by graduation day to be married, a speech arguing for the overriding importance of the very role to which the great majority of young listeners looked forward must have been welcome.

Just eight years after Stevenson's speech, *The Feminine Mystique* would so affect public consciousness concerning women's role that his remarks would quickly become antiquated. Yet with hindsight one can discern a natural progression from Stevenson's speech to Betty Friedan's book. What he dimly perceived, she articulated. What he wanted to deny yet could not bring himself to ignore entirely, she brought into the open for all to see, feel, and abhor. Attempting to convince a twentieth-century audience of the validity of what was essentially Wollstonecraft's philosophy of women's education and women's place, Stevenson tried to make the problem of the mismatch between Emily's liberal education and her domestic role disappear by arguing for the importance of the traditional female role. Perceiving and caring about the damage that role was doing women, Friedan showed her readers how Stevenson's address fit squarely within "the logic of the feminine mystique" and exhorted them to reject the very life-style he extolled for women.[2]

"Here's where you come in," Stevenson had said in his speech:

> to restore valid meaningful purpose to life in your home: to beware of instinctive group reaction to the forces which play upon you and yours, to watch for and arrest the constant gravitational pulls to which we are all exposed, your workaday husband especially, in our specialized, fragmented society that tend to widen the breach between reason and emotion, between means and ends.

He added, perhaps a bit too facetiously, that "this assignment for you, as wives and mothers, has great advantages. In the first place, it is home work—you can do it in the living room with a baby on your lap, or in the kitchen with a can opener in your hands." Stevenson cited the second advantage in dead earnest, however:

> It is important work worthy of you, whoever you are, or your education, whatever it is—even Smith College because we will defeat totalitarian, authoritarian ideas only by better ideas; we will frustrate the evils of vocational specialization only by the virtues of intellectual generalization. Since Western rationalism and Eastern spiritualism met in Athens and that mighty creative fire broke out, collectivism in various forms has collided with individualism time and again. This twentieth-century collision, this "crisis" we are forever talking about, will be won at last not on the battlefield but in the head and heart.

Stevenson told the Smith seniors he had large notions about what they would have to do and warned them not to get caught, whether in the kitchen or the nursery, by the steady pressures surrounding them. "Educated women," he insisted,

> have a unique opportunity to influence us, man and boy, and to play a direct part in the unfolding drama of our free society. But, I am told that nowadays the young wife or mother is short of time for the subtle arts, that things are not what they used to be; that once immersed in the very pressing and particular problems of domesticity, many women feel frustrated and far apart from the great issues and stirring debates for which their education has given them understanding and relish. Once they read Baudelaire. Now it is the Consumers' Guide. Once they wrote poetry. Now it's the laundry list. Once they discussed art and philosophy until late in the night. Now they are so tired they fall asleep as soon as the dishes are finished. There

is, often, a sense of contraction, of closing horizons and lost opportunities. They had hoped to play their part in the crisis of the age. But what they do is wash the diapers.

"I hope I have not painted too depressing a view of your future," said Stevenson. Fearing that he had, Stevenson reassured his listeners that "the vocation of marriage and motherhood" would put them in the very center of the great issues of the day and would place upon them a deeper responsibility "than that borne by the majority of those who hit the headlines and make the news." Catharine Beecher's sentiments exactly, although, because of the exclusion from public learning of her philosophy, Stevenson would not have known this. Nor would he have known that the tension he exposed so clearly between the by then accepted educational practice of providing a liberal education for women and the prevailing expectation that women would be traditional wife-mothers is to be found in Wollstonecraft's philosophy. Unaware of the very existence of Beecher and Wollstonecraft, denied the opportunity to listen to the conversation being reclaimed here, probably not even cognizant that such a conversation had ever taken place, Stevenson approached his topic de novo.

Women's Education and Public Learning

Would Stevenson have given a significantly different address had the topic of women's education regularly appeared on lists of "great issues"; had *Republic,* book 5, *Emile,* book 5, *A Vindication,* Beecher's *Treatise,* and *Herland* routinely been considered major texts; had philosophical conversation across time and space about the education of women been incorporated into the "mainstream of Western thought?" Would he have challenged the adequacy of Emily's education? Might he have looked to Sarah's instead? We cannot know, in part because we do not know enough about Stevenson, but also because we do not know what a world would look like in which women were included in public learning as both the objects and subjects of educational thought. Who can say that in such a world the very education given women at U.S. colleges in 1955 would not have been significantly different? That in such a world most college women would have been expecting to spend the rest of their lives as traditional wife-mothers?

One can speculate, however, that if Stevenson had had the benefit of the wisdom of Plato, Rousseau, Wollstonecraft, Beecher, and Gilman, his own solution to the problem of mismatch between a liberal education and the traditional role of wife and mother would have been less shallow. In a letter to the English scientist and philosopher Robert Hooke, Sir Isaac Newton wrote: "If I have seen further (than you and Descartes) it is by standing upon the shoulders of giants."[3] That even this genius attained his fundamental insights into nature only because he was acquainted with what others before him had discovered suggests the dangers inherent not only in Stevenson's ignorance of what his predecessors had said about female education but in our own.

It is commonplace that a prepared mind is essential to creative insight and genuine discovery. This condition does not and cannot obtain when what has been said on a subject is not a part of public learning. Stevenson's commencement speech is a fine illustration of what happens when each generation has to start afresh. Of course, he did not approach his topic with an utterly blank slate, but having no access to what the great thinkers of the past had said about women's education and women's place, Stevenson is to be admired for even perceiving the problem of mismatch between a Smith College education and women's traditional role. He can hardly have been expected to have provided a well-developed solution to it.[4]

Although the metaphor Newton used certainly served his purpose, the imagery of standing on the shoulders of giants is not acceptable. Its defect is not merely that because of common expectations, if not actual dictionary definitions, the reference to giants conjures up visions of male human beings, whereas so many of those who have had the most to say about women's education are female. Implicit in the image of standing taller, and hence seeing farther, is a conception of theory construction in particular, and of the attainment of knowledge more generally, which does not at all capture the nature of educational thought.[5] Standing on Hooke's shoulders, Newton could presumably see what that giant saw and more besides. Someone else then standing on Newton's shoulders— Einstein, for instance—would presumably see what Newton and Hooke had seen, and more. The picture is one of linear progress with knowledge portrayed as cumulative, each new theory incorporating the discoveries of earlier ones and consequently being more inclusive than its predecessors.

The conversation reclaimed here reveals the inadequacy of a cumulative conception of the history of educational theory and philosophy. Having read *Republic,* book 5, Rousseau saw *differently* from Plato, not farther than he. Having read *Emile,* book 5, Wollstonecraft did not extend Rousseau's vision, she altered it. *A Vindication* is not more inclusive than *Emile* and *Republic* in the sense of incorporating the theories of both Rousseau and Plato. How could it be when their theories contradict each other? Thus, while Beecher's *Treatise* develops ideas contained in both *Emile* and *A Vindication,* it does not and could not possibly provide a unifying theory subsuming the views of both Rousseau and Wollstonecraft. Similarly, although *Herland* speaks directly to the concerns of both Plato and Rousseau, Gilman's perspective on her subject, informed as it is by her insights into the oppression of women and into the values of mother love, is at such variance with theirs that it makes little sense to consider her vision as somehow including theirs.

We need to know what thinkers of the past have had to say about women's education, but not in order to stand on anyone's shoulders. Whose shoulders would we choose? Each of the five historical parties to our conversation has insight into our topic, but each one's theory also contains serious flaws. Moreover, none speaks in a late-twentieth-century tongue. What we want is acquaintanceship and conversation, not discipleship and dogma. We need the opportunity to attend to what the participants in this conversation have said and to enter into it ourselves. Taking into account both the insights and the mistakes of others, and perhaps most of all allowing our imaginations to be kindled by the interchange of radically different ideas, how much more intelligently and creatively we will be able to think about our topic than Stevenson could.

When each individual and each generation has to ponder anew an issue as complex as the education of women, the resultant ideas tend to be reactive rather than creative, to represent the rejection of some clear evil rather than the adoption of a well-developed alternative. Recoiling from Sophie and her modern counterparts, we find ourselves opting for Emile's education, never stopping to appreciate Sophie's positive contributions both to his life and that of his society. Denying the validity of a strict gender-based division of natures, we find ourselves endorsing coeducation without contemplating the problems posed by genderized traits for both Emily and Plato's female guardians. Fearing that even today women may be kept from equal participation in the productive processes of society, we find ourselves claiming an education devoted solely to preparation for these functions, not for a moment considering that education is also needed if society's reproductive processes are to be performed well.

The fallacy of the false dilemma—either Sophie's education or Emile's, either an education based solely on gender or one having nothing to do with gender, either preparation solely for carrying on the productive processes of society or solely for carrying on the reproductive processes—is a natural consequence of our ignorance of alternative ideals of the educated woman. Resulting from a failure of imagination, this fallacy flourishes where tongues are silenced.

Fresh, creative thinking about women's education is to be desired, but it is not to be confused with de novo thinking. If it does not derive from discipleship, neither will it emerge without acquaintanceship, especially when the assumptions with which we approach our problem are so deeply entrenched in the culture that we do not even recognize their existence. Those who do not know the past run the risk not only of repeating its mistakes but of taking as givens their society's most fundamental—yet not necessarily valid—educational assumptions.

The Identity Postulate is one such assumption we never think to question. Another one, the source of which is also the *Republic,* is that preparation for carrying on the productive processes of society is education's sole concern. A corollary of this second assumption—one Beecher tried valiantly to discredit—is the belief that education for carrying on the reproductive processes of society is not necessary, if not because of women's instincts, then because those processes are the domain of feeling and emotion rather than reason. By accepting these assumptions uncritically, we end up exchanging one kind of lopsided female education—Sophie's—for another—Emily's. Moreover, consciously or not, we give our support to the hierarchy of values, rejected by both Beecher and Gilman but with us still today, that places society's productive processes above its reproductive ones. And in supporting this we also endorse the social vision, challenged by Gilman, that places a greater value on traits the culture associates with males than on ones associated with females.

To think and act intelligently and creatively in claiming an education for women, we must begin to question propositions that to many may seem self-evident. In so doing, we run the risk of being accused by those who themselves commit the fallacy of the false dilemma of looking backward: of placing women in the home, in the fashion of Rousseau; of making domesticity women's work, in the manner of Beecher. There is no doubt that some today who ask us to value the reproductive processes of society and their associated traits do embrace the traditional family structure, with its gender-based division of roles grounded in a gender-based division of natures. But giving the reproductive processes of society their due in educational theory and philosophy does not necessarily entail a return to Rousseau or Beecher.

One of the lessons to be learned from our conversation is that institutions, roles, tasks, traits are detachable from one another and from gender. Thus, to call Sophie's gentleness a virtue does not mean consigning women to the home, as Rousseau did; nor does it commit one to educational programs in which this virtue is developed in one sex rather than in the other. Similarly, to point to the importance of Sophie's child-rearing activities and to the positive role she plays within her family does not entail the preservation of the traditional wife-mother role; indeed, it does not even commit one to a position on who should do the child rearing.

The present task of reclamation is intended to encourage critical examination of programs and proposals concerning education today, and that must include questioning some of our most basic assumptions. It must be remembered, however, that ours is but one part of a much larger conversation waiting to be reclaimed and that there is no reason to suppose that the five historical parties to it are the only theorists from whom we can learn about the education of females. Our conversational circle needs to be enlarged so that more ideals of the educated woman can be discussed and alternative formulations of ideals already introduced can be explored. Among the promising candidates are Mary Astell, John Dewey, François Fénelon, Margaret Fuller, Emma Goldman, Florence Howe, John Locke, Mary Lyons, Margaret Mead, B. F. Skinner, and Emma Willard.

It will not be enough simply to increase the circle's size, however; we must also reclaim conversations about the education of females that are different from the one reconstructed here. Although Plato, Rousseau, Wollstonecraft, Beecher, and Gilman all address the difference of sex, they do not entertain the many questions of difference arising within gender categories. Yet race, ethnicity, and economic status should be discussed seriously, too. It is imperative, also, that we examine the heterosexual assumptions of the parties to our conversation and trace the implications for education of alternative constructions of female sexuality.[6]

Redefining the Educational Realm

The larger effort of reclamation—even the conversation reclaimed here—has important implications for the content, methodology, and structure of the history of educational thought. Earlier I raised the question of why this discipline has censored conversation about the education of half the world's population. Now that we know the subject matter of that conversation, we are in a position to answer the question. We have heard Plato, Rousseau, Wollstonecraft, Beecher, and Gilman repeatedly discuss marriage, home, family, child rearing, and domestic management. Of course, they also addressed political and economic issues, but no matter what sort of education our five philosophers were claiming for women, they could not ignore the reproductive processes of society and their associated traits, tasks, functions, and institutions. Historians of educational thought consider these topics to be none of their concern, however.

Lorenne Clark has shown that from the standpoint of political theory the consignment of women, children, and the family to the ontological basement—that is, their apolitical status—is due not to historical accident or necessity but to arbitrary definition.[7] The reproductive processes of society, broadly interpreted to include the rearing of children to more or less independence, are excluded by fiat from the political domain, which is defined in relation to the world of productive processes—political, social, and cultural as well as economic. Since the subject matter of political theory is politics, and since the reproductive processes have traditionally been assigned to women and have taken place within the family, it follows that women and the family are excluded from the subject matter of the discipline.

The analogy between political theory and educational thought is striking. Despite the fact that the reproductive processes of society, broadly understood, are largely devoted to child rearing and include the transmission of skills, beliefs, feelings, emotions, values, and even world views, they are not considered to belong to the educational realm. Thus education, like politics, is defined in relation to the productive processes of society, and the status of women and the family is every bit as "a-educational" as it is apolitical. No wonder Sophie is overlooked by historians of educational thought. Unless the borders of the educational realm are altered, Emily, Sarah, and Ellador will be, too.

To be sure, the education Plato prescribes for his female guardians is designed to equip them to carry on that most important productive process, ruling. If my explanation of the way the history of educational thought defines its subject matter is correct, why is the education of these women neglected by the field? Two reasons come to mind. In the first place, Plato's female guardians constitute an anomaly for the field's definition of itself: productive processes fall within the educational realm; women fall outside it. One way to resolve the problem posed by Plato's women is to ignore them; another is to discuss their education but treat as irrelevant the fact that they are women. Furthermore, to understand and evaluate Plato's theory of female education, one must take into account his views on the institutions of private marriage, home, family, and child rearing. Since these fall outside the educational realm, it is easy enough to perceive the education of his female guardians as falling there, also.

If conversation about women's education is to be incorporated in the history of educational thought, the definition of that discipline's subject matter must be expanded to include the processes of society with which women's lives have historically been intertwined. If the conversational circle is to be enlarged and the discussion enriched, the methods of this field will also have to become more inclusive.

The five theories of female education reclaimed here were reconstructed from the pages of books. Although the last three of the works I have drawn on—*A Vindication, A Treatise, Herland*—are not part of the established canon of educational theory and philosophy, my approach has nonetheless been one of looking to books for data. Recall, however, that one of the books—*Herland*—was originally published in serialized form in a popular magazine. Had it not been for Ann Lane's retrieval, *Herland,* independent of its subject matter, might have been considered a suspect source to use in the reconstruction of the history of educational thought. Thus if we are finally to be able to listen to the full range of our conversation, we will have to change our notion not only of what counts as a bona fide topic of study but also of what counts as a bona fide source of data.

The general expectation that any educational theory worth recording is readily accessible in books or academic journals becomes unreasonable when the objects or the subjects of educational thought are considered marginal. Marginal people do not normally have access to established channels of communication, and those channels rarely give equal time to topics concerning marginal people. Yet marginal is precisely what society has considered women to be. Thus, as the larger effort of reclamation proceeds, we will have to look to sources of data that the history of educational thought regards as far from standard: to personal letters, diaries, pamphlets, newsletters, pieces of fiction, and to oral sources as well.

As our conception of sources is affected by the entrance of women into the educational realm, so too will be our conception of the discipline's techniques. Historians of educational thought are accustomed to having their philosophers and their sources handed to them ready-made— Dewey's *Democracy and Education,* Whitehead's *The Aims of Education*—so that the investigator's task is the relatively straightforward one of interpretation and evaluation. Occasionally a new work or a new thinker will be discovered and made a part of the canon. Occasionally a person's philosophical thought will be reconstructed from lecture notes rather than polished essays. It is rare, however, for a historian of educational thought to become a historian in the more primary sense of digging up the sources and, in the process, determining whether the author is indeed to be considered an educational philosopher. Yet this is precisely what will be required of those engaged in the larger reclamation effort concerning the education of women—on the one hand, if letters, pamphlets, and the like are even to serve as sources for a reconstructed conversation and, on the other, if we are to discover which individuals in our past have actually constructed theories of female education.

Even this way of putting the problem, however, is a function of present conceptions of methodology, in particular of what counts as an author or creator of an educational philosophy. It is normally assumed that the educational thought of the past worth preserving has been created by individuals. When the topic of study is women's education, this assumption too must be questioned.

Wollstonecraft, Beecher, Gilman: we must not be misled by the fact that these women wrote philosophical works into supposing that women in general have had access to the social, economic, and educational resources philosophy requires. The life stories of the three female participants in our conversation testify to the enormous difficulties even the most successful women have had to overcome in order to do the sort of intellectual labor reclaimed here. Although our three are by no means the only women in history to have attained philosophical authorship in the field of education, we need to follow Wollstonecraft's lead. Just as she refused to ground her case for women's rationality on the existence of the extraordinary women of her time, so we should refuse to ground our larger effort of reclamation on the existence of the relatively few extraordinary women—and those men—who have written extensively on female education. Rather, we must understand that some of the most interesting and significant theories of female education may have been authored not by single individuals but by groups of individuals—for instance, those founding and running schools—and others may have simply emerged out of social movements.

When our conception of authorship changes, historians of educational thought will have to take on the role of anthropologist. Just as the reconstruction of Hopi ethics required the skills of both philosopher and anthropologist,[8] so the reconstruction of the philosophy of education of a school or social movement may require the skills of these two professions and of the primary historian besides. The standard philosophical processes of analysis, criticism, interpretation, and evaluation will continue to be essential activities. Otherwise the very policies and practices whose "value, virtue, veracity, and validity" have never been enlightened by philosophy will continue to be denied this needed source of illumination. Nevertheless, when half of the world's population and with it the reproductive processes of society are admitted into the subject matter of a discipline, some very real methodological and substantive changes will occur. The extent of these changes cannot be predicted, but the shape and structure of the narrative of educational thought will undoubtedly be affected.

Once the absence of women from the standard texts and anthologies has been recognized, can we not simply add sections about female education to existing chapters on Plato and Rousseau and introduce new chapters on Wollstonecraft, Beecher, and Gilman? Whatever methodological adjustments may be required, are not revised editions all that we need?

The history of educational thought is no exception to the rule dis-

covered by scholars in a wide range of fields that a simple additive solution to the problem of the inclusion of women will not work. Consider
Sophie. As we have seen, it is not just that the accepted interpretation of
Rousseau's thought does not mention her education. Sophie's education
constitutes an anomaly for that interpretation since what Rousseau says
about her stands in contradiction to it. Of course, it is possible to add a
section about Sophie to a chapter on Rousseau, but the result will be
unsatisfactory: Rousseau will be made to look the fool who spent the
last hundred pages of *Emile* contradicting the first three hundred. And
Rousseau was no fool. Moreover, the additive approach obscures the
important fact that when book 5 of *Emile* is taken seriously, our reading
of books 1–4 changes.

How tempting it is to think of women's entry into the educational
realm as requiring, if not simply brief addenda to the history of educational thought, then at most the introduction of a second and separate
narrative strand. Taking female education as its object of study, would
not a second strand complement the already existing one, now acknowledged to constitute a narrative only of the education of males? The
suggestion may sound promising, but the separate-strand approach to
the history of educational thought is self-defeating: once the female narrative is constructed, the inadequacy of the original strand for even the
limited task of tracing theories about the education of boys and men
becomes apparent.

Again Sophie is a case in point. Since Rousseau ties her education
so closely to her societal role, it is all but impossible to understand *Emile,*
book 5, unless concepts like the ones employed in reclaiming the present
conversation are introduced. Whether or not the interpretive framework
ultimately adopted for Sophie's education is the one used here, it is necessary in capturing Rousseau's intent to introduce such notions as the
wife-mother role, domesticity, the patriarchal family, and the reproductive processes of society, which have no place at all in the intepretations
that currently constitute the history of educational thought. Home, family, marriage, children: the original narrative strand has nothing to say
about such phenomena. Given a second narrative strand in which they
figure prominently, the silences of the original narrative will become in-
tolerable. If Sophie is educated for marriage to Emile, the question of his
education for marriage to her inevitably arises. If she is educated to be
his "other half," questions about the extent and nature of his self-sufficiency can no longer go unasked.

Sophie's case is instructive. Since we have seen in the conversation reclaimed here the standard interpretation of both Rousseau's and Plato's philosophies of education brought into question, the hypothesis that the inclusion of women in the educational realm will have little if any effect on the accepted narrative of the field lacks credibility. When it is understood that females can carry out the guardian duties to Plato's satisfaction only because he has stripped his guardian class of private home, marriage, and family and of all responsibility for the reproductive processes of society, the one-sidedness of the education he prescribes for the guardians is revealed. When his educational ideal of self-disciplined, self-contained individuals is juxtaposed with Gilman's ideal for mother love, the inadequacy of the Platonic scheme for achieving the communal feelings he believes to be essential for unity is exposed. From the examples of Plato and Rousseau one must conclude that those who listen to and engage in conversation about women's education can expect to find enlightenment not only about the education of females but also about that of males.

In a two-sex society it is to be expected that theories of male and female education are mutually illuminating. But the major reason for rejecting the two-strand approach is not that the theoretical separation of females and males keeps out badly needed light, although it does. The more important fault is its failure to recognize that in our two-sex society, educational theory and philosophy must place males and females in one world—a world in which the sexes live together interdependently. Only when Sophie and Emile are seen to be interdependent individuals and their education is interpreted in light of their relationship to each other is an adequate understanding of Rousseau's educational thought possible. Only when the reproductive processes of society are seen to stand in relation to the productive ones is an adequate understanding of Plato's educational thought possible.

Of the parties to our conversation, both Plato and Rousseau understand that so long as the societies they envision contain males and females, the theories of education they construct will have to take both sexes into account. Rousseau, in particular, understands the importance of developing an educational theory that recognizes the ways in which the sexes interact. It is no accident that Sophie is educated for dependence: that is the relation in which she is supposed to stand to Emile. It is no accident that he is educated to be his own legislator: that is the relation in which he, as citizen, is supposed to stand to the state and he, as husband, is supposed to stand to Sophie. To be sure, if Emile is educated according to plan, he may not in fact acquire the loving qualities he must possess if his union with Sophie is to flourish. But this is because Rousseau is mistaken about what a harmonious marriage involves, not because he does not realize that males and females must be educated to live in the same world.

As a woman who had founded a highly successful female seminary, Beecher had ample justification for directing her attention specifically to the education of females. Yet it must not be forgotten that in Beecher's philosophy Sarah requires a husband who acknowledges her competence. Beecher's ideal society could perhaps incorporate legal sanctions to force men to give way to their wives in domestic affairs, but it certainly would run more smoothly and happily if, instead, the early education of males instilled in them a willingness to accept the judgment of professionals of both sexes.

Given her desire to extend the rights of men to women, Wollstonecraft also had good reason to develop a theory of female, not male, education. Yet her daughters require husbands who will treat them as equals in marriage and politics, and there is no reason to suppose that without reeducation the men they marry will do so. Of course, by extending to women the education she takes to be suitable for men, in *A Vindication* Wollstonecraft indirectly takes a stand on the education of males. But if she really wants to educate a new woman, she cannot realistically advocate the same old education for men. Just as Plato must reeducate his male guardians to respect and treat as equals the females he would educate to be rulers, so to transform the marriage relation and to add to women's traditional wife-mother role that of citizen, Wollstonecraft must reeducate her sons as well as her daughters.

Wollstonecraft is correct that Sophie is an artifact of society. What she fails to note is that Emile is socialized, too, and that so long as his socialization and formal education remain unchanged, the new educational program she constructs for Emily will be insufficient. Will men treat Emily as an equal citizen—will they, indeed, allow her to be a citizen—if they continue to believe that Sophie represents every woman? Will Emily be willing or able to reject Sophie if the man in her life continues to desire a toy rather than a friend and colleague? Will she derive the anticipated benefits from the male education extended to her if Sophie remains the norm in male eyes?

So long as Sophie represents the norm for femininity, Emily will be evaluated negatively for her rationality and independence.[9] Thus even as Wollstonecraft educates her daughters to be citizens and rational wives-mothers, she must educate her sons to see Sophie as she does. She can hope that, because of their own rationality, without her intervention her Emiles will appreciate her Emilys once they get to know them, but she had best not count on their relinquishing voluntarily their monopoly in political affairs and their ultimate authority in marriage. For this end to be realized, Wollstonecraft's sons must come to see the world—and women in particular—differently. Even as Wollstonecraft extends men's formal education to women, she must change men's informal education so as to transform their consciousness.

Moreover, if men's *formal* education remains unchanged, Wollstonecraft's social and political program for women will not succeed. In extending to females the liberal education traditionally limited to males, Wollstonecraft makes the mistake Plato makes of initiating both sexes into cognitive perspectives according to which women are viewed as the Other, as beings defined and differentiated by reference to men.[10] Surely the exclusion or distortion of the lives, works, and experiences of women from the subject matter of the theoretical disciplines is not a modern phenomenon. Philosophers did not begin portraying women as less rational than men in the nineteenth and twentieth centuries. With few exceptions, Greek, medieval, Renaissance, and Enlightenment philosophies all contain a vision of women as creatures both alien and inferior. And until the past two decades historians have tended to overlook the accomplishments of individual women and to ignore entirely topics having to do specifically with female experience. Thus, unless Wollstonecraft takes measures to transform the content of the liberal education she extends to both males and females, there is little reason to expect the males to view the females as their equals in the state or in the home, or for that matter for the females to consider themselves their husbands' equals.

Beecher is guilty also of prescribing a liberal education for women in which they are either seen through male eyes or not seen at all. Gilman, as we know, gets around this problem by constructing a one-sex society in which women have created their own forms of knowledge. That she does not endow Herland with the ready-made disciplines of her own society suggests that she perceived their male biases. Furthermore, Gilman's treatment of the intrusion of the three American males, and especially her differentiation of the views of women held by Terry, Jeff, and Van, indicate that she was well aware of both male socialization and the need for male reeducation. Still, Gilman does not provide us with a two-sex philosophy of education in which these insights are fully incorporated.

Educating Our Sons

"What do we want for our sons?" asks Adrienne Rich in *Of Woman Born.* "We want them to remain, in the deepest sense, sons of the mother, yet also to grow into themselves, to discover new ways of being men even as we are discovering new ways of being women."[11] If she could have one wish for her own sons, Rich continues, it is that they should have the courage of women: "I mean by this something very concrete and precise: the courage I have seen in women who, in their private and public lives, both in the interior world of their dreaming, thinking, and creating, and the outer world of patriarchy, are taking greater and greater risks, both psychic and physical, in the evolution of a new vision" (p. 215).

Rich's new vision includes the assimilation of males into a full-time, universal system of child care that would change not only the expectations of both sexes about gender roles but "the entire community's relationship to children." A latter-day Charlotte Perkins Gilman in her insistence that "the mother-child relationship is the essential human relationship" and simultaneously that "the myth that motherhood is 'private and personal' is the deadliest myth we have to destroy,"[12] Rich makes clear the need men will have for "a kind of compensatory education in the things about which their education as males has left them illiterate."[13]

The realm of illiteracy Rich has in mind is populated by the virtues of Sophie and Sarah: a well-developed capacity for sympathetic identification, a denial of the separation between love and work, a desire and an ability to nurture children. One need not adopt Rich's social vision—in which children are no longer "mine" and "thine," the mother-child relationship is placed at the very center of society, and child rearing is a universal responsibility—to agree that in the late twentieth century men should be claiming for themselves an education in Sophie's and Sarah's virtues as well as Emile's. Family living and child rearing are not today, if they ever were, solely in the hands of women. Males and females alike have responsibility for making the reproductive processes of society work well. Thus, men must claim an education that does justice to those processes even as they claim one that gives the productive processes their due.

The reproductive processes are of central importance to any society. It is no small matter, then, to insist that men as well as women be educated to carry them on. It would be a terrible mistake, however, to suppose that in our own society the virtues of Sophie and Sarah have no relevance beyond marriage, home, family, and child rearing. Ours is a country in which one out of four women is raped at some time in her life, one out of four girls and one out of ten boys is sexually abused before the age of eighteen, and some $4–6 billion per year are grossed by the pornography industry.[14] Our country belongs to a world on the brink of nuclear and/or ecological disaster. Efforts to overcome these problems, as well as the related ones of poverty, economic scarcity, and racial injustice, flounder today under the direction of people who do not know how to sustain human relationships or respond directly to human needs, indeed, do not even see the value of trying to do so. We should not suppose that education can solve the world's problems. Yet if there is to be any hope of the continuation of life on earth, let alone of a good life for all, those who carry on society's productive processes must acquire the nurturing capacities and ethics of care Rousseau attributes to Sophie's nature.

Unfortunately, easy as it is to say that men's education must take Sophie and Sarah into account, and convincing as it may sound, our Platonic heritage stands between us and this goal. A case study of what almost everyone today would consider American education at its best reveals the extent to which Plato's educational vision persists in our own time and the damage it does.

In his educational autobiography *Hunger of Memory,* Richard Rodriguez tells of growing up in Sacramento, California, the third of four children in a Spanish-speaking family.[15] Upon entering first grade he could understand perhaps fifty English words. For half a year he resisted his teachers' demands that he speak English. When asked questions, he mumbled; otherwise he sat waiting for the bell to ring. One Saturday morning three nuns descended upon his house: "Do your children speak only Spanish at home?" they asked his mother. "Is it possible for you and your husband to encourage your children to practice their English when they are at home?" In an instant, Rodriguez's parents agreed, in his words, "to give up the language (the sounds) that had revealed and accentuated our family's closeness." An astounding resolve, but it bore fruit. Within a year Rodriguez was a fluent speaker of English; a short while later he graduated from elementary school with citations galore and entered high school having read hundreds of books; he next attended Stanford University; and, twenty years after the nuns' visit, he sat in the British Museum working on a Ph.D. dissertation in English literature.

Rodriguez, having learned to speak English, went on to acquire a liberal education in history, literature, science, mathematics, philosophy. His is a story of the cultural assimilation of a Mexican-American, but it is more than this, for by no means do all assimilated Americans conform to our image of a well-educated person. Rodriguez does because, to use the terms philosopher R. S. Peters employs in his analysis of the concept of the educated man, he did not simply acquire knowledge and skill.[16] He acquired conceptual schemes to raise his knowledge beyond the level of a collection of disjointed facts and to enable him to understand the reason for things; moreover, the knowledge he acquired is not inert, but characterizes the way he looks at the world and involves the kind of commitment to the standards of evidence and canons of proof of the various disciplines that comes from "getting on the inside of a form of thought and awareness."

Quite a success story; yet *Hunger of Memory* is notable primarily for being a narrative of loss. In the process of becoming an educated man Rodriguez loses his fluency in Spanish, but that is the least of it. As soon as English becomes the language of the Rodriguez family, the special feeling of closeness at home is diminished. As his days are devoted more and more to understanding the meaning of words, it becomes increasingly difficult for Rodriguez to hear intimate family voices. When it is Spanish-speaking, his home is a noisy, playful, warm, emotionally charged environment; with the advent of English the atmosphere becomes quiet and restrained. There is no acrimony. The family remains loving. But the experience of "feeling individualized" by family members is now rare, and occasions for intimacy are infrequent.

Thus, Rodriguez tells a story of alienation: from his parents, for whom he soon has no names; from the Spanish language, in which he loses his childhood fluency; from his Mexican roots, in which he loses interest; from his own feelings and emotions, which all but disappear in the process of his learning to control them; from his body itself, as he discovers when, after his senior year in college, he takes a construction job.

John Dewey spent his life trying to combat the tendency of educators to divorce mind from body and reason from emotion. Rodriguez's educational autobiography documents these divorces and another that Dewey deplored, that of self from other. *Hunger of Memory,* above all, depicts a journey from intimacy to isolation. Close ties with family members are dissolved as public anonymity replaces private attention. Rodriguez becomes a spectator in his own home as noise gives way to silence and connection to distance. School, says Rodriguez, bade him trust "lonely" reason primarily. And there is enough time and "silence," he adds, "to think about ideas (big ideas)."

What is the significance of this narrative of loss for those who want to claim the best possible education for their sons? Not every American has Rodriguez's good fortune of being born into a loving home filled with the warm sounds of intimacy; yet the separation and distance he ultimately experienced are by no means unique to him. On the contrary, they represent the natural end point of the educational journey Rodriguez took.

Dewey repeatedly pointed out that the distinction educators draw between liberal and vocational education represents a separation of mind from body, head from hand, thought from action. Since we define an educated person as one who has profited from a liberal education, these splits are built into our ideal of the educated person. Since most definitions of excellence in education derive from that ideal, these splits are built into them as well. A split between reason and emotion is built into our definitions of excellence, too, for we take the aim of a liberal education to be the development not of mind as a whole but of rational mind. We define this in terms of the acquisition of knowledge and understanding, construed very narrowly. It is not surprising that Rodriguez acquires habits of quiet reflection rather than noisy activity, reasoned deliberation rather than spontaneous reaction, dispassionate inquiry rather than emotional response, abstract analytic theorizing rather than concrete storytelling. These are integral to our ideal of the educated person, an ideal familiar to readers of the *Republic.*

Upon completion of his educational journey Rodriguez bears an uncanny resemblance to the guardians of the Just State. Granted, not one of Plato's guardians will be the "disembodied mind" Rodriguez says he became. Yet Plato designs for his guardians an education of heads, not hands. (Presumably the artisans of the Just State will serve as their hands.) Furthermore, holding up for the guardians an ideal of self-discipline and self-government he emphasizes inner harmony at the expense of outward connection. If his guardians do not begin their lives in intimacy, as Rodriguez did, their education, like his, is intended to confirm in them a sense of self in isolation from others.

Do the separations bequeathed to us by Plato matter? The great irony of the liberal education that comes down to us from Plato and still today is the mark of an educated man or women is that it is neither tolerant nor generous. As Richard Rodriguez discovered, there is no place in it for education of the body, and since most action involves bodily movement, this means there is little room in it for education of action. Nor is there room for education of other-regarding feelings and emotions. The liberally educated man or woman will be provided with knowledge about others but will not be taught to care about their welfare or to act kindly toward them. That person will be given some understanding of society, but will not be taught to feel its injustices or even to be concerned over its fate. The liberally educated person will be an ivory-tower person—one who can reason but has no desire to solve real problems in the real world—or a technical person—one who likes to solve real problems but does not care about the solutions' consequences for real people and for the earth itself.

The case of Rodriguez illuminates several unhappy aspects of our Platonic heritage while concealing another. No one who has seen Fred Wiseman's film *High School* can forget the woman who reads to the assembled students a letter she has received from a pupil in Vietnam. But for a few teachers who cared, she tells her audience, Bob Walters, a subaverage student academically, "might have been a nobody." Instead, while awaiting a plane that is to drop him behind the DMZ, he has written her to say that he has made the school the beneficiary of his life insurance policy. "I am a little jittery right now," she reads. She is not to worry about him, however, because "I am only a body doing a job." Measuring his worth as a human being by his monetary provision for the school, she overlooks the fact that Bob Walters was not merely participating in a war of dubious morality but was taking pride in being an automaton.

High School was made in 1968, but Bob Walters's words were echoed many times over by eighteen- and nineteen-year-old Marine recruits in the days immediately following the Grenada invasion. Readers of *Hunger of Memory* will not be surprised. The underside of a liberal education devoted to the development of "disembodied minds" is a vocational education whose business is the production of "mindless bodies." In Plato's Just State, where, because of their rational powers, the specially educated few will rule the many, a young man's image of himself as "only a body doing a job" is desirable. That the educational theory and practice of a democracy derives from Plato's explicitly undemocratic philosophical vision is disturbing. We are not supposed to have two classes of people, those who think and those who do not. We are not supposed to have two kinds of people, those who rule and those who obey.

The Council for Basic Education has long recommended and some people concerned with excellence in education now suggest that a liberal education at least through high school be extended to all.[17] For the sake of argument, let us suppose that this program can be carried out without making more acute the inequities it is meant to erase. We would then presumably have a world in which no one thinks of him- or herself as simply a body doing a job. We would, however, have a world filled with unconnected, uncaring, emotionally impoverished people. Even if it were egalitarian, it would be a sorry place in which to live. Nor would the world be better if somehow we combined Rodriguez's liberal education with a vocational one. For assuming our world were then peopled by individuals who joined "head" and "hand," reason would still be divorced from feeling and emotion, and each individual cut off from others.

The Platonic divorce of reason from feeling and emotion and of self from other is built into our prevailing theories of liberal and vocational education as well as into our very definition of the function of education. For Rodriguez, the English language was a metaphor. In the literal sense of the term he had to learn English to become an educated *American*, yet in his narrative the learning of English represents the acquisition not so much of a new natural language as of new ways of thinking, acting, and being, which he associates with the public world. Rodriguez makes it clear that the transition from Spanish to English for him represented the transition almost every child in our society makes from the "private world" of home to the "public world" of business, politics, and culture.

He realizes that Spanish is not intrinsically a private language and English a public one, although his own experience made it seem this way. He knows that the larger significance of his story lies in the fact that whether English is one's first or second language, education inducts one into new activities and processes. His autobiography thus reveals that it is not just historians of educational thought and philosophers who define education as preparation solely for carrying on the productive processes of society.

Needless to say, the liberal education Rodriguez received did not fit him to carry on *all* productive processes of society. Aiming as it did at the development of a rational mind, his liberal education prepared him to be a consumer and creator of ideas, not an auto mechanic or factory worker. A vocational education—had he received one—would have prepared him to work with his hands and use procedures designed by others. Very different kinds of education, yet both kinds are designed to fit students to carry on productive, not reproductive, societal processes.[18]

Rodriguez's perception that the function of education is to induct us into the public world and its productive processes is of great consequence. Yet although this function harks back to Plato and constitutes an implicit presupposition of almost all educational thought in our own time, it has never been explicitly acknowledged and so its implications have not been traced. *Hunger of Memory* contains a wonderful account of Rodriguez's grandmother taking him to her room and telling him stories of her life. He is moved by the sounds she makes and by the message of intimacy her person transmits. The words themselves are not important to him, for, as he makes clear, he perceives the private world in which she moves—the world of child rearing and homemaking—to be one of feeling and emotion, intimacy and connection, and hence a realm of the nonrational. In contrast, he sees the public world—the world of productive processes for which his education fit him—as the realm of the rational. Feeling and emotion have no place in it, and neither do intimacy and connection. Instead, analysis, critical thinking, and self-sufficiency are the dominant values.

Rodriguez's assumption that feeling and emotion, intimacy and connection are naturally related to the home and society's reproductive processes and that these qualities are irrelevant to carrying on the productive processes is commonly accepted. But then, it is to be expected that their development is ignored by education in general and by liberal education in particular. Since education is supposed to equip people for carrying on productive societal processes, from a practical standpoint would it not be foolhardy for liberal *or* vocational studies to foster these traits?

Only in light of the fact that education turns its back on the reproductive processes of society and the private world of the home can Rodriguez's story of alienation be properly understood. His alienation from his body will reoccur as long as we equate being an educated person with having a liberal education. His journey of isolation and divorce from his emotions will be repeated as long as we define education exclusively in relation to the productive processes of society. But the assumption of inevitability underlying *Hunger of Memory* is mistaken. Education need not separate mind from body and thought from action, for it need not draw a sharp line between liberal and vocational education. More to the point, it need not separate reason from emotion and self from other. The reproductive processes *can* be brought into the educational realm, thereby overriding the theoretical and practical grounds for ignoring feeling and emotion, intimacy and connection.

If we define education in relation to *both* kinds of societal processes and then act upon our redefinition, future generations will not have to experience Rodriguez's pain. The dichotomies upon which his education rested—and which he never questions—must be questioned if we want our sons to be educated well. We must recognize, however, that to challenge the productive/reproductive dichotomy is to call for a basic rethinking of education.

Toward a Gender-Sensitive Ideal

It is no accident that in *Hunger of Memory* the person who is the embodiment of nurturing capacities and an ethics of care is a woman—Rodriguez's grandmother. The two kinds of societal processes, productive and reproductive, are gender-related, and so are the traits our culture associates with them. According to our cultural stereotypes, males are objective, analytical, rational, interested in ideas and things; they have no interpersonal orientation; they are not nurturant or supportive, empathetic or sensitive. Women, on the other hand, possess the traits men lack.[19] Education is also gender-related. Our definition of the function of education makes it so. For if education is viewed as preparation for carrying on processes historically associated with males, it will inculcate traits the culture considers masculine. If the concept of education is tied by definition to the productive processes of society, our ideal of the educated person will coincide with the cultural stereotype of a male human being, and our definitions of excellence in education will embody "masculine" traits.

The conversation reclaimed here has shown that it is possible for members of one sex to possess personal traits our cultural stereotypes attribute to the other. Thus, the fact that the traits incorporated in our educational ideal are genderized in favor of males does not mean that girls and women cannot or do not acquire them. It does mean, however, that when females today embark on Rodriguez's journey of becoming educated, they experience hardships that Rodriguez did not. That our daughters do regularly travel the route taken by Rodriguez cannot be doubted. It may have been premature for Virginia Woolf to call Wollstonecraft's philosophy her "commonplace,"[20] but in late-twentieth-century America, Wollstonecraft's proposal to extend Emile's education to Emily has been accomplished.

Having pondered the fate of both Emily and the female guardians of the Just State, we have some idea of the difficulties girls and women encounter when their education is guided by ideals developed for boys and men. Because women today participate in the productive processes of society, they must acquire the traits that are functional for carrying them on. Because they are responsible also for performing at least some of the reproductive processes, they must, as Beecher argued, apply those "masculine" traits of rationality and self-government in this area, too, if these processes are to be performed well.

In claiming their education women would be well advised to reject the Platonic mold placed on Rodriguez, but in doing so they should not deny themselves access to all the traits our culture associates with males. While opting for a new ideal that joins reason to feeling and emotion and self to other, women must make such qualities as critical thinking, abstract reasoning, and self-government their own as they claim both Sophie's and Sarah's virtues for themselves.

Do girls and women today really need to claim an education in Sophie's virtues? Doesn't Nancy Chodorow's thesis that women develop nurturing capacities just because they are mothered by women imply that no education for females in an ethics of care is required? And is Carol Gilligan's finding of "a different voice" proof that at least this kind of education need not be claimed for females? The answer to these questions must be no: Chodorow's theory does not rule out education in nurturance, nor has Gilligan suggested that all females possess Sophie's virtues. The moral to be drawn from the new scholarship on women is not that females have no need for an education in nurturance but rather that an education in Sophie's virtues for females may have to proceed differently from one designed for males. Where the different voice exists it may simply need to be fostered; where it does not exist it must be constructed.

Insofar as we contemplate, as Plato did, an education for both sexes in traits and tasks associated with the productive processes of society, and insofar as we contemplate, as Gilman did, an education for both sexes in traits and tasks associated with the reproductive processes—we should not make the mistake of uncritically accepting the Identity Postulate. The educational treatment given males and females may have to be different if equivalent results are to be achieved. Before I became a participant in the conversation reclaimed here I assumed, as many people do, that the sole alternative to separate gender-bound ideals of education such as Rousseau's was one that, like Plato's, remained gender-blind. Once I entered into this conversation, however, I began to see that there is another alternative—namely, a *gender-sensitive* educational ideal.

In a society in which traits are genderized and socialization according to sex is commonplace, an educational philosophy that tries to ignore gender in the name of equality is self-defeating. Implicitly reinforcing the very stereotypes and unequal practices it claims to abhor, it makes invisible the very problems it should be addressing. So long as sex and gender are fundamental aspects of our personal experience, so long as they are deeply rooted features of our society, educational theory—and educational practice, too—must be gender-sensitive. This does not mean that we must, in the manner of Rousseau, hold up different ideals for the two sexes. It does not mean that we should agree with him that sex is the difference that makes all the difference. What it does mean is that we must constantly be aware of the workings of sex and gender because in this historical and cultural moment, paradoxically they sometimes make a big difference even if they sometimes make no difference at all.

When education is defined solely in relation to the productive processes of society, trait genderization is seen as "a woman's problem." Once we redefine education so as to give the reproductive processes of society their due, once the virtues of nurturance and care associated with those processes are fostered in both males and females, educated men can expect to suffer for possessing traits genderized in favor of females, as educated women do now for possessing traits genderized in favor of males. This is not to say that males would be placed in the double bind educated females find themselves in now, for males would continue also to acquire traits genderized in their own favor, whereas the traits educated females must acquire today are *all* genderized in favor of males. On the other hand, since traits genderized in favor of females are considered by our culture to be lesser virtues, if virtues at all, and the societal processes with which they are associated are judged relatively unimportant, males would be placed in the position of having to acquire traits both they and their society consider inferior. Because his hands were soft Rodriguez worried that his education was making him effeminate. Imagine his anxieties if he had been educated in those supposedly feminine virtues of caring and concern and had been taught to sustain intimate relationships and to value connection.

When we claim Sophie's and Emile's virtues for both sexes, trait genderization becomes everyone's problem. Yet despite the fact that males as well as females can be made to feel abnormal if they acquire traits genderized in favor of their "opposites"—and that, as Elizabeth Janeway has pointed out, "natural" and "abnormal" are our equivalents of what being "damned" meant to our ancestors[21]—the issues genderized traits raise for males and females differ. Educate our daughters according to an ideal incorporating "masculine" traits and, whatever damage done them, they can at least console themselves that the qualities they acquire are considered valuable and the societal processes to which these traits are attached are considered worthwhile. Educate our sons in Sophie's and Sarah's virtues and they will have no such consolation.

The existence of genderized traits makes sensitivity to gender a prerequisite of sound educational policy and so does the persistence into our own time of the value hierarchy Beecher tried to overturn. Assigning greater importance to its productive than its reproductive processes, our society places a higher value on the masculine than the feminine gender. Those who remain blind to gender will not see this disparity and consequently will not address it explicitly. Yet our policymakers must address it or the prospects of extending to our sons the education they deserve will remain slight.

What is to be done by those who believe that humanity's fate and that of the earth itself require that boys and girls, women and men, should all possess Sophie's and Sarah's virtues as well as Emile's? One essential first step is to raise to consciousness the hidden curriculum of schooling: its denigration of women and the tasks, traits, and functions our culture associates with them.[22] The subject matter of the liberal curriculum is drawn from disciplines of knowledge—history, literature, science—that give pride of place to male experience and achievements and to the societal processes associated with men. Implicitly, then, this curriculum is the bearer of bad news about women and the reproductive processes of society.

At college and university campuses across the country programs in women's studies thrive and projects incorporating the ever increasing body of scholarship on women into the liberal curriculum as a whole are underway. Such efforts must be undertaken at all levels of schooling, for it is too little, too late, and too elitist to postpone until the college years the revelations of the new research. Taking our cue from Plato, moreover, we must acknowledge that our schools and colleges are not our only educative—or in this instance miseducative—institutions, and we must expand our sights accordingly. Even as we work directly to change the negative messages about women and the reproductive processes of society transmitted by religious and secular, popular and high culture, we should raise to a conscious level in all students the hidden value hierarchy of society itself.

Another essential step is to build nurturing capacities and an ethics of care into the curriculum itself. I do not mean by this that we should fill up school time with courses in the 3Cs of caring, concern, and connection. In an education that gives Sophie, Sarah, and the reproductive processes of society their due, Compassion 101a need no more be listed in a school's course offering than Objectivity 101a is now. Just as the general curricular goals of rationality and individual autonomy derive from the productive processes of society, so too the reproductive processes yield general goals. And just as rationality and autonomy are posited as goals of particular subjects, such as science, as well as of the curriculum as a whole, so nurturance and connection can become overarching educational goals as well as the goals of particular subjects.

In making nurturance, caring, concern, and connection goals of education, we must beware of replicating within the curriculum the split between the productive and reproductive processes of society. If education links nurturing capacities and the 3 Cs only to subjects such as home economics that arise out of the reproductive processes, we will lose sight of the *general* moral, social, and political significance of these traits. So long as rationality and autonomous judgment are linked exclusively with the productive processes of society, the reproductive ones will continue to be devalued. Thus, we must find ways of incorporating Sophie's and Sarah's virtues into our science, math, history, literature, and auto mechanics courses, even as we emphasize theoretical knowledge and the development of reason in the teaching of nutrition or family living.

Essential as these measures are, however, consciousness raising, the setting of new goals, and the integration of the new scholarship on women into the curriculum are only the first steps in the transformation of the journey of becoming educated. We should not underestimate the changes to be wrought by redefining the function of education and restructuring the ideal of an educated man or woman. When the productive/reproductive dichotomy and its accompanying hierarchy of values is rejected, teaching methods, learning activities, classroom atmospheres, teacher-pupil relationships, school structures, attitudes toward education may all be affected. As a matter of fact, we cannot even assume that our definitions of the virtues of Sophie and Emile will remain the same. Combine his rationality and objectivity with her nurturance and caring and who knows—his "masculine" qualities and her "feminine" ones may both be transformed.

The details of these changes must be worked out, but I can think of few tasks as important or exciting. Too seldom do we perceive education to be the creative endeavor it really is. The subjects taught in our schools are not God-given; the way our schools are organized and children learn is by no means writ in stone; our educational ideals and our view of the function of education are not immutable truths.[23] We should not delude ourselves that education can be created anew: as a social institution it has a history and traditions, and it is bound by economic and cultural constraints. Nevertheless, old habits of educational thinking can change, long-standing assumptions can be discarded, and fresh vision can improve practice. One of the unanticipated rewards of bringing women into the educational realm is that the study of the education of the "other" half of the population enables us to see all of education differently. The changed vision resulting from acquaintance with the conversation reclaimed here makes our own journey of transforming the education of our sons and daughters possible. If we let it, it will also enable us to discern ways to bring educational practice into tune with the full range of people's lives and with the present perils to life on earth.

Notes

Chapter One

1. I realize that although individual feminist thinkers have tended to neglect questions of educational philosophy, the women's studies movement is directly concerned with just such issues. The extent to which this movement has explored alternative educational *ideals* is a question that requires further investigation.

2. Adrienne Rich, "Claiming an Education," in *On Lies, Secrets and Silence* (New York: W. W. Norton & Co., 1979), p. 231.

3. Ibid., p. 232.

4. Jane Roland Martin, "Excluding Women from the Educational Realm," *Harvard Educational Review* 52 (1982):133–48.

5. To say that a discipline such as the history of educational thought has not achieved epistemological equality is to comment on the nature of the knowledge produced by that discipline, not on the nature of practitioners of the discipline and not on, for example, the hiring practices within the profession.

6. This new scholarship on women is too extensive to be cited in its entirety here. For reviews of it, see the journal *Signs*. See also anthologies such as Julia A. Sherman and Evelyn Torton Beck, eds., *The Prism of Sex* (Madison: University of Wisconsin Press, 1979); Elizabeth Langland and Walter Gove, eds., *A Feminist Perspective in the Academy* (Chicago: University of Chicago Press, 1983); Sandra Harding and Merill B. Hintikka, eds., *Discovering Reality* (Dordrecht: D. Reidel Publishing Co., 1983).

7. Israel Scheffler, "Philosophy of Education: Some Recent Contributions," *Harvard Educational Review* 50 (1980):402–06.

8. Rich, "Claiming an Education," pp. 233–34.

9. Dale Spender says: "While men take it for granted that they can build on what has gone before, selecting, refining, adapting the knowledge they have inherited to meet their needs, women are constantly required to begin with a blank sheet" (*Invisible Women: The Schooling Scandal* [London: Writers and Readers Publishing Cooperative Society, 1982], p. 17).

10. Israel Scheffler, Preface to *Three Historical Philosophies of Education*, by William F. Frankena (Chicago: Scott, Foresman & Co., 1965).

11. Paul Nash, *Models of Man* (New York: John Wiley & Sons, 1968), p. vii;

Henry J. Perkinson, *Since Socrates: Studies in the History of Western Educational Thought* (New York: Longman, 1980), p. xi.

12. Recent reports on American education reflect this same focus. See, for example, Mortimer J. Adler, *The Paideia Proposal* (New York: Macmillan, 1982); Ernest L. Boyer, *High School* (New York: Harper & Row, 1983); John I. Goodlad, *A Place Called School* (New York: McGraw-Hill Book Co., 1984); Theodore R. Sizer, *Horace's Compromise* (Boston: Houghton Mifflin Co., 1984).

13. For more on the distinction between productive and reproductive societal processes, see Lorenne Clark, "The Rights of Women: The Theory and Practice of the Ideology of Male Supremacy," in *Contemporary Issues in Political Philosophy*, ed. Wiliam R. Shea and John King-Farlow (New York: Science History Publications, 1976), pp. 49–65.

14. For a thorough discussion of these topics, see Wini Breines and Linda Gordon, "The New Scholarship on Family Violence," *Signs* 8 (1983):493–507.

15. Jonathan Schell, *The Fate of the Earth* (New York: Avon, 1982), p. 175.

Chapter Two

1. *Plato's Republic*, trans. G. M. A. Grube (Indianapolis: Hackett Publishing Co., 1974), (369b). References to this work will henceforth appear in parentheses in the text.

2. On this point, see Lynda Lange, "The Function of Equal Education in Plato's *Republic* and *Laws*," in *The Sexism of Social and Political Theory*, ed. Lorenne M. G. Clark and Lynda Lange (Toronto: University of Toronto Press, 1979), pp. 3–15.

3. Some interpreters of Plato would argue that Socrates discerns certain natural talents or aptitudes in people and then designs a state to fit them, whereas others would say that he assumes a parallelism between human nature and societal needs. The account of education contained in the *Republic*, however, supports the interpretation given here.

4. Nicholas P. White abstracts from *Republic*, book 2, a principle of the natural division of labor that encompasses what I am calling the Postulate of Specialized Natures and the Postulate of Correspondence. For the present purpose, however, it is important to keep these postulates separate. See White, *A Companion to Plato's Republic* (Indianapolis: Hackett Publishing Co., 1979), pp. 84–85.

5. Lorenne M. G. Clark, "The Rights of Women: The Theory and Practice of the Ideology of Male Supremacy," in *Contemporary Issues in Political Philosophy*, ed. William R. Shea and John King-Farlow (New York: Science History Publications, 1976), pp. 49–65.

6. In other dialogues, however, characteristics of the good artisan or craftsman are made clear. See Terence Irwin, *Plato's Moral Theory* (Oxford: Clarendon Press, 1977).

7. For a discussion of these misunderstandings, see Christine Pierce, "Equality: *Republic* V," *Monist* 57 (1973):1–11.

8. See, for example, Christine Garside Allen, "Plato on Women," *Feminist Studies* 2 (1975):131–38; Julia Annas, "Plato's *Republic* and Feminism," in *Women in*

Western Thought, ed. Martha Lee Osborne (New York: Random House, 1971), pp. 24–33; Jean Bethke Elshtain, *Public Man, Private Woman* (Princeton: Princeton University Press, 1981), chap. 1; Lange, "Function of Equal Education"; Pierce, "Equality."

9. Susan Moller Okin, *Woman in Western Political Thought* (Princeton: Princeton University Press, 1979), chap. 1.

10. On this point, see Sheila Tobias, *Overcoming Math Anxiety* (New York: W. W. Norton and Co., 1978), chap. 3; Eleanor Emmons Maccoby and Carol Nagy Jacklin, *The Psychology of Sex-Differences* (Stanford: Stanford University Press, 1974), chap. 3; Lynn H. Fox, Linda Brody, and Diane Tobin, eds., *Women and the Mathematical Mystique* (Baltimore: Johns Hopkins University Press, 1980). Note that my argument here does *not* rely on the thesis that females would *by nature* be unable to complete the guardian curriculum satisfactorily.

11. See book 7 of the *Republic,* especially 540c. Compare, Elshtain, *Public Man, Private Woman.* Dale Spender, in *Invisible Women* makes this same point about women's education today.

12. The distinction between sex and gender is relevant to Plato's thesis in the following way. It is possible that biological sex per se—that is, having the biological attributes of a male or female—makes no difference to learning (or to doing or being something), but that because we are gendered—that is, because we have the cultural attributes of masculinity or femininity—and gender is closely correlated in our culture with biological sex, being born male or female does after all make a difference. Neither Plato nor the other parties to our conversation seems fully aware of this distinction. None of them, of course, uses the term *gender* in its contemporary meaning. In reconstructing this conversation, I have made no attempt to put this term in their mouths, although I do use it myself. I hope the reader will at all times keep in mind that insofar as I question Plato's thesis about the difference of sex, I do so because of its correlation with gender.

13. Adrienne Rich, "Taking Women Students Seriously," in *On Lies, Secrets and Silence* (New York: W. W. Norton & Co., 1979), p. 243.

14. Alexandra G. Kaplan and Mary Anne Sedney, *Psychology and Sex Roles: An Androgynous Perspective* (Boston: Little, Brown & Co., 1980); Rosemary Deem, *Women and Schooling* (London: Routledge & Kegan Paul, 1978); Nancy Frazier and Myra Sadker, *Sexism in School and Society* (New York: Harper & Row, 1972); Ann Oakley, *Sex, Gender and Society* (New York: Harper & Row, 1972).

15. Rich, "Taking Women Students Seriously," p. 243.

16. Ibid., p. 241.

17. See *NCTV News* 4 (May 1983) for an extensive bibliography on this subject.

18. Plato, *Timaeus* (91) in *The Dialogues of Plato,* trans. B. Jowett (New York: Random House, 1937), p. 67.

19. Frazier and Sadker, *Sexism in School and Society;* Spender, *Invisible Women;* Kaplan and Sedney, *Psychology and Sex Roles.*

20. See, for example, Nancy Schrom Dye, "Clio's American Daughters: Male History, Female Reality," in *The Prism of Sex,* ed. Julia Sherman, and Evelyn Torton Beck (Madison: University of Wisconsin Press, 1977), pp. 9–31; Carl N. Degler,

"What the Women's Movement Has Done to American History," in *A Feminist Perspective in the Academy,* ed. Elizabeth Langland and Walter Gove (Chicago: University of Chicago Press, 1981), pp. 67–85; Joan Kelly-Gadol, "The Social Relation of the Sexes: Methodological Implications of Women's History," *Signs* 1 (1976):809–23.

21. See, for example, Carol Gilligan, *In a Different Voice* (Cambridge, Mass.: Harvard University Press, 1982); Naomi Weisstein, "Psychology Constructs the Female," in *Women in Sexist Society,* ed. Vivian Gornick and Barbara K. Moran (New York: Basic Books, 1970), pp. 133–46.

22. See, for example, Evelyn Fox Keller, *Reflections on Gender and Science* (New Haven: Yale University Press, 1985); Carolyn Merchant, *The Death of Nature* (New York: Harper & Row, 1980).

23. Janice Moulton, "A Paradigm of Philosophy: The Adversary Method," in *Discovering Reality,* ed. Sandra Harding and Merill B. Hintikka (Dordrecht: D. Reidel, 1983), pp. 149–64.

24. Merchant, *Death of Nature,* p. 10.

25. Arlene Saxenhouse, "The Philosopher and the Female in the Political Thought of Plato," *Political Theory* 4 (1976):196.

26. Elshtain, *Public Man, Private Woman,* p. 38.

27. Allen Bloom, trans., *The Republic of Plato* (New York: Basic Books, 1968), p. 384.

28. Elizabeth Beardsley, "Traits and Genderization" in *Feminism and Philosophy,* ed. Mary Vetterling-Braggin, Frederick A. Elliston, and Jane English (Totowa, N.J.: Littlefield, Adams, 1977), pp. 117–23. Beardsley uses the term *genderization* to refer to language. I will be using it to refer to the traits themselves.

29. Lynn Z. Bloom, Karen Coburn, and Joan Pearlman, *The New Assertive Woman* (New York: Delacorte, 1975), p. 12.

30. James D. Watson, *The Double Helix* (New York: New American Library, 1968); see also Ann Sayre, *Rosalind Franklin and DNA* (New York: Norton, 1975); Ruth Hubbard, "Reflections on the Story of the Double Helix," *Women's Studies International Quarterly* 2 (1979):261–73; Horace Freeland Judson, *The Eighth Day of Creation* (New York: Simon & Schuster, 1974). It should be noted that there is more than one story of Rosalind Franklin to be told. My interest here is in how others perceived this woman scientist, not in the ways in which being a woman may have affected her actual research. Compare, Elizabeth Janeway, *Man's World, Woman's Place* (New York: Morrow, 1971), pp. 102–04.

31. Watson, *Double Helix,* p. 51.

32. Ibid., p. 20. Sayre, in *Rosalind Franklin,* reports that even family and close friends did not call Franklin "Rosy."

33. Rich, "Taking Women Students Seriously," p. 241. See also Spender, *Invisible Women;* Roberta M. Hall, "The Classroom Climate: A Chilly One for Women?" (Washington, D.C.: Project on the Status and Education of Women, 1982); Pat Mahoney, "How Alice's Chin Really Came to Be Pressed against Her Foot: Sexist Practices of Interaction in Mixed-Sex Classrooms," *Women's Studies International Forum* 6 (1983):107–15.

34. Rich, "Taking Women Students Seriously," author's emphasis.

Chapter Three

1. Jean-Jacques Rousseau, *Emile,* trans. Allan Bloom (New York: Basic Books, 1979), p. 6. Page references will henceforth appear in parentheses in the text.

2. Irving Berlin, "The Girl that I Marry" from *Annie Get Your Gun* (New York: Irving Berlin Music Corp., 1946).

3. These might well be considered two distinct roles, or perhaps even three—wife, mother, homemaker. (See Elizabeth Janeway, *Man's World, Woman's Place* [New York: William Morrow & Co., 1971], pp. 85 ff.) Rousseau clearly views them as a single role, however.

4. See Robert Ulich, *History of Educational Thought* (New York: American Books, 1945) and *Three Thousand Years of Educational Wisdom* (Cambridge, Mass.: Harvard University Press, 1948); Robert S. Brumbaugh and Nathaniel M. Lawrence, *Philosophers on Education: Six Essays on the Foundations of Western Thought* (Boston: Houghton Mifflin Co., 1963); Robert R. Rusk, *The Doctrines of Great Educators,* 3d ed. (New York: St. Martin's Press, 1965); Paul Nash, Andreas M. Kazamias, and Henry J. Perkinson, eds., *The Educated Man: Studies in the History of Educational Thought* (New York: Wiley, 1965); Kingsley Price, ed., *Education and Philosophical Thought,* 2d ed. (Boston: Allyn & Bacon, 1967); Paul Nash, ed., *Models of Man: Explorations in the Western Educational Tradition* (New York: Wiley, 1968); and Steven M. Cahn, ed., *The Philosophical Foundations of Education* (New York: Harper & Row, 1970).

5. See Carol Gilligan, *In a Different Voice* (Cambridge, Mass.: Harvard University Press, 1982).

6. See, for example, Zillah Eisenstein, *The Radical Future of Liberal Feminism* (New York: Longman, 1981), chap. 4; Jean Bethke Elshtain, *Public Man, Private Woman* (Princeton: Princeton University Press, 1981), chap. 4; Lynda Lange, "Rousseau: Women and the General Will," in *The Sexism of Social and Political Theory,* ed. Lorenne M. G. Clark and Lynda Lange (Toronto: University of Toronto Press, 1979), pp. 41–52; Carole Pateman, " 'The Disorder of Women': Women, Love and the Sense of Justice," *Ethics* 91 (1980):20–34; Susan Moller Okin, *Women in Western Political Thought* (Princeton: Princeton University Press, 1970), chaps. 5–8. See also Ron Christianson, "The Political Theory of Male Chauvinism: J. J. Rousseau's Paradigm," *Midwest Quarterly* 13 (1972):291–99; Victor G. Wexler, " 'Made for Man's Delight': Rousseau's Anti-feminism," *American Historical Review* 81 (1976):266–91.

7. See Lynda Lange, "Rousseau and Modern Feminism," *Social Theory and Practice* 7 (1981):245–77, for an interpretation of other aspects of Rousseau's ideas that also attempts to show that he is consistent in his treatment of men and women.

8. Jean-Jacques Rousseau, *The Social Contract* (New York: Hafner, 1947), book 2, chap. 2 ff.

9. Rousseau's defense of majority rule vitiates his solution, however. See Robert Paul Wolff, *In Defense of Anarchism* (New York: Harper & Row, 1970).

10. See also John Plamenatz, "Ce Qui Ne Signifie Autre Chose Sinon Qu'on Le Forcera d'Être Libre," in *Hobbes and Rousseau,* ed. Maurice Cranston and R. S.

Peters (New York: Doubleday, 1972), p. 362; Roger D. Masters, *The Political Philosophy of Rousseau* (Princeton: Princeton University Press, 1968), p. 42; J. H. Broome, *Rousseau: A Study of His Thought* (London: Edward Arnold, 1963), chap. 5.

11. On this point, see Lange, "Rousseau: Women and the General Will." She argues, moreover, that the obvious strategy of eliminating the sexism of Rousseau's theory of the General Will by eliminating the patriarchal family is not feasible.

12. Okin, *Women,* p. 135.

13. "The first education ought to be purely negative. It consists not at all in teaching virtue or truth but in securing the heart from vice and the mind from error" (*Emile,* p. 93). Judith N. Shklar argues that this "negative education" is necessary because Emile is to be educated to be his real self. She forgets that since Emile is to be educated apart from society, there is no need for the tutor to be so protective against society. See "Rousseau's Image of Authority," in *Hobbes and Rousseau,* ed. Cranston and Peters, p. 360; see also Shklar, *Men and Citizens* (Cambridge: Cambridge University Press, 1969), p. 148.

14. Daniel Pekarsky, "Education and Manipulation," in *Philosophy of Education 1977: Proceedings of the 33rd Annual Meeting of the Philosophy of Education Society,* ed. Ira S. Steinberg (Urbana: University of Illinois, 1977), p. 356.

15. For accounts of open classrooms, see Joseph Featherstone, "The British Infant Schools," in *Radical School Reform,* ed. Ronald and Beatrice Gross (New York: Simon & Schuster, 1969), pp. 195–205; Charles H. Rathbone, ed., *Open Education* (New York: Citation Press, 1971); Ewald B. Nyquist and Gene R. Hawes, eds., *Open Education* (New York: Bantam, 1972); and Charles E. Silberman, ed., *The Open Classroom Reader* (New York: Vintage, 1973).

16. Some readers may wonder how principles of teaching and learning that were advocated by proponents of open classrooms can be compatible with the model of education I am attributing to Rousseau. A production model does not entail the harsh methods of teaching and rigid structures that radical school reformers rejected. Since the Identity and Difference postulates are purely formal, the methods to be used in equipping people for a given role or function in society can be harsh, but they can also be humane; moreover, they can be employed in a wide range of contexts, the traditional school being only one.

17. Israel Scheffler, *The Language of Education* (Springfield, Ill.: Thomas, 1960), p. 37. I am assuming here the "naive" conception of gardening spelled out by Scheffler since it is the one employed in the standard interpretation of *Emile.* Rousseau's manipulative principle might well be compatible with a different conception of that activity.

18. Ibid., p. 50.

19. On this issue, see Wexler, "Rousseau's Anti-feminism," p. 274; Broome, *Rousseau,* pp. 98–101; Joel Schwartz, *The Sexual Politics of Jean-Jacques Rousseau* (Chicago: University of Chicago Press, 1984).

20. Marabel Morgan, *The Total Woman* (Old Tappan, N.J.: Fleming H. Revell, 1973), p. 80.

21. Ibid., p. 71.

22. On this issue, see Okin, *Women*; Larry Blum, Marcia Homiak, Judy Housman, and Naomi Scheman, "Altruism and Women's Oppression," in *Women and Philosophy*, ed. Carol C. Gould and Marx W. Wartofsky (New York: G. P. Putnam's Sons, 1976), pp. 222–47.

23. Adrienne Rich, in *Of Woman Born* (New York: Bantam Books, 1977), p. 213, says: "One of the most insidious patterns between the sexes is the common equation, by women, of man with child. It is infantilizing to men, and it has meant a trapping of female energy which can hardly be calculated."

24. George Eliot, *Middlemarch* (Boston: Houghton Mifflin Co., 1956), p. 147.

25. John Charvet, "Individual Identity and Social Consciousness in Rousseau's Philosophy," in *Hobbes and Rousseau*, ed. Cranston and Peters, pp. 462–83. For other discussions of this issue, see Lange, "Rousseau and Modern Feminism," pp. 247–48; Elizabeth Rapaport, "On the Future of Love: Rousseau and the Radical Feminists," in *Women and Philosophy*, ed. Gould and Wartofsky, pp. 195 ff.

26. Elshtain, *Public Man, Private Woman*, p. 165.

27. For a review of recent studies of family violence, see Wini Breines and Linda Gordon, "The New Scholarship on Family Violence," *Signs* 8 (1983):490–543. In *The Social Contract*, pp. 169ff, Rousseau maintains that a father's duties are dictated by natural feelings and that to do what is right in a family he need only consult his heart. We are told in *Emile*, however, that Sophie serves as the link between her children and Emile, that "she alone makes him love them" (p. 361). There is not necessarily a contradiction here. Emile can know by nature what his familial duties are without by nature loving and feeling attached to his wife and children.

28. Aristotle, *The Politics*, trans. T. A. Sinclair, rev. ed. (Harmonsworth, England: Penguin Books, 1981), book 2, pp. ii–v.

29. According to Lange, "Rousseau and Modern Feminism," p. 236, the relation of mother and child is the prototype of the particular attachment Rousseau wants individuals to have to the state. Lange does not, however, reveal the problems Rousseau's philosophy faces when the female role of wife and mother becomes the model for the male role of citizen. Compare, Pateman, " 'Disorder of Women.' "

30. For a discussion of Rousseau's ambivalence on this issue, see Judith N. Shklar, "Rousseau's Images of Authority," in *Hobbes and Rousseau*, ed. Cranston and Peters, p. 358.

31. Nancy Chodorow, *The Reproduction of Mothering* (Berkeley: University of California Press, 1979).

32. Gilligan, *In a Different Voice*.

33. Carole Pateman, in " 'The Disorder of Women,' " p. 29, noted that Rousseau is surprisingly unaware of the problem the family poses the state; that he fails to see that the family is a sectional institution that threatens justice. She points out that husbands and fathers may well place the family's interest above the public interest. Her argument is rather different from the one presented here, but she delineates beautifully the paradox in Rousseau's viewing women at one and the same time as the guardians of order and morality in the family, which for him is the foundation of social life, and as inherently subversive because they are incapable of developing a sense of justice. On the issue of the family's threat to the state, see also Okin, *Women*, pp. 189 ff.

34. Okin, *Women*, p. 180.

35. Rapaport, "On the Future of Love"; Eisenstein, *Radical Future*, pp. 64 ff.

36. Eisenstein, *Radical Future*, pp. 81 ff. See Schwartz, *Sexual Politics*, chap. 4, for an interpretation of Emile's dependency based on Rousseau's assertion: "Woman and man are made for one another, but their mutual dependence is not equal. Men depend on women because of their desires; women depend on men because of both their desires and their needs" (p. 364). Rousseau's two-track system of education belies this statement, however.

37. Eisenstein, *Radical Future*; Elshtain, *Public Man, Private Woman*, p. 165.

38. Brian Clark, *Whose Life Is It Anyway?* (New York: Avon, 1978). It should be noted that although the two faces of autonomy are logically independent, they may be related to each other empirically.

39. Eisenstein, *Radical Future*, pp. 62 ff.; Elshtain, *Public Man, Private Woman*, p. 159; Okin, *Women*, pp. 148 ff. See also Schwartz, *Sexual Politics*, chap. 4.

40. Adrienne Rich, "Taking Women Students Seriously," in *On Lies, Secrets, and Silence* (New York: Norton, 1979), p. 240.

Chapter Four

1. Virginia Woolf, "Mary Wollstonecraft," reprinted in Mary Wollstonecraft, *A Vindication of the Rights of Woman*, ed. Carol H. Poston (New York: W. W. Norton & Co., 1975), pp. 224–25. Page references will henceforth appear in parentheses in the text. For other works by Wollstonecraft as well as biographies and critical analyses, see the selected bibliography in Barbara H. Solomon and Paula S. Berggren, eds., *A Mary Wollstonecraft Reader* (New York: New American Library, 1983). See also Katherine M. Rogers, *Feminism in Eighteenth Century England* (Urbana: University of Illinois Press, 1982).

2. Ferdinand Lundberg and Marynia Farnham, "Mary Wollstonecraft and the Psychopathology of Feminism," in Wollstonecraft, *A Vindication*, ed. Poston, p. 226.

3. Ibid., p. 229.

4. Edith Wharton, *The House of Mirth* (New York: Berkley Books, 1981), p. 301.

5. Mary Wollstonecraft, *A Vindication of the Rights of Woman*, ed. Charles W. Hagelman, Jr. (New York: W. W. Norton & Co., 1967).

6. Eleanor Flexner says that Wollstonecraft "never really substantiates her basic assumption, that all women, or even most women, are as she describes them: trivial, deceiving, pleasure-loving, and weak in character, morals, brain, and body." "Ideas in *A Vindication of the Rights of Woman*" in Wollstonecraft, *A Vindication*, ed. Poston, p. 234. Wollstonecraft's argument does not require that this assumption be substantiated, however.

7. Wollstonecraft has no fear that this outcome will obtain. Throughout *A Vindication* she refuses to argue from the existence of the knowledgeable, intelligent women of her own day to the rationality of women in general, but she knows that their existence guarantees the success of the experiment she proposes.

8. D. W. Winnicott, *Mother and Child: A Primer of First Relationships* (New York: Basic Books, 1957), p. vii.

9. Jane Austen, *Sense and Sensibility* (New York: Dell, 1959), p. 30. Page references will henceforth appear in parentheses in the text.

10. Zillah Eisenstein, *The Radical Future of Liberal Feminism* (New York: Longman, 1981), p. 106.

11. Margaret Drabble, "With All My Love, (Signed) Mama," in *Motherhood: A Reader for Men and Women*, ed. Susan Cahill (New York: Avon, 1982), p. 7.

12. Adrienne Rich, *Of Woman Born* (New York: Bantam, 1977), pp. 1–2.

13. Literary critics seem to be divided on this issue. See, for example, Douglas Bush, *Jane Austen* (New York: Macmillan Co., 1975); Marilyn Butler, *Jane Austen and the War of Ideas* (Oxford: Clarendon Press, 1975); Claire Lamont, Introduction to *Sense and Sensibility*, by Jane Austen (London: Oxford University Press, 1970).

14. Jane Austen, *Persuasion* (New York: Dell, 1959), p. 274.

15. George Eliot, *Middlemarch* (Boston: Houghton Mifflin Co., 1956), p. 582.

16. For a discussion of a political treatment of the soul, see Elizabeth V. Spelman, "Aristotle and the Politicization of the Soul," in *Discovering Reality*, ed. Sandra Harding and Merill B. Hintikka (Dordrecht: D. Reidel, 1983), pp. 17–30.

17. See, for example, Eisenstein, *Radical Future*, chap. 5; Carolyn Korsmeyer, "Reason and Morals in the Early Feminist Movement: Mary Wollstonecraft," in *Women and Philosophy*, ed. Carol C. Gould and Marx W. Wartofsky (New York: C. P. Putnam's Sons, 1976), pp. 97–111; Miriam Brody Kramnick, Introduction to Wollstonecraft, *A Vindication* (London: Penguin, 1975), p. 57. This scholarship also points out the class bias in her work.

18. Helen B. Andelin, *Fascinating Womanhood* (Santa Barbara, Calif.: Pacific Press, 1963), p. 206.

19. Elizabeth Badinter, *Mother Love: Myth and Reality* (New York: Macmillan Co., 1981), p. 109. Page references will henceforth appear in parentheses in the text.

20. It is important to keep the structure of Wollstonecraft's preferred society in mind here, for given a very different philosophy of home, family, and child rearing—for example, that of the kibbutz—these traits might not be associated with good mothers but rather with others in the society. See Bruno Bettelheim, *Children of the Dream* (New York: Avon Books, 1970); see also Sara Ruddick, "Maternal Thinking," *Feminist Studies* 6 (1980):342–67.

21. Nancy Chodorow, *The Reproduction of Mothering* (Berkeley: University of California Press, 1978), p. 7. Page references will henceforth appear in parentheses in the text.

22. For critical discussions of Chodorow's book, see Judith Lorber, Rose Laub Coser, Alice S. Rossi, and Nancy Chodorow, "On *The Reproduction of Mothering*: A Methodological Debate," *Signs* 6 (1981):482–514; Iris Marion Young, "Is Male Gender Identity the Cause of Male Domination?" in *Mothering: Essays in Feminist Theorizing*, ed. Joyce Trebilcot (Totowa, N.J.: Rowman & Allenheld, 1984); Roger S. Gottlieb, "Mothering and the Reproduction of Power," lecture presented at the University of Massachusetts, Boston, 1983; Pauline Bart, "Review on Chodorow's *The Reproduction of Mothering*" in *Mothering*, ed. Trebilcot, pp. 147–52.

23. Adrienne Rich, "Taking Women Students Seriously," *On Lies, Secrets, and Silence* (New York: W. W. Norton & Co., 1979), pp. 244–45.

24. Emma Goldman, "On Mary Wollstonecraft," *Feminist Studies* 7 (1981): 115.

Chapter Five

1. Catharine Beecher, *A Treatise on Domestic Economy* (New York: Schocken Books, 1977). Page references will henceforth appear in parentheses in the text.

2. Kathryn Kish Sklar, *Catharine Beecher: A Study in American Domesticity* (New Haven: Yale University Press, 1973), pp. 152, 153.

3. Beecher's naiveté with respect to workers' options in a capitalistic society is apparent here. The discussion to follow will bracket this issue, however, in order to concentrate on her apparent optimism about women's options in respect to marriage. For a discussion of Beecher's class, racial, and ethnic prejudices, see Gerda Lerner, ed. *The Female Experience* (Indianapolis: Bobbs-Merrill Co., 1977), pp. 262–63.

4. Which is not to say that patients have no knowledge to contribute to the healing process or that clients ought not to be consulted in matters of law.

5. Apart from citing the authority of Tocqueville, however, Beecher gives no reasons for supposing that a sex-based division of labor is efficient, let alone that it is more efficient than some other organization of labor.

6. Jean-Jacques Rousseau, *The Social Contract* (New York: Hafner Publishing Co., 1947), pp. 6, 15–16. A close examination of the role Beecher gives Sarah vis-à-vis the state suggests that our political vocabulary is not adequate to the task of describing women's place. One certainly has to use circumlocutions here to get at what Beecher is saying. Of a woman in the early years of the American Republic, Linda K. Kerber says: "She was a citizen but not really a constituent" (*Women of the Republic* [Chapel Hill: University of North Carolina Press, 1980], p. 283). See also Mary Beth Norton, *Liberty's Daughters: The Revolutionary Experience of American Women, 1750–1800* (Boston: Little, Brown & Co., 1980), p. 299.

7. Barbara Welter bases her account of the Cult of True Womanhood in large part on these materials ("The Cult of True Womanhood: 1820–1860," in *The American Family in Social-Historical Perspective*, ed. Michael Gordon, 2d ed. [New York: St. Martin's, 1978]).

8. Ibid., p. 313.

9. See, for example, Nancy F. Cott, ed., *Roots of Bitterness* (New York: Dutton, 1972), pp. 11–12; Lerner, ed., *The Female Experience*, pp. 121–22; Mary P. Ryan, *Cradle of the Middle Class* (Cambridge: Cambridge University Press, 1981), p. 189. Judith A. McGaw, in "Women and the History of American Technology," *Signs* 7 (1982):816, refers to the assumption of scholars "that Beecher and Stowe were traitors to their sex who consigned women to tedious housework."

10. Louisa M. Alcott, *Little Women* (Boston: Little, Brown, & Co., 1936), p. 167.

11. Sklar, *Catharine Beecher*, pp. 158–61.

12. For discussions of Beecher's role in creating the subject home economics, see Charlotte E. Biester, "Prelude—Catharine Beecher," *Journal of Home Economics* 51 (1959):549–51; James M. Fitch, "When Housekeeping Became a Science," *American Heritage* 12 (1961):34–37. For a general discussion of the construction of school subjects, see Jane Roland Martin, "Two Dogmas of Curriculum," *Synthese* 51 (1982):5–20.

13. Joan N. Burstyn, "Catharine Beecher and the Education of American

Women," *New England Quarterly* 47 (1974):388. Page references will henceforth appear in parentheses in the text.

14. This is not to say that Beecher gives Sarah the last word in all domestic matters; on most occasions, for example, Sarah will do as the doctor directs. However, she must exercise judgment in all matters, even those in relation to which her expertise is limited.

15. Carol McMillan, *Women, Reason and Nature* (Princeton: Princeton University Press, 1982), p. x.

16. Barbara M. Cross, ed., *The Educated Woman in America* (New York: Teachers College Press, 1965), p. 13.

17. George Eliot, *Adam Bede* (New York: New American Library, 1961), p. 88.

18. This does not mean that the king should blindly follow the physician's advice and accept no responsibility for his own recovery. See Norman Cousins, *Anatomy of an Illness as Perceived by the Patient* (New York: Norton, 1979).

19. John Heinrich Pestalozzi, *Leonard and Gertrude*, trans. Eva Channing (Boston: Heath, 1885), p. 43.

20. Sara Lawrence Lightfoot, *Worlds Apart* (New York: Basic Books, 1978), chap. 2.

21. Elaine Heffner, *Mothering* (New York: Doubleday, 1978), chap 9.

22. Letty Cottin Pogrebin, *Family Politics* (New York: McGraw-Hill, 1983), p. 31.

23. Alcott, *Little Women*, p. 65.

24. For a discussion of the mother's educative function as that of raising patriotic sons, see Kerber, *Women of the Republic*, chap. 9.

25. Adrienne Rich, *Of Woman Born* (New York: Bantam, 1976), p. 250.

26. Recall, however, the overlap between Sarah's education and her husband's. To say that an educational theorist embraces the Difference Postulate is not to say that for different societal roles he or she prescribes entirely different educational programs.

27. Rich, *Of Woman Born*, p. 248. It should be noted that Beecher's rigorous program of physical education for females is designed to promote the health of women's bodies—something sadly neglected in her day—if not actually an affection for their bodies.

28. The home economics profession is, of course, based on Beecher's premise.

Chapter Six

1. Charlotte Perkins Gilman, *Herland* (New York: Pantheon Books, 1979), p. v. Page references will henceforth appear in parentheses in the text.

2. Sara Ruddick, "Maternal Thinking," *Feminist Studies* 6 (1980):361. Page references will henceforth appear in parentheses in the text.

3. Adrienne Rich, *Of Woman Born* (New York: Bantam Books, 1977), pp. 352 ff.

4. Ibid., p. 223.

5. That these are all examples of relationships in nuclear families should not be taken to mean that I am committed to the preservation of the modern nuclear family

212 / Notes to Pages 153–71

or, indeed, of the institution of private family more generally. These examples are meant simply to elucidate the force of Gilman's metaphorical use of the family in *Herland*.

6. George Eliot, *Middlemarch* (Boston: Houghton Mifflin Co., 1956), p. 190.

7. For treatments of this topic by psychologists, see Carol Gilligan, *In a Different Voice* (Cambridge, Mass.: Harvard University Press, 1982); Nona Plessner Lyons, "Two Perspectives: On Self, Relationships, and Morality," *Harvard Educational Review* 53 (1983):125–45.

8. Eliot, *Middlemarch,* pp. 186–87.

9. Eamonn Callan, "Education for Democracy: Dewey's Illiberal Philosophy of Education," *Educational Theory* 31 (1981):168.

10. Ann Oakley, *Woman's Work* (New York: Vintage Books, 1976), p. 233.

11. See, for example, Bruno Bettelheim, *Children of the Dream* (New York: Avon Books, 1970); Urie Bronfenbrenner, *Two Worlds of Childhood: U.S. and U.S.S.R.* (New York: Russell Sage, 1970).

12. Barbara Ehrenreich and Deirdre English, *For Her Own Good* (New York: Anchor Books, 1979), p. 324.

13. They could not have known of this relation because *Herland* was not published in book form until after *For Her Own Good* appeared. This is not to say that they would necessarily agree with the way Gilman works this vision out: with her total rejection of private home, family, child rearing; with her Rousseauian methods of education; with the value she places on efficiency and specialization.

14. Charlotte Perkins Gilman, *The Home: Its Work and Influence* (Urbana: University of Illinois Press, 1972), p. 80.

15. See Charlotte Perkins Gilman, *Women and Economics* (1898. Reprint. New York: Harper & Row, 1966).

16. See, for example, Ehrenreich and English, *For Her Own Good,* p. 21. Compare, Dolores Hayden, *The Grand Domestic Revolution* (Cambridge, Mass.: MIT Press, 1981), pp. 4–5; Ann Palmeri, "Charlotte Perkins Gilman: Forerunner of a Feminist Social Science," in *Discovering Reality,* ed. Sandra Harding and Merill B. Hintikka (Dordrecht: D. Reidel, 1983), pp. 92–119.

17. Charlotte Perkins Gilman, *The Man-Made World* (New York: Charlton Co., 1911. Reprint. Johnson Reprint Corp., 1971), p. 156. References henceforth appear in parentheses in the text.

18. Ursula K. LeGuin, *The Dispossessed* (New York: Avon Books, 1975), p. 297.

19. Evelyn Fox Keller, "Science and Power for What?" in *Science and Utopia: Social Studies of Science Yearbook 1984,* ed. Helga Nowatny and Everett Mendelson (Dordrecht: Reidel, 1984).

20. Marguerite Duras, "From an Interview," in *Motherhood: A Reader for Men and Women,* ed. Susan Cahill (New York: Avon Books, 1982), p. 9.

21. Compare Bettelheim, *Children of the Dream;* Elizabeth Janeway, *Man's World, Woman's Place* (New York: William Morrow & Co., 1971), chap. 12.

Chapter Seven

1. Adlai E. Stevenson, Smith College commencement, June 6, 1955. Reprinted in *Smith Alumnae Quarterly.*

2. Betty Friedan, *The Feminine Mystique* (New York: Dell Publishing Co., 1963), p. 54.

3. John Bartlett, *Bartlett's Familiar Quotations,* 14th ed. (Boston: Little, Brown & Co., 1968).

4. It is not the fact that Stevenson extolled domesticity that makes this solution seem simplistic. Beecher extolled it, too, and whatever the defects of her solution, it cannot be considered shallow. In the 1970s Elizabeth Janeway described the problem Stevenson discerned as follows: " 'What am I doing here?' graduates of the Seven Sisters were asking themselves as they sorted the laundry or put the vacuum cleaner together to give the venetian blinds a thorough going-over. Perhaps even more often the question was, 'What was I doing there—listening to lectures on Seventeenth Century French Poetry, Organic Chemistry, and Money and Banking—when I was fated by the Destiny of Anatomy to end up here?' For the decade of the fifties was not one in which the graduates of even the most prestigious women's colleges easily contemplated a change in their fate, their status, or their occupation. Married they must aspire to be, housewives they must expect to become" (*Women on Campus: The Unfinished Liberation* [New Rochelle: Change Magazine, 1975], p. 10).

5. Many would argue that it does not capture the nature of scientific thought, either. See, for example, Thomas S. Kuhn, *The Structure of Scientific Revolutions* (Chicago: University of Chicago Press, 1962).

6. Since *Herland* portrays a single-sex society, it would seem that its philosophy could not presuppose heterosexuality. Yet one cannot help but suspect that the reason the women of Herland have no erotic ties to one another and are such asexual beings in general is that Gilman is assuming that the only proper kind of sexual relationship is a heterosexual one. As for Plato, although the foundation of his philosophy has been said to be "a series of homoerotic temptations not yielded to" (Jean Bethke Elshtain, *Public Man, Private Woman* [Princeton: Princeton University Press, 1981], p. 28), for the guardians of the Just State only heterosexual alliances are tolerated and these only for the purpose of procreation; moreover, the homoerotic impulses to be controlled appear to belong solely to males.

7. Lorenne M. G. Clark, "The Rights of Women: The Theory and Practice of the Ideology of Male Supremacy," in *Contemporary Issues in Political Philosophy,* ed. William R. Shea and John King-Farlow (New York: Science History Publications, 1976), pp. 49–65.

8. Richard Brandt, *Hopi Ethics* (Chicago: University of Chicago Press, 1954).

9. Consider the following excerpts from interviews conducted in 1969–70 with members of the senior class of an Ivy League male college: "I enjoy talking to more intelligent girls, but I have no desire for a deep relationship with them. I guess I still believe that the man should be more intelligent." "I may be frightened of a man who is superior to me in some field of knowledge, but if a girl knows more than I do, I resent her" (Mirra Komarovsky, "Cultural Contradictions and Sex Roles: The Masculine Case," in *Changing Women in a Changing Society,* ed. Joan Huber (Chicago: University of Chicago Press, 1973), p. 112.

10. Simone de Beauvoir, in *The Second Sex* (New York: Bantam, 1961), provides an extended discussion of woman as the Other.

11. Adrienne Rich, *Of Woman Born* (New York: Bantam, 1977), p. 210.

12. Adrienne Rich, "The Contemporary Emergency and the Quantum Leap," in *On Lies, Secrets, and Silence* (New York: Norton, 1979), p. 271.

13. Rich, *Of Woman Born*, p. 216.

14. Allen Griswold Johnson, "On the Prevalence of Rape in the United States," *Signs* 6 (1980):136–46; Bernice Lott, Mary Ellen Reilly, and Dale R. Howard, "Sexual Assault and Harassment: A Campus Community Case Study," *Signs* 8 (1982):296–319; Jack Thomas, "Subject: Child Abuse," *Boston Globe*, September 15, 1984, p. 18; "The Pornographic Industry," *Boston Globe*, February 13–18, 1983.

15. Richard Rodriguez, *Hunger of Memory: The Education of Richard Rodriguez* (Boston: David B. Godine, 1982).

16. R. S. Peters, *Ethics and Education* (London: Allen & Unwin, 1966); "Education and the Educated Man" in *A Critique of Current Educational Aims,* ed. R. F. Dearden, P. H. Hirst, and R. S. Peters (London: Routledge & Kegan Paul, 1972).

17. See, for example, Mortimer J. Adler, *The Paideia Proposal* (New York: Macmillan Co., 1982); Ernest L. Boyer, *High School* (New York: Harper & Row, 1983).

18. Home economics is the exception to this generalization. However, the chances that Rodriguez would have studied this subject are slight.

19. For discussions of our male and female stereotypes, see, for example, Alexandra G. Kaplan and Joan P. Bean, eds., *Beyond Sex-role Stereotypes* (Boston: Little, Brown & Co., 1976); Alexandra G. Kaplan and Mary Anne Sedney, *Psychology and Sex Roles* (Boston: Little, Brown & Co., 1980).

20. Virginia Woolf, "Mary Wollstonecraft," reprinted in Mary Wollstonecraft, *A Vindication of the Rights of Women,* ed. Carol H. Poston (New York: Norton, 1975), p. 221.

21. Elizabeth Janeway, *Man's World, Woman's Place* (New York: Morrow, 1971), p. 96.

22. Jane Roland Martin, "What Should We Do with a Hidden Curriculum When We Find One?" *Curriculum Inquiry* 6 (1976):135–51.

23. Jane Roland Martin, "Two Dogmas of Curriculum," *Synthese* 51 (1982):5–20.

Index